Institutions of Isolation
Border Controls in the Soviet Union and
Its Successor States, 1917–1993

Until Mikhail Gorbachev came to power in 1985, the Soviet Union was one of the most restrictive and powerful states in the world, and border controls were one of the most important symbols of the Soviet repressive apparatus – as the phrase "Iron Curtain" attests. In *Institutions of Isolation* Andrea Chandler traces the evolution of the USSR's extremely restrictive border-control system.

Chandler provides a comprehensive examination of border controls from the Bolshevik Revolution of 1917 to the collapse of the USSR in 1991 and shows the continued importance of border controls for the newly independent Soviet successor states. She reveals the changing nature of Soviet border-control policy, from the extreme Stalinist isolation of the 1930s to liberalization – and eventual instability – during *perestroika* in the late 1980s.

Chandler argues that Communist ideology was not the only reason for the self-imposed isolation of the state and explores a complex, ever-changing set of political, inter-bureaucratic, and economic factors that combined to influence the Soviet Union's closed-border policies. She draws on social science theories of comparative institutional change and state formation to illuminate policies within the Soviet state, which has often been regarded as a unique case.

By exploring why a political system that originally prided itself on its internationalism devoted such intense efforts to seal its society from the outside world, *Institutions of Isolation* provides a revealing case-study of the strengths and weaknesses of the Soviet state.

ANDREA CHANDLER is assistant professor of political science, Carleton University.

Institutions of Isolation

Border Controls in the Soviet Union and Its Successor States, 1917–1993

ANDREA CHANDLER

McGill-Queen's University Press
Montreal & Kingston · London · Buffalo

© McGill-Queen's University Press 1998
ISBN 0-7735-1717-0

Legal deposit first quarter 1998
Bibliothèque nationale du Québec

Printed in Canada on acid-free paper

This book has been published with the help of a grant
from the Humanities and Social Sciences Federation of
Canada, using funds provided by the Social Sciences
and Humanities Research Council of Canada.

McGill-Queen's University Press acknowledges the support of the Canada Council for the Arts for its
publishing program.

Canadian Calatoguing in Publication Data

Chandler, Andrea, 1963–
    Institutions of isolation: border controls in the
    Soviet Union and its successor states, 1917–1993

    Includes bibliographical references and index.
    ISBN 0-7735-1717-0
    1. Soviet Union – Boundaries.   2. Former Soviet
    republics – Boundaries.   3. Soviet Union – Foreign
    relations.   4. Soviet Union – Politics and government.
    I. Title.

    DK66.C43 1998   327.47   C98-900023-0

This book was typeset by True to Type in 10/12 Sabon.

To my grandparents,
Bram and Dorothy Chandler, and
Graham and Mildred Millar;
and to my parents,
Joan Chandler and Brian M. Chandler

Contents

Preface

This manuscript began as a dissertation, a dissertation in which there were many doubts, not the least of which were my own. I began the dissertation at Columbia University in 1990, at a time when Soviet border control was a decidedly unfashionable topic, and found that I met with a certain amount of scepticism. The Soviet Union, it seemed, was undergoing democratization: why focus on its methods of coercion, the tools of a former "evil empire"? Indeed, my interest in the topic had originally been sparked at Carleton University when, in the mid-1980s (the height of the so-called "New Cold War"), I began my MA research essay on Soviet Jewish emigration. Was I simply out of step with the times? Yet, nothwithstanding the monumental changes in the USSR under Gorbachev, my belief was that Soviet borders offered more than met the eye and that historical exploration of this aspect of Soviet state-building could provide insight into the problems coming to the fore under *perestroika*: the Soviet Union was opening up its political system from within, but how quickly was it opening up to the outside world? Still, at the beginning I didn't foresee just how interesting the topic would become. As *perestroika* progressed, political unrest emerged in Soviet border areas, and republics began to set up their own border controls in defence of their new claim to independent statehood. When the Soviet Union collapsed, to be replaced by fifteen independent states, I had the rare privilege of seeing my subject-matter fragment and multiply just as I was completing research and writing. The dissertation's chronological end-point was the end of 1991; subsequently, the newly independent states' development of their own border controls provided a fertile subject for the last chapter of this study. Consequently, the scope of my analysis here extends to approximately the end of 1993.

Following independence, the state institutions of the post-Soviet republics proved increasingly complex and differentiated but remained fragile and contentious. Border controls were no exception. None the less, today's border controls show signs of substantive change, although whether those are irreversible is anybody's guess. This is not to say that the new states have their border regulations under control or that their personnel know what the rules were: an unpleasant encounter I had with Ukrainian border guards while trying to travel to Kyïv with a valid visa in the spring of 1994 convinced me there is much room for improvement.

A NOTE ON SOURCES

In this study I take a historical, archival approach to the collection of evidence in order to trace the development and changes in Soviet border institutions and policies over time. I have relied extensively on published and unpublished primary sources: edited collections of documents such as the four-volume *Pogranichnye Voiska SSSR*, edited by P. Zyrianov et al., including compilers E.I. Solov'ev, A.I. Chuganov, and others; published collections of documents; Soviet laws, statutes, and decisions; newspapers and journals, including both central sources and local border-area newspapers; archives, including the Smolensk Archive materials on microfilm, the Nicolaevsky Archive of the Hoover Institution, the Bakhmeteff Archive at the Rare Book and Manuscript Library, Columbia University, and Soviet archives, which provided insights into the real workings of the relevant Soviet state bureaucracies rather than the ideological explanations of Soviet politics common to Soviet published sources; and memoir literature and emigré sources.

The opening of the former Communist Party Archives in the fall of 1991 provided new sources of information that until then had been considered politically sensitive. All the same, the occasional gap in information existed at the time of my research on many aspects of Soviet policy, particularly for the 1930s. In contrast, the scholar interested in the perestroika and post-Soviet periods can be overwhelmed with data, as the newly independent states began to produce a large array of laws and decrees, many of which were never properly implemented. This of course makes for a certain methodological unevenness, as the availability, nature, and quality of research material varies considerably across time and region. None the less, the striking feature is the continuity of the trends this evidence reveals.

As the system of Communist rule in the USSR fell, Soviet archives were greatly affected. In the past few years archives have often been reorganized and renamed. I have chosen to refer to the archives by the names they had at the time of my research (primarily spring and fall 1991), for two reasons. First, I assume that this system will provide a more accurate citation. Secondly, the upheavals in the former Soviet Union have not ended, and I see no reason to assume that the naming process will not continue in the future. It is up to scholars to be aware of changes and to follow them accordingly. The bibliography provides a complete listing of archives consulted and their various name changes.

For transliteration from the Russian, I follow the Library of Congress system, except for variations that are commonly recognized in the West (e.g., Trotsky, *glasnost*, Yeltsin, *oblast*). In the endnotes, translations of Russian source titles have generally been provided, except where they are very brief or easily recognized.

Acknowledgments

This book began as a PhD dissertation completed in 1992 at Columbia University. I was fortunate to receive support for my doctoral studies and research from a number of sources. From 1987 to 1990 I received a Doctoral Fellowship from the Social Sciences and Humanities Research Council of Canada. I received Barton Scholarships for my doctoral research and writing from the Canadian Institute for International Peace and Security in 1990–91 and in 1991–92. At various points during my five years of study at Columbia I also received fellowship support from Columbia University, where I was a student in the Department of Political Science, and the Harriman Institute. My three trips to the Soviet Union during the course of my research were made possible respectively by the Variable Term Research Program of the American Council of Teachers of Russsian, and a grant from the Pepsico Foundation offered through the Harriman Institute for a trip to Moscow in the spring of 1991; the Canada-USSR Academic Exchange of the Association of Universities and Colleges of Canada for research in the fall of 1991; and the Republican Association of Ukrainists in Kyïv, Ukraine, where I was able to do some research in the summer of 1990 while attending the International Summer School for Ukrainists. I would like to thank the Russian State Humanities University (RGGU, formerly the Moscow State Historical Archive Institute) for hosting me in Moscow on my two research trips, and the RGGU staff and faculty members, who were very helpful and kind to me.

During the writing of the dissertation various people provided me with advice and guidance. I would like to thank Alexander J. Motyl for his cheerful support, his careful and prompt readings of various drafts, and his advice throughout the dissertation process. Lisa Anderson and Mark von Hagen gave invaluable suggestions, perceptive criticisms, and encouragement at all stages of the dissertation. Two other scholars sat on my dissertation committee, Thomas P. Bernstein and the late John Hazard, both of whom provided thorough comments. As a graduate student I benefited from my opportunity, courtesy of the Social Science Research Council, to participate in their 1990 and 1991 Summer Workshops on Soviet Domestic Politics and Society. In addition, the organizers and participants in the workshops made many helpful comments, particularly Thane Gustafson, Peter Solomon, and Susan Solomon. Villiam Smirnov of the Institute of State and Law in Moscow helped me to find materials and access in Moscow. A number of individuals who are both dear friends and respected colleagues provided great moral and intellectual support; in particular I would like to thank Bridget Welsh, Frances Bernstein, Paul Lerner, and Charles Steinwedel. Finally, David Millar and Barbara Roberts offered practical advice and moral support.

I would like to thank the Centre for Research on Canadian-Russian Relations (formerly Research Centre for Canada and the Soviet Successor States) and its director, Professor J.L. (Larry) Black, at Carleton University. My post-doctoral fellowship at the Centre in 1992–93 allowed me the time to consider how to turn the dissertation into a manuscript, which I continued to rewrite after I became a member of the faculty of the Department of Political Science at Carleton University in July 1993. Chapter 9 of this study is adapted from a paper entitled "An End to Isolation? *Perestroika*, Reform and the Fate of Border Control Institutions in the Soviet Successor States," which I presented to the Annual Meeting of the American Association for the Advancement of Slavic Studies, Honolulu, Hawaii, in November 1993. Roger Kangas, who was panel discussant, provided helpful comments on the paper as well as encouragement before and after.

I alone bear responsibility for the content of this work and for any errors or omissions that appear.

Some of the ideas developed in depth in chapter 8 were initially explored in preliminary form in Andrea Chandler, "The Iron Curtain and Gorbachev: Recent Changes in the Soviet System of Border Control," in *Soviet Observer* (a former publication of students of the Harriman Institute, Columbia University), 1, no. 1 (Apr. 1990): 4–6.

I am grateful for the criticisms and suggestions I received from the anonymous reviewers who read either the original manuscript or the revised manuscript, or both. Their comments aided me greatly in making the necessary improvements for the revised version. I would like to thank the Aid to Scholarly Publications Committee; Joan McGilvray, of McGill-Queen's University Press, for her helpfulness and her quick responses regarding the final editorial work; and Susan Kent Davidson for her expert copy-editing.

I would like to thank Henri Jarque for his understanding and helpful suggestions during the process of rewriting the manuscript.

Finally, I thank Nick Aylott for his English breakfasts and wisdom beyond his years.

Institutions of Isolation

1 The Paradox of Socialist Isolation: Ideology and Territory in the Construction of Soviet Border Controls

In 1985 the Soviet Union was one of the most restrictive and powerful states in the world, such that it was still commonly described as a "totalitarian" political system. In the short decades following the tumultuous Bolshevik Revolution of 1917 the Soviet Communist Party elite had established an impressive form of rule: the size of the Soviet state bureaucracy, its investment in military and police capacities, and its involvement in socio-economic affairs were unparalleled. Among the noteworthy features of the Soviet state were its border controls; they severely restricted its citizens' ability to emigrate or travel abroad while also making it difficult for foreign influences or visitors to enter the country. Border controls epitomized the power of the Communist party-state, its control of both society and the domestic economy. These border controls complemented the Soviet Union's strong territorial defences, its strict internal surveillance regime, and its state-planned economy, which asserted control over human as well as material resources; border restrictions performed both economic and internal-security functions. Border controls, as exemplified in the phrase "Iron Curtain," were one of the most important symbols of the power of the Soviet repressive apparatus – they were one of the ways in which the Soviet state supposedly "worked." They had a reputation for maintaining airtight, impermeable boundaries by which the Soviet state was able to prevent mass emigration, exposure to foreign ideas, and travel. By the time Mikhail Sergeevich Gorbachev came to power in 1985, the Soviet system was widely perceived as a viable, albeit repressive, system of government. Border controls were one of the visible images that propagated the myth that the USSR was a strong state.

Yet only six years later the Soviet Union collapsed. With the fall of the Communist system, the country split apart, and its fifteen constituent republics became independent states. As a part of this process, instability and conflict emerged on the Soviet Union's once-rigid borders, creating a situation that in some ways resembled the territorial upheaval of the young Bolshevik state after the Revolution of October 1917. The uncertain situation on the borders of the former Communist state graphically illustrated that, as the founding leaders of the Commonwealth of Independent States (CIS) declared in December 1991, the Soviet Union no longer existed as a state.[1]

If the Soviet Union during the Cold War had one of the most restrictive systems of border control in the world, this was partly because its borders throughout this century have been the site of extraordinary contestation and volatility. In view of this instability, the question of Soviet border controls as a characteristic and problematic aspect of the Soviet political system are worth examining in their own right. The Soviet Union's border controls have rarely been studied in depth; they tend to be taken for granted as an essential feature of the Communist system. Often forgotten is that aspects of the Soviet system such as border controls were distortions of Marxist ideology that ran counter to many of its original precepts. Karl Marx stressed that the modern capitalist state was essentially a repressive tool of the ruling classes and that the common interests of workers transcend international borders, themes echoed in some of Lenin's works. The USSR's border controls seize the imagination because on the surface they defied, even violated Marxist ideological principles. They represented the idea of the socialist state as a fragile piece of land whose inhabitants needed to be protected from capitalists and reactionary nationalists lurking outside its frontiers; they were symptomatic of both the political struggle at the edges of the young Soviet state and the importance that states in general at that point in history attached to such crude manifestations of strength as border controls. Far from a necessary outgrowth of Communism, border controls were one of the Soviet Union's essential paradoxes.

PURPOSES OF BORDER CONTROLS

This study poses two essential questions: why was the Soviet system of border control established and maintained, and how was it involved in the collapse of the Soviet Union? The formation of the Soviet border-control apparatus, a process that began with the Bolshevik Revolution and was strengthened throughout the Stalin era into the 1950s, is a formidable example of a new state's successful use of a coercive strategy of state building. For Soviet leaders the isolation imposed by border controls was an act of affirmation of the state. The Soviet border was closed, and the right to travel or cross the border was an isolated privilege available to a fortunate few, not a right of society as a whole.

The Soviet elite's concern with borders was not unprecedented. Uncertainty and conflict over boundaries have been recurring themes in the history of the Eurasian region since tsarist times, continuing into Soviet history.[2] In part this is a consequence of the vast territorial borders of the country, as Russian and Soviet leaders defined them, and cataclysmic wars that have been accompanied by rival territorial claims and mass population movements. The Soviet Union came into being in a world where borders were a source of political conflict, where control of territory and military power were considered crucial to a state's survival, and where societies were polarized and fragmented. The border became a physical symbol of resistance to the international bourgeoisie and to capitalism. To the Bolsheviks, and especially to V.I. Lenin's successor Joseph Stalin, the capitalist enemy was at the gates, and the Soviet Union's leaders knew that control of knowledge, information, and contact with the outside world was power. The Soviet Union was vulnerable at its borders, where its military security was in question, as was the loyalty of its borderland population. So it built the state from the outside in, from the border to the centre, as well as from the top of the Communist Party down to the Soviet population. In addition, the Soviet Union was trying to build an alternative, self-sufficient society. Soviet leaders believed that they needed to "protect" a society they considered too immature to be able to choose socialism of its own free will. The new state's first leaders wanted to build a totally self-contained economy, as autonomous as possible, in which all resources needed to be mobilized for the good of the state and society. No resources could be allowed to escape because the war with capitalism would ultimately be a war of attrition. Finally, control of borders was not just a triumph of military policy; it was a triumph of bureaucracy over the chaos of the Russian Revolution and Civil War. The bureaucratic priorities, rules, and procedures associated with border controls tended to become more elaborate, more convoluted, and more prohibitive over time.

Interestingly, the people who actually lived on the borders of the Soviet Union were the people the Bolsheviks considered the most untrustworthy. Border controls were in part the result of a confrontational interaction between the state and local society in Soviet border areas, often directed against peasants and other rural populations considered to be ill disposed towards the Bolshevik government. The Soviet Union's international boundaries cut across and through multi-ethnic populations, dividing ethnic groups and separating Soviet peoples from those groups and power centres with whom they might have more in common than they had with Moscow. For example, border controls intercepted contact between Soviet Ukrainians and the Galician Ukrainians under Polish rule until 1939; border controls also prevented Central Asian peoples and Tatars from connecting with Muslims or Turks abroad, Belarusans from conversing with Poles, and Armenians on both sides of the Soviet border from engaging in dialogue. As Soviet territory expanded in the 1930s and 1940s, the location of the border changed, whereupon border controls were extended to new sites. This happened not just because the borderland peoples were often genuinely hostile to Bolshevism and to being part of the Soviet state but also because they were, for the most part, peasants. They were often people of non-Russian ethnicity who, in the view of the leadership, needed to be sealed off from the bad influence of their bourgeois or reactionary compatriots across the border, since these people were assumed to put ethnic identity first.

In a study of border controls it is essential to deal with the role and legacy of Stalin. There is no doubt that Stalin further restricted and politicized the Soviet system of border control. Yet Stalin did not initiate extreme border controls. Much of the apparatus was in place by the late and even the mid-1920s. The development of the centrally planned economy, the peasant resistance to collectivization, and Stalin's increasing terror against supposed political threats from the population all served to make border controls more important because Stalin considered the world outside the Soviet Union to be plotting and scheming to conquer his government from without and overthrow it from within. At the height of the purges in 1936–39 Stalin accused large numbers of people of being agents of foreign governments; any contact an individual had with a foreign country, no matter how trivial, could be perceived as proof of treason. Border controls served to police the domestic population and keep the foreign enemy at bay, yet ironically they were quickly overcome when Nazi Germany invaded the Soviet Union in 1941. Even after Stalin's death, when border-control restrictions were slightly modified in order to permit a trickle of emigration and expanded travel opportunities for a lucky few, the regime continued to justify its border controls on the grounds that Soviet territory and society needed to be protected; controls were depicted as a proud symbol of the Soviet Union's ability to protect itself, both from the untrustworthy outside world and from the citizen whose motives to travel abroad were always suspect. The most rigorous controls continued in place to ensure that the right to travel and have contact with the West was an option – and a reward – only for the most loyal and reliable of the Communist Party's allies.

The Soviet border-control system served the purposes for which it was originally designed. It helped to maintain central control over the economy; it ensured that foreign trade and population movements were consistent with the objectives of Soviet leaders. It also proved useful for maintaining the internal security and public order that are so important to authoritarian rulers. It limited Soviet citizens' vulnerability to "undesirable" foreign influences, and it helped to ensure that the defences of the country's territorial integrity were carefully maintained. Moreover, by making foreign travel and foreign goods the exclusive privilege of the Communist elite, it created an incentive for curious citizens to support the status quo actively.

Border controls affected several types of social groups. On the local level they negatively affected small peasants and traders, and their ability to trade for gain and survival. They imposed hardships on families divided by state borders, who were subsequently unable to make contact with each other. They affected non-Russian-nationality populations, whose way of living and trading were affected by arbitrary boundaries and who perceived border controls as an instrument of central domination; and they also hurt national minorities such as Jews, who felt persecuted by the regime and sought emigration as a recourse.

Border controls were extremely secure, but they were also rigid. The mass flight from the USSR during the Second World War suggests that border controls had acted merely to restrain rather than resolve state-society problems. Over the long term, until the initiation of *perestroika*, border controls simply contained societal evasion or resistance – what Albert O. Hirschman has called "exit"[3] – but they became a resented part of the Soviet repressive apparatus, which ultimately could not keep out all foreign influences.

In addition, the institutional apparatus itself was costly. Border controls responded to the Soviet Union's particular problems of government, a consequence of particular political choices; but they eventually became evidence of the USSR's problems in *controlling* the size and responsibility of the government bureaucracy. The Soviet border-control system also, by the time Gorbachev launched his first reforms, seemed unnecessarily extreme, since it served to prohibit rather than regulate cross-border contact. In the country at large there had grown a sense that the state's prohibitive, monopolizing role was producing too few returns. *Perestroika* can be understood in part as an attempt to initiate a transition from a punitive and controlling state to an order that promoted the exchange of ideas, which in turn would involve ceding part (but not all) of the state's monopoly on economic resources.

Perestroika was also intended to devolve more responsibilities for redistribution and social services from the central government to the republic and local level.[4]

Under *perestroika* the Soviet leadership and legislature in relatively short order set about to create a streamlined, more open system that would encourage trade and travel, with a much more minimalist conception of the state's security needs. The border-control apparatus continued to function, although in places it was disrupted or shaken by national unrest, because it continued to be seen by society as an instrument of power. Moreover, the isolation that had accompanied the old system proved a stumbling block to reform under *perestroika*. A more serious issue was the increasingly secessionist tendencies of some of the Soviet Union's fifteen constitutuent republics (especially the three Baltic republics, plus Georgia and Ukraine), who proposed to set up their own border-control forces to back up their claims of sovereignty.

Border control continued to be a controversial issue for the Soviet successor states. Among the problems accompanying the breakup of the USSR are a series of boundary-related challenges. The republics were pulled into a powerful momentum to set up customs posts on what had previously been open, intra-Soviet republican boundaries. The successor states have been left with their predecessor's shaky and conflict-ridden borders, some of which are now contested. Cross-border smuggling and mass refugee movements proliferated in the uncertain environment of the collapse of the USSR. Although the former Soviet states would like to join the international community, they inherited the remains of the convoluted Soviet network of restrictive border controls. Indeed, some of the most pressing issues in post-Soviet society since 1991 have to do with loosely construed border issues: territorial disputes between states, uncertainty over military jurisdiction, separatist claims by ethnic minorities, and struggles for authority between central governments and localities. Some of the severe crises that the republics face now are similar to those that led to such extreme responses by the Soviet state; some of their responses to date echo those of their predecessor, while others reflect efforts to create a more open and democratic system. However, because the Soviet state controlled everything, post-Soviet leaders have great difficulty differentiating between state powers that are excessive and those that are appropriate to a functioning state. They vacillate between avoiding "normal" uses of coercive power and using it indiscriminately to compensate for past laxity. As I argue in my final chapter, their border-control policies at the time of writing suffer simultaneously from arbitrariness, ambivalence, and bureaucratic confusion.

The successor states seem attached to border controls as a psychological symbol of sovereignty inherited from the old "Iron Curtain." This reflects a desire to carve out territory to remove it from contestation, as borders have become the site of so much conflict and unrest. Of course, many of the problems in the successor states today are reactions against the Soviet state, and efforts to contain border problems are related to various Soviet legacies, whether defensive reactions, common responses to similar problems, or desires to right past wrongs or gain new resources.

Perhaps there was some kind of cause and effect between the isolation of border controls and the stability of the Soviet system, and a relationship between the collapse of the USSR and the removal of border controls. Yet in some ways the successor states, including Russia, sometimes appear to be reverting to old patterns. The state retains strong control over the economy; xenophobic rhetoric has emerged again where nationalist movements have gained influence; from 1991 to 1995 Boris Yeltsin resorted more than once to force, rather than democratic methods, in order to resolve political problems. The case of border controls demonstrates that political structures, institutions, and old habits remain in the system.

INSTITUTIONS OF ISOLATION

This study examines the development and change of Soviet border-control institutions from 1917 to 1991, and concludes with a comparative exploration of the role of those institutions in the Soviet successor states to date. Soviet border controls developed through several historical phases. Chapter 2 examines the relationship between the state and borders, placing the Soviet state in a comparative and theoretical context. Chapter 3 discusses the early crises of the Soviet state during the revolutionary and Civil War period, and the use of border controls as a response to this crisis, while chapter 4 explores the relationship of border controls to the emerging economic policies of the Soviet state. Chapters 5 and 6 examine the increasingly coercive nature of border controls in the late 1920s and 1930s as a result of Stalinist policies, security concerns over nationality relations in border areas, and the expansion of the Soviet bureaucracy. Chapter 7 looks at the solidification of the border-control system in the post–Second World War period, leading into a discussion of Gorbachev's early reforms aimed at opening the Soviet system to international contacts and influences. Chapter 8 examines the role that border controls played in aggravating tensions between the Soviet government and the republics, and chapter 9 outlines the steps that the republics have taken since independence to establish their own border controls.

By spanning all of Soviet history – from 1917 to its end-point in 1991 and beyond – this study offers an opportunity to explore the chronological evolution of one aspect of the Soviet state and to compare it with the state-building problems and opportunities of the Soviet successor states as they attempt to break the cycle of autarky. While border controls by themselves cannot be held responsible for the Soviet decline, they suffered from some of the same problems as did other state institutions and provide a manageable case-study for an examination of the problems of the Soviet state throughout its history. Obviously, the collapse of the Soviet state is a very large topic; only Philip G. Roeder's ambitious overview has as yet attempted to look at the Soviet Union's institutional failures in an integrated way.[5] Yet examinations of individual state sectors provide a useful way to gain insight into Soviet institutions in general.

Border controls provide a useful case-study of changes in the Soviet state for two reasons. First, since Soviet boundaries were by definition located in the country's territorial periphery, border controls reveal the dynamics of the state-building process in borderland territories, which were often inhabited by non-Russian nationalities who were hostile to Soviet rule. Secondly, border controls are a measure of a state's attitude towards the outside world and its desire to monopolize international transactions. In the Soviet Union, border controls maintained the political economy of isolation. As a result, they were one of the institutions that *perestroika* aimed to change in order to liberalize the country's foreign trade and expand its access to international ideas and communications. While border controls did not "make or break" the USSR, and were an outgrowth of other state policies, they represent a manageable, concrete section of the state bureaucracy that was a point of intersection of various diverse, vital state decisions.

The research in this study was guided by a series of assumptions, first of all that the Soviet state was dynamic, not static: state policies and the institutions created to implement them changed over time. Such respected historians as Moshe Lewin and Lewis Siegelbaum have pointed out the political and social limitations that influenced Soviet policy,[6] while Jack Snyder has called for attention to international pressures on the Soviet Union in its early days.[7] The contention that Soviet state responses varied according to the changing goals and purposes of state institutions is not meant to imply that Soviet leaders adjusted "rationally" to changing demands; indeed, as scholars have argued, the failure to modernize was one of the key failings of the Soviet state.[8] Moreover, territorial factors, political conflict in border areas, and the international environment constrained Bolshevik policy and influenced the development of state institutions.[9]

This line of argument leads to the question of whether the Bolsheviks were doctrinaire totalitarian ideologues or pragmatic and flexible (albeit imperialist) political strategists. Conventional Sovietology, in particular the influential "totalitarian model," has often stressed the critical importance of Communist ideology in determining Soviet policy. Controversy has emerged over whether ideology on the one hand, or pragmatic political concerns on the other were the most important factors influencing Soviet decision-making. Social scientists have also debated whether ideology should be seen as a set of beliefs that inspire actions or whether ideology is mainly used to justify a particular course of action.[10] The collapse of the Soviet Union has led to a renewed, vigorous discussion of the meaning of Soviet ideology.[11] For the purposes of this study the most convincing approach seems to accept that for Soviet leaders, Leninist ideology provided a common set of principles and goals, and a flexible framework for interpreting events.[12] Evidence suggests that in the case of border controls, Soviet leaders wrote about the problems of the border primarily in political and strategic terms, focusing more on situational and territorial concerns than on ideological discourse. The discussion of border controls was couched in a statist language that stressed strength, order, economic normalization, and political loyalty. Nevertheless, their coolly realist perceptions of economic and security problems were always guided by ideology, in the sense that they perceived protection of Soviet territory and the economy as synonymous with defence of the revolution.

As an interesting aside to the discussion of the role of ideology in both the USSR and the successor states, unstable borders contributed to decisions to impose border controls. This observation is not intended to minimize or apologize for Soviet state policies, nor to deny that state leaders voluntarily and consciously chose particular state strategies in response to these conditions. To recognize that coercion was a response to political unrest is not to condone it as a justifiable or advisable policy of state management. Border controls did, however, reflect the Soviet government's fear of restiveness in borderland areas, which was seen as an issue requiring constant, vigilant attention in order to be contained.

With these assumptions in mind, a few caveats are necessary. This study focuses on the Soviet Union's *international* borders rather than the boundaries internal to the Soviet state. The Soviet Union, as a purportedly federal (but actually highly centralized) system, was divided into fifteen union republics, each of which theoretically had its own constitution and the right to secede from the union, was granted jurisdiction over certain areas of government, and represented a particular major ethnic group.[13] To make matters more complicated, the Soviet system contained further ethnic-territorial subdivisions such as autonomous republics, autonomous *oblasts, krais,* and *okrugs.* These units were ascribed various levels of autonomy and ethnic status and were distinguished from the regular administrative sub-units of the Soviet system, which included regions (*oblasts*) and localities. As scholars have argued, this administrative system involved a complex process of drawing and redrawing boundaries in order to map out a convoluted and unequal division of powers between the central government and the lower levels of government; the implications of these arrangements are the subject of a great deal of current interest among students of post-Soviet studies.[14] The question of boundary formation *within* the USSR is an important one and is integrally related both to the emergence of nationalism in the late Soviet period and to the renegotiation of federalism today within the Russian Federation. As some scholars have noted, borders within the USSR were artificially created and reinvented by the Soviet state, with lasting consequences for the ethnic divisions this created.[15]

The borders between republics were political and had political consequences. Like international borders, they divided and ordered people, and created different, sometimes arbitrary conditions for people on one side or another. Like international borders, they sometimes divided people of the same ethnic group and were sites of internal controversy, which would become relevant once the republics began to seek sovereignty. Moreover, internal passports and labour controls prevented totally free migration or contact between republics. Finally, internal borders sometimes took on significance when two neighbouring republics were treated unequally. For example, historians of Ukraine have argued that the famine in that Soviet republic in 1931–32 was an artificial famine resulting from the Soviet state's desire to export Ukrainian grain abroad, and did not affect Russian agriculture as severely.[16] Another example of the importance of internal boundaries has been raised in connection with Central Asia and the Caucasus, where ethnic groups were divided in a most convoluted way among administrative units.[17] This would create the widely discussed potential for irredentism once the Soviet Union collapsed into fifteen newly independent states. Border controls existed on the Soviet Union's international boundaries, those separating Soviet republics from foreign states; they did not exist as such on the internal boundaries between individual Soviet republics until those republics began to assert their sovereignty in the early 1990s.

This study looks at *international* border controls, which limit contact and movement between independent states, not at the administrative or federal boundaries that exist within states, however significant they may have become once the Soviet republics became interested in pursuing sovereignty. The Soviet Union's boundaries between republics and regions may have been politicized, but they were none the less boundaries between Soviet citizens whom the regime considered to be politically unified under socialism. Therefore, this study as a whole does not focus on the fascinating yet complex intricacies of the boundaries between Soviet republics, autonomous republics, or regions, except in the very final section, which treats the period when the borders between Soviet republics suddenly became international boundaries.

Of course, internal boundaries became extremely important under *perestroika,* when the admininistrative boundaries between republics suddenly became the politicized points of contact between aspiring secessionist states and when the republics, in the act of declaring greater sovereignty, attempted to claim the right to control international borders, thus rejecting Soviet authority over borders and wreaking havoc over formerly rigid Soviet boundaries. As discussed in chapter 8, border controls of the Soviet Union actually became a focus of resistance, which demonstrated both that in themselves they had become a grievance of national and social movements (as evidenced earlier in the dissident movement, perhaps worth mentioning) and that republics and regions – and Soviet people in general – had absorbed a potent message: that border controls were a visual symbol of the power of the sovereign state. The right to act as one's own gatekeeper, to limit the people who could enter and the valuables that could leave, became identified with the right to self-determination. The key question of course is why territory becomes so important and why there is such a fixation on the "gates" of sovereignty. This conviction is not unique to the Soviet Union, by the way. Although the West may not have had the stark physical barriers of the USSR, Western countries are just as attached to their role as gatekeepers, even though they may use it in a more nuanced way.

A second caveat is that this study does not purport to be an exhaustive study of either the Soviet state or state-building, nor does it seek to exaggerate the role that border controls played in the system. It seeks to provide a case-study of a particular sector of the state bureaucracy, and will not substitute for further study or research of other aspects of the Soviet state bureaucracy; much work remains for others to explore other institutions. We still have a great deal to learn about the USSR, and as new archival research comes to light, more will be revealed that may alter our previous understanding. Moreover, the discussion of trends in the Soviet successor states is tentative, given the infancy of these polities at this writing. However, in the interim it is important to produce generalizations that can be either refuted or corroborated by future research.

Lastly, this study incorporates comparative analysis and social-science theory of the state, which are useful in understanding the Soviet Union. However hermetically sealed its leaders might have wished it to be, the Soviet state was not built in a vacuum; rather, it was profoundly influenced by the shape of power relations between states that prevailed at that time. The Soviet system also displayed some common concerns of new, multi-ethnic states that are created in a bitter political environment. Despite its unusual preoccupation with border security, the Soviet Union was not the only state to experience political conflict over boundary issues. Internationally, difficult problems and choices revolve around problems of borders and border claims. Around the world the relationship between borders and the state is volatile and changing. The disintegration of Soviet boundaries is a particularly extreme example of the lack of consensus over state boundaries, one that was undoubtedly rooted in the unresolved tensions in Soviet society. Yet perhaps it is in some way symptomatic of a generalized problem of the *fin de siècle* political environment: the co-existence of widespread secessionist tendencies with pressures favouring transnational integration is a commonly noted paradox.[18] New boundaries are being created as states split up, while other states become integrated such that their boundaries are less relevant: witness Yugoslavia on the one hand and the European Union on the other. The Soviet case could help us to understand the stresses that fragment states at their borders and the reactions of "society" to the borders that they do not always have reason to respect.

Finally, the Soviet Union's border controls provide a way for Western observers to learn about themselves. The Western gaze upon the Soviet system was until recently tinted by the Cold War mystique of the Iron Curtain and filtered through the symbolism of the grimly mechanized Soviet border, sometimes with a moralistic intent to distinguish between "us" and "them," at other times with a call to appraise the progressive achievements of the society behind the curtain. While border controls were rightly perceived as a violation of Soviet citizens' human rights, it is important to transcend moral denunciation and try to understand why they were in place. Now that we are able to distance ourselves from the Cold War, we may also be able to demystify the Soviet experience and examine it as a state-building experiment that happened in a particular context with its own successes and failures, and some ironic results. We might venture so far as to say that border controls, contrary though they seemed to the principles of a proletarian state, were designed to avert precisely those scenarios that happened under *perestroika*.

2 States, Regimes and Border Controls: The Link between Communism and Isolation

Recent scholarly writing on the state has been preoccupied with some of the same kinds of questions that today are asked about the Soviet Union: How are states built? Why do they decline? Why are some states more effective than others? And why do states change? What kind of state *was* the Soviet Union? The Soviet Union has often been seen as a different kind of state that has to be analysed on its own terms, distinct from the Western or third-world polities that are the central focus of literature on the state.[1] This was because of the extremely centralized nature of the Soviet system and the Communist Party's monopoly on power and resources. As a result, the USSR was often characterized as a "totalitarian" system, a concept that emphasized its essentially hierarchical and authoritarian flow of power from the top down.[2] Certainly, the hostility of the Bolsheviks to liberal democracy and their adoption of state-sponsored economic mobilization have been well documented, and border controls have tended to be seen as one of the Soviet Union's most characteristic "totalitarian" features.

Some scholars regarded the Soviet Union's unusual preoccupation with border controls and internal security as manifestations of the country's repressive political system.[3] The Soviet political system sought to inhibit communication, movement, and exchange with states, groups, and individuals in other countries, and a strong coercive apparatus existed to ensure this goal.[4] Alexander J. Motyl listed closed borders as one of the instruments of coercion of the Soviet state.[5] Both Jerry Hough and Ken Jowitt considered "protectionism," or isolation, to be essential features of the Soviet regime.[6] The Soviet border-control system and its accompanying restrictions on travel can be seen as part of the entire Soviet passport system's regimentation of citizens' rights to movement and choice of domicile, which had historical roots in the tsarist period.[7]

Border controls were rarely explored in any depth; rather than being the subject of investigation in their own right, they were often perceived as a secondary characteristic of a totalitarian, Communist regime.[8] From this perspective they appeared mainly to be yet another instrument of a totalitarian regime intent on enforcing its monopoly of ideas.[9] Alan Dowty, for example, argued that restrictive border-control regimes result from the "modern state's" capacity, and the totalitarian regime's will, to engineer the lives of its citizens.[10] Similarly, Iurii Felshtinskii wrote a legal-historical study of the evolution of some aspects of Soviet border control up to the 1930s. He too saw what he called the Soviet "closed society" as a product of the fundamental malevolence of socialism, the result of an ideology that divided the world into two class camps, and a means towards the end of eliminating the country's internal enemies and creating a monolithic society. Restrictions on emigration and immigration were a manifestation of the Bolsheviks' goal of controlling all communications with foreign countries.[11]

This thesis has its limitations, although it has some validity. First, it does not explain the existence of socialist states that did not close their borders, such as post-Tito Yugoslavia.[12] Secondly, it neglects the fact that, historically, new states (whether "totalitarian" or not) have imposed border controls over society. Finally, the totalitarian thesis doesn't explain how state capacity was developed: it accepts a strong coercive state as a given but is less informative in explaining how and why these institutions were developed. To understand the problem further we need to see border control as a case-study in state-building and consider the Bolsheviks' rationales and strategies for building a strong border-control apparatus over time.

The emergence of a Soviet state with unprecedented bureaucratic scope and coercive capacity was, if not an unintended result, then at least an ironic outcome. Bolshevik Marxism assumed that an international proletarian revolution would create a world socialist order in which states and borders would no longer be necessary.[13] The historical outcome should rightly be seen as puzzling rather than inevitable. In "The State and Revolution," written shortly before the Russian Revolution, V.I. Lenin argued that with the achievement of socialist revolution a "semi-state" controlled by the workers would replace the bourgeois state, which he considered to be an essentially repressive institution that served capitalist interests. The state itself would gradually be abolished under socialism, since it would no longer perform its essential function of ensuring the domination of one social group over all others.[14] Yet the Bolsheviks came into their own in a world of hostile, even predatory states, and therefore the Soviet state, ostensibly in place in order to realize the achievement of socialism, ushered in a period of statist expansion. The Soviet Communist elite had several basic goals: the redistribution of property, the defence of Bolshevik territory, and the administration of society and the economy. Increasingly leaders realized, somewhat reluctantly, that the socialist state structure provided the instrument to achieve those goals.

In the absence of world revolution, Bolshevik Russia – and later the Soviet Union with its constituent republics – aimed to create a workers' state that would stand fast against the capitalist states of the world. In the process the class struggle against the bourgeois capitalist enemy was transferred to the state level; as Jean-Yves Calvez writes, the idea of the defence of socialist property was extended to the establishment of strongly guarded state territory, with sharply defined and controlled borders.[15] Other countries, embodying in Bolshevik eyes the persistence of capitalism and hostility to Soviet Marxism, thus came to be perceived as the class enemy, and "socialism in one country" summed up the philosophy of the need to fight capitalism as an international force with the controlled internationalism of the Soviet state. Later, under Stalin, the success of the Soviet Revolution was seen as leading to an intensification of the class struggle, which was to require greater vigilance against the increasingly treacherous infiltration of the state by the capitalist enemy.[16]

Border controls were among the features of the Soviet political system that were intended to serve the interests of the country's internal economic and military security. The Soviet Union's authority over its borderlands, which became battlegrounds of conflicting allegiances during the Civil War, remained precarious in the first few decades of Bolshevik rule. The expansion of border controls throughout the 1920s and 1930s reflects the hardening statism of the Soviet regime amid the realities of "socialism in one country." Preserving the socialist state as a fortress would allow for the achievement of ideological norms: the dispossession of the capitalist and landed classes, the equitable redistribution of wealth, and the material prosperity afforded by scientific progress.

Border controls go hand in hand with the idea of the modern state as a piece of territory that is vulnerable to the attacks and encroachments of warring powers. Prior to its collapse, the USSR was all too often seen as a unique case that could not be meaningfully compared to non-communist states, or to which Western social-science theory had little relevance. However, with respect to its concerns over geopolitics and internal security, the Soviet state was by no means unique. Moreover, the Soviet Union was influenced by the political climate of the time. Its early development was influenced by the prevailing international environment between the two world wars and by the policies that were commonly used by states in that particular historical period. The Soviet state faced an uncertain international environment of "capitalist encirclement" by hostile states.[17]

To those of us who have become accustomed to hearing about the many supposed advantages of contemporary globalization, the Soviet border-control system seems excessive or even unnecessary. Yet the Bolshevik state was born in the sobering aftermath of the First World War, when military power still prevailed as a way to resolve disputes and expand state resources and when states' concerns for their internal security reached a peak. Since the prevailing view in the literature today assumes that the USSR collapsed because of its shortcomings as a state, it is important to look at the state in general and the Soviet system in particular in some detail.

Notwithstanding the unique features of the Soviet political system, current literature on state formation will aid our understanding of the Soviet experience. First, it explores the relationship between a state, its territory, and its borders in the modern era and the way in which the modern state evolved in Europe. Secondly, it examines the influence of the international environment upon the policies and institutions of a particular state. Territorial, class, and ethnic factors influence the choices of state leaders. Thirdly, the literature on state formation argues that new states tend to behave in particular ways. Finally, it suggests that states that do not adapt over time may face a difficult struggle for survival later on. These notions are worth examining in detail for their relevance to understanding the Soviet state, which began its life in a world in which territory was virtually synonymous with power and in which nationalism was stirring among the many East European and Asian ethnic groups that had hitherto been ruled by the great European empires.

BORDER CONTROL AND THE STATE

Drawing on Max Weber's influential definition, we shall consider the state as a permanent administrative organization that claims the right to enforce its laws within its territory, and to extract resources from the population (mainly through taxation) to support its activities.[18] There are two important dimensions to this understanding of the state: the structure of state organization, which gives rise to a complex bureaucracy; and the notion that the state uses force (namely the military, police, and prisons) in order to control the population and resources of a defined piece of territory over which it has exclusive claims. Much has been written in the theoretical literature about the state as a hierarchical organization, concentrating on the bureaucracy of its central power structures, but recently more attention has been paid to the state as a spatial entity in which power is dispersed across a defined expanse of land.[19] As Michael Mann points out, a state is a

territorially centralized form of organization. ... Only the state is inherently centralized over a delimited territory over which it has authoritative power. Unlike economic, ideological or military groups in civil society, the state elite's resources radiate authoritatively outward from a center but stop at defined territorial boundaries.[20]

This territorial quality is essential to the state, whose external boundaries encircle the residents over which the state rules. State policy, law, and obligations to the state are binding on all citizens.[21] Borders are the point at which the state's authority ceases; hence, they become a place where the state's power is vulnerable. Border controls arise from the state's attempt to address this vulnerability.

Border controls can be defined as the sum of a state's institutions to regulate the movement of people, communication, and goods across its international frontiers.[22] All modern sovereign states have some form of border controls to regulate who or what goods are allowed to enter and leave their territory: this is one of the key prerogatives of state sovereignty.[23] In fact, border controls can be seen as an important coercive mechanism for assuring the state's authority, by preventing citizen evasion of state policies such as taxation or the payment of tariffs through, for example, smuggling or flight. Albert O. Hirschman has discussed this as the state's struggle against "exit."[24] Following the work of Michel Foucault, Anthony Giddens discusses the importance of control of space and boundaries for state power: it provides enclosure, which helps to permit the exercise of vital state functions such as surveillance.[25] Border controls help to create the image of a powerful and forbidding state.[26]

Modern governments employ border controls to perform several functions: they help to maintain the state's territorial vigilance against military aggression; they monitor, for national security purposes, the traffic of people and goods entering and leaving a country; and they maintain the state's economic interests, such as maintaining customs prohibitions and tariff barriers. The degree of border control in states varies along a continuum from open borders, which hypothetically would allow free movement of people, goods, and ideas across state borders, and closed borders, which would impose extreme restrictions, limits, and state-imposed monopolies on the same. Most states fall somewhere on the continuum between these extremes. In this sense the USSR was not qualitatively different in its closed-border regime. But its coercive monopolies were far more sweeping and more efficient than those of most other states; the Soviet state had greater scope and technological power for overt coercion than, for instance, the early European states.[27]

Four aspects of scholarship on the state are particularly relevant to the issue of border controls and cross-boundary contacts of states. They focus, respectively, on the role of borders in the formative period of new states; the influence of the international environment; the pressures of borderland ethnic minorities, especially when the state is attempting to rein in recalcitrant periphery regions in an ethnically heterogenous population; and the development of bureaucracy. All these factors are potentially relevant to the Soviet state, which developed restrictive border controls early in its formative period as a multi-ethnic state, after several years of civil war, intervention, and military threats from foreign powers and after relying upon the Red Army to secure power over a number of restive nationalist borderland territories.

Social science thought on state formation emphasizes that international and domestic pressures on the state influence the types of institutions that the state adopts. The literature on state formation was pioneered by authors such as Charles Tilly, who explores the origins and development of European nation-states. The state-building model has also been applied to Third World countries to explain the particular problems of post-colonial states.[28] In general, the literature has sought to identify the role that the early period of state formation played in determining the nature and survival of the state. For instance, one view has stressed the international environment as crucial to state-building, as pressures from the international environment and the presence of security threats from powerful states influence the development of a would-be state.[29] Another view has emphasized the importance of the development of capitalism and relations of political leaders with various social classes.[30] Still another stresses the ability of state leaders to amass economic resources, by negotiation and persuasion as well as by force.[31] Finally, the successful development and deployment of military force has been considered one of the most crucial variables for state formation.[32] Yet all these factors are important and interrelated in state-building: as Tilly argues, amassing military force and capital are the driving state-building processes. A strong defence allows the state to resist foreign threats and gain new potential sources of wealth through conquest, while a military's upkeep requires sources of funding and an ability to solicit contributions from the population.[33] The literature also aims to account for variations between states, suggesting that their differences are caused by the particular social struggles and coalitions that emerge in the state-formation process.[34] Intense domestic political struggles often lead to the development of politicized coercive institutions.[35] Different forms of revenue collection influence political relations within the state: for instance, if the state finances itself by avenues other than taxation of citizens, then that might free regimes inclined towards authoritarianism from a sense of obligation to provide democratic rights to its citizenry.[36]

The literature on state formation also suggests that internal coercion, including border control, is useful for the purposes of establishing authority in outlying areas, enforcing state economic monopolies, and demarcating national identity. At a crucial early phase of this state-building process, border controls are introduced.[37] Hirschman suggests that in response to the assertion of authority by a new state, populations could resist through *exit*, that is to say by evading state control (for example, through emigration or secession), or through *voice*, by protesting and making political demands. States must be able to command compliance and obedience from the population so that citizens cannot simply evade or ignore any obligation the state imposes. New states thus might try to prevent exit, in a literal sense, by preventing populations from leaving or developing outside alliances.[38] Populations with ready access to the border could evade state control by fleeing to a neighbouring state whenever they broke the law, smuggled, or wished to evade military service or taxation.[39] To cope with these challenges, states develop varying approaches to "boundary-building," depending on the advantages and disadvantages of instituting various controls of movement between local populations across borders.[40] Hirschman notes that in Europe efforts to control exit require an extremely high concentration of coercive resources, and extends his paradigm to Stalinist Russia, noting its suppression of both exit and voice.[41] Yet over the long term the suppression of exit has costs: "The closure of boundaries tends to discourage investments, cause higher costs, and generally have depressing effects on economic activities, while open boundaries and energetic interactions with the environment tend to attract people and capital."[42]

The absolutist state's ability and desire to suppress exit, according to Hirschman, is tempered by capitalism and the existence of private "movable property," as it is in the state's interest to promote private capitalism and prevent capital flight.[43] The repressive mechanisms and methods adopted during the period of state formation, including border control, will be softened as the population recognizes the authority of the state and as capitalist trade develops. This approach suggests that we should try to ascertain whether the Soviet Union developed border controls as a defence mechanism to help contain the potential resistance of a restive population and to put up barriers to the perceived possibility of foreign encroachment from countries whose regimes were hostile to Communism or who sought to take advantage of the Bolshevik state's vulnerable territorial peripheries.

This leads to the hypothesis that a state is influenced by the type of political organization that prevails in the world around it. Since border controls by definition are instruments of both foreign relations and domestic policy, we must first take into account the international environment. There are times when states in general are more "autarkic" than at others, when there is a crisis of the international monetary system, or when upheavals bring waves of political refugees that other countries do not want to accept.[44] Peter Gourevitch has described how, in times of a difficult international economic situation, states may try to restrict transborder trade, as seemed to be the trend of the late nineteenth and early twentieth centuries.[45] States throughout the West and Latin America were also increasing their border controls for economic purposes in the interwar period.[46] Moreover, some scholars have noted that passport controls and restrictions of human movement across borders have been a twentieth-century phenomenon associated with the experience of great wars, which generated the need to control transborder movement for political security and health reasons, concurrent with the growth in the contemporary state's capacity to enforce such policies.[47] The Soviet Union was formed at a time when border controls in general seemed to be increasing, and its contrary stance to the capitalist world further strongly influenced its imposition of border controls. Today, by contrast, some interpret the growth of international trade and modern communications in the post–Second World War period as evidence that borders are becoming somehow less relevant.[48] Such diverse innovations as air travel, nuclear-security arrangements, economic organizations, and the computer revolution are, scholars argue, mediating influences that cut across state boundaries, allow for cross-border mobilization, and hence erode states' control over their borders.[49]

A further hypothesis holds that multi-ethnic states have particular concerns in imposing border controls, especially when an international border divides an ethnic group between two or more states. At boundaries, ethnic divisions between states become blurry, as often a border population shares cultural and linguistic traits with those just across the border in a neighbouring state.[50] Maintaining borders is of particular concern when an ethnic group's population is dispersed on both sides of the border between two states. This means that the population in the peripheral area near the border might find more in common with inhabitants across the border than with the representatives of the central authorities, and could lead the state to adopt measures to prevent secessionism and irredentism.[51] In multi-ethnic states, border controls provide a particularly important state-building function by helping to prevent territorial secession and to "create" separate national identities for potentially irredentist nationalities.[52] The historian Peter Sahlins writes that, in the case of France, arbitrarily drawn and enforced state boundaries eventually created a local population that had fewer contacts with, and saw themselves as a culturally distinct nation from, the inhabitants of northern Spain. Hence, boundaries were used by the state to help to shape national identity. This identity could be imposed solely by coercive means, but the state also co-opted local interests and drew local society at the border into a sense of nationhood.[53]

A series of hypotheses can be derived from the above theoretical literature. First, a state that is isolated internationally and is trying domestically to create a socio-economic regime different from that of its neighbours may close its borders to preserve its national interest. Secondly, a new state is likely to feel a need to assert border controls in order to establish its authority over the population in its territorial periphery and consolidate itself against foreign threats. Because border controls seal off internal oppositions from foreign contacts and support, states may impose them in order to contain the contacts and resources of secessionist movements and domestic political oppositions and to neutralize the influence of hostile foreign powers. Finally, economic factors are important: if a state establishes itself as the monopolistic controller over physical and human resources, then border controls will be necessary to enforce those monopolies. They are likely to be particularly valuable to state leaderships that pursue both monopolistic control over the economy and economic self-sufficiency. Given a combination of both domestic political-security threats and a state-centred, autarkic economy, a state will face intense pressures to create tight border controls. But an additional factor is necessary to create a strong border-control regime: effective state institutions capable of enforcing it. To be fully effective, border-control institutions must be geographically comprehensive across all border areas, and they must have bureaucracies that regulate all aspects of cross-border movement.

The Soviet Union was established as a consequence of the Russian

Revolution, a reality that compels us to consider the importance of border-control policy to the radical Bolshevik leadership. Post-revolutionary states seek first to consolidate power and then to initiate programs of socio-economic change.[54] Leninist-type regimes, which claim a strict monopoly over all state resources, have a great need not only to re-establish control over those resources as post-revolutionary systems but also to establish themselves as polities that possess a state-centred economic system.[55] There is a link between border control and state-sanctioned dramatic socio-economic change. Border controls can help to ensure that the state controls the commerce within its jurisdiction, and can enable the internal economy to preserve its autonomy from international capitalist market forces. In the Soviet case, border controls made it prohibitively difficult for individuals to profit from cross-border trade, move their wealth abroad, or import goods from the West.

The three approaches mentioned above are all relevant to the Soviet state. Border controls developed at a relatively early point in Soviet state-building, and the emphasis on border controls shares the pattern of early state formation described by Hirschman, Samuel E. Finer, and Stein Rokkan. The Bolshevik Revolution occurred in an international environment where the state system was the prevailing means of political organization; being political realists, Soviet leaders consolidated their rule in the form of the state, facing strong pressures from the international environment.[56] Surrounded by autonomous, compact states that prioritized military power and were mostly ill disposed towards them, the Bolsheviks moulded their ideology and socialist goals in an international context when border controls seemed necessary and where the autarkic command economy depended on border controls to facilitate the conservation and development of resources.

Finally, the question of national identity, especially in the so-called borderlands of the USSR, constituted one of the Bolsheviks' most pressing security concerns, and created a potential for irredentism at various points along the Soviet border. Historically, empires have been threatened when peripheral social movements come in contact with international forces such as the spread of nationalist ideas.[57] Some scholars have argued that Soviet leaders, concerned over the proximity of ethnic groups to national movements in neighbouring countries, appropriated the principle of national self-determination in order to gain control over the non-Russian nationalities.[58] For example, as Paul Austin has argued in the case of the Karelian Finns, the Soviet Union's language and alphabet policy sometimes served to deny links with ethnic groups abroad and to promote ties with Russia.[59] Meanwhile, scholars have also argued that inter-republican boundaries helped to promote divisions within ethnic groups, in order to prevent the threatening emergence of broader unions against Soviet rule such as pan-Turkism and *jadidism* among Central Asians and Tatars, a rising movement in the late nineteenth and early twentieth centuries.[60] This problem could affect internal boundaries as well: administrative boundaries were particularly complex and cumbersome in the North Caucasus, where the Sufi Islamic movement known as Muridism and the leadership of Shamil had helped to unify the peoples of the North Caucasus to unite to fight Russian expansion in the nineteenth century.[61] Nationalism is rightly considered to have been one of the Soviet government's biggest problems. A case in point was the Ukrainian nationalist movement, which had sought to establish links with the Galician Ukrainians, formerly under the rule of the Austro-Hungarian Empire and who came under Polish rule after the First World War. The Galician Ukrainians had developed more advanced nationalist traditions and cultural institutions than the Eastern Ukrainians of the former Russian Empire.[62] The Soviet Union thus had an obvious interest in suppressing communication with Western Ukraine, Turkey, Finland, and Poland. Border controls in this context could serve to thwart the prospective nation-building processes of groups who spanned the Soviet border and prevent their access to potentially hostile foreign governments.

Due to the particularly politicized nature of border areas during the revolution, border control was a high priority of the new Bolshevik state. Border areas were highly strategic and sensitive for the Bolshevik leaders, but they were also remote and difficult to penetrate. This postrevolutionary dilemma proved to be greatly problematic, and border restrictions resulted in part from the Soviet state's problems in assimilating the border areas and the territorial periphery in general. The post-revolutionary Soviet regime had to re-establish state control over peripheral areas of territory and to rebuild state institutions that had broken down with the fall of the tsarist empire.[63] The link between these states and internal oppositions in the USSR was a strong motivation for border controls. Moreover, the Soviet Union's revolutionary policies themselves created upheaval that led to mass dislocations and migrations; border controls responded to the ensuing need for stabilization. The Bolshevik leadership, particularly Stalin, bear responsibility for this resistance.[64]

By the late 1930s the Soviet Union's border-control system was sufficiently strong to serve the state's monopolies over resources and to exercise the degree of coercion and surveillance needed for this purpose. Border controls were enforced over all aspects of international movements: for internal security, restriction of migration and travel, trade, and communications. Since private trade and mass travel were not permitted, border controls took on a prohibitive character. Their main function was to prevent the transfer of goods, people, and ideas to and from foreign countries and to maintain the state's exclusive right to select, limit, and benefit from all such transfers. In addition, official ideology *reinforced* the system. Political and state-building dilemmas, and domestic and international resistance to the construction of a redistributive socialist state, contributed to the creation of a new ideology of isolation.

Secondly, border control followed from particular economic and political choices undertaken by the Soviet leadership.[65] It is important to specify exactly what these choices were and how central initiatives led to concrete state structures. Soviet leaders aimed to create a state-controlled, self-sufficient socialist economy. Jerry Hough has correctly assessed the Soviet political-economic system as "protectionist." Hough sees the "Iron Curtain" as an accompaniment to the protectionist economy and anti-Western nationalism of the Bolsheviks.[66] The ideologically based nationalizations of private property and foreign trade had extremely important consequences for the adoption of border-control policies. The regimentation and conservation of labour, the concentration of state resources and currency, and the collectivization of agriculture all in their turn contributed in some way to the development of border controls. As the Soviet state adopted dramatic policies of rapid industrialization and collectivization of the land, the border-control system, like Stalinism in general, underwent a qualitative change to reach a new level of restrictiveness.[67]

A final important factor to consider is the nature of the growth and capacity of Soviet state institutions. Over time, a border-control apparatus developed in the USSR that was increasingly impenetrable, backed by state resources, coercive power, and numerous levels of restrictions. Many state organizations were involved in it, duplicating and monitoring each other's functions, in a way that served to enforce its restrictiveness. Meanwhile, the power of the secret police over border control and the use of terror under Stalin helped to entrench a set of norms and procedures based on the view that allowing emigration and travel was a political risk.[68] The multifaceted institutional network of the border-control system, like other parts of the Soviet bureaucratic system, had so many layers that it became difficult to change, and the piecemeal partial liberalizations of Khrushchev and Brezhnev did little to penetrate it.

Therefore, what is noteworthy about Soviet border controls is not merely their creation and intensification during the formative years under the leadership of Lenin and Stalin but their persistence decades after the Second World War, even as the Soviet Union became a super-power. As Peter J. Katzenstein has noted, "the factors that create polit-ical regimes are not identical with those that maintain them."[69] The Soviet Union's attachment to coercion and state control long defied political science theories that, in the long term, states must adapt to change and accomodate the demands of citizens.[70] The ability to change and to respond to new situations has been identified as crucial to a state's long-term viability. Samuel P. Huntington argues that the ability to adapt to changed circumstances was one of the four essential characteristics of a strong, stable political system.[71] Not all state bureaucracies are able to adapt smoothly to changed horizons: institu-tions build up their own rules and vested interests and can block reform initiatives even when political leadership demands their imple-mentation.[72] States tend to develop institutions that respond to politi-cal struggles and cleavages at their earliest phases of development, such that a mature state may still possess institutions that reflect the needs of earlier times.[73] When these needs are outgrown, the organizations that serve them are not always re-examined in a timely way: institu-tions tend to maintain their existing rules and behaviour rather than adapt to new circumstances; the choice of certain types of institutions leads to the entrenchment of values that shape future political options, and thus to the creation of complex structures that are difficult to change easily.[74] The more fundamental the change in the system, the more complex and expensive institutional reform will be.[75] Therefore, the institutional choices that a new state's leaders make will have a last-ing impact for the direction of that state, and a state may remain vigi-lant against its earliest challenges, even when they no longer exist.

The Soviet Union was a state whose leaders were highly preoccupied with maintaining national unity through coercive power. The exces-siveness of this power, and the bureaucracy's stubborn resilience despite reform attempts, are often seen today as contributing to the Soviet Union's ultimate downfall.[76] The Soviet border-control regime was one component of that restrictive, prohibitive state bureaucracy. However, the fall of the USSR has attracted attention *because* the Bol-shevik regime's post-revolutionary consolidation and expansion of power after the 1917 Revolution was so spectacular. While as narrow an issue as border control cannot explain the entire rise and fall of the USSR, it can reveal over a long historical span the strengths and weak-nesses of this particular state sector in microcosm. The USSR's border controls were a product of the interaction of three elements: first, seri-ous internal security threats and political instability in the country's territorial peripheries; second, autarkic and resource-mobilizing strate-gies of economic and political development chosen by Soviet leaders;

and third, the existence of effective bureaucratic and coercive state capacities to which responsibilities for border control were delegated – institutions whose autonomy from society, extensive deployment in border areas, and intra-bureaucratic complexity were uniquely capable of strictly limiting cross-border movement. These three factors reinforced each other: the presence and intensity of all three contributed to the development and maintenance of a strong border-control regime. The development of highly coercive border-control institutions was an instrument of the state-building process and was designed to a great extent to fulfil an internal function, to extend state control inward towards the interior. Therefore, let us turn our attention to the case-study, beginning with the 1917 Bolshevik Revolution.

3 Borderland Sovereignty Struggles and the Creation of the Soviet State, 1917–1922

The Bolshevik Revolution of October 1917, led by Vladimir Ilyich Lenin, established a radical Marxist-inspired government in Soviet Russia that immediately embarked on a program of radical socialist redistribution. However, amidst the upheaval of the First World War, the Bolsheviks faced a chaotic economic situation and a burgeoning refugee problem; in order to establish their workers' state, they would have to consolidate their power over a territory whose communications networks and political loyalties had become extremely fragmented. They also found that the nationalization of property created resistance, in the form of emigration, capital flight, and open military challenges. Both these sets of problems led the Bolsheviks to regard the establishment of firm borders as crucial to establishing and maintaining their power. In addition, Soviet leaders confronted the need to make decisions about the form of border controls to adopt, whether local or central governments would administer them, and exactly which state organs should control them. This chapter lays out the process of setting up border controls that evolved during the Soviet state's earliest moments of state-building.

Until the 1917 Revolution the Bolsheviks never really considered details of border or customs controls. Prior to their seizure of power, the Bolsheviks saw customs agents, military installations, and restrictions on emigration and immigration as routinized elements of coercion that bolstered bourgeois capitalist states, or identified them with the oppressive tsarist regime. According to Leonid Krasin, the People's Commissar of Foreign Trade under Lenin's regime, the Bolsheviks upon coming to power had very little use for border control even as an economic instrument. Customs control (*tamozhniia*) was seen as a mechanism used by the bourgeois state to protect capitalist industry. Hence the Bolsheviks planned, after the Revolution, to abolish existing customs institutions, and even talked of converting the Moscow Customs House into a public bath-house.[1] Yet, as former émigré subversives themselves, the Bolsheviks were particularly aware of the potential danger of the subversion of the state from abroad.[2] While Lenin's leadership faced pressures to institute border controls, they developed in a rather haphazard manner.

Generally, Bolshevik leaders offered few ideological justifications for the imposition of border controls. At the Seventh All-Russian Conference of the RSDRP (Russian Social Democratic Workers' Party) Lenin claimed that, notwithstanding the Bolshevik Revolution, Russia still needed to observe and protect its state borders.[3] An appeal to a local border population stated that people must understand that even Communists needed to uphold state borders in the interim period of socialist transition, but that they would be dispensed with as soon as the world revolution came.[4] Another document rationalized, "We are not fighting on the Czechoslovak front, but the class front."[5] According to one Soviet scholar, Lenin initially advocated "democratic" state borders, to be determined according to the principles of self-determination; however, with the treaty of Brest-Litovsk there was an increased *Realpolitik* awareness that borders would separate the Soviet republic from aggressive imperialism.[6] State borders thus were given a class character following the Bolshevik Revolution; the Soviet Union's international borders became the dividing line between capitalist and socialist social systems. They were no longer just the borders between states but between competing social systems.[7]

Marxist ideology influenced the political struggles between the Bolsheviks and their opponents, which led to the desire for politically secure borders. At the same time, "internationalist" ideology was also used to justify open contacts with other Communist parties, cultural exchanges, and the like, but with the proviso that these exchanges were to be sponsored by the state. The Soviet state emerged from the idea of revolutionary sovereignty, which posited the state as the territorial unit that constituted the revolution. The Bolsheviks became determined to establish their rule over the territory of the former tsarist empire, even if this involved expansionism into non-Russian areas, in order to defend against the spread of capitalism.[8] Once the revolution had to be defended, military and border-control institutions represented the territorial dimension of the revolution. Exit controls originated not to choke off travel and emigration for its own sake but from the desire to limit and regulate them to encourage positive forms of "international-ism" rather than the negative international contacts associated with capitalism and counter-revolution. In addition, Soviet policy observed these internationalist ideals by permitting the immigration of *bona fide* political refugees and sympathizers as immigrants.[9] A decree of the All-Russian Central Executive Committee of 5 March 1918 allowed foreigners to come to the USSR as refugees.[10] As the first self-defined workers' state, the USSR became a sort of a haven for "fellow-travellers" and victims of political persecution. But there was increasing concern to screen incomers who might secretly harbour opposition towards the regime.

There were five main problems in the early post-revolutionary period that contributed to the Bolsheviks' creation of border controls: the determination of state borders in a hostile international environment; the struggle with White oppositions to Soviet rule, especially in border territories; mass population movements in and out of Soviet territory; the question of national self-determination in former tsarist border-lands versus centralized state control over territories of the old empire; and finally, the economic crises variously created and inherited by the Bolsheviks. Corresponding to the first factor described in chapter 2, these all constitute parts of the immediate structural problems facing the Soviet regime in its state-building phase, problems that led the regime to establish border-control mechanisms. The long-term structural dilemmas facing the Soviet regime on its peripheries, which contributed to the increasingly restrictive nature of Soviet border controls in the 1930s, will be explored in chapter 5. But it is necessary to discuss the Soviet regime's early context, the conditions under which its territorial authority was formed.

First of all, the uncertainty of borders, and the fragility of Bolshevik state structures during the Civil War, led to confusion over exactly what the Soviet state's borders were and who controlled them. Different organs of authority operated on different territories of what had been the Russian Empire. The structures of the former tsarist state that served to hold it together territorially had broken down or been severed: its transportation and communications systems, its networks of economic exchange, and its military forces.[11] Recent scholarship on the Bolshevik Revolution and the Civil War has vividly described the degree of turmoil in the country, the breakdown of authority, and the difficulties of re-establishing functioning political institutions in the chaotic situation at hand.[12] It apparently took tsarist border troops operating in remote parts of the country some time to realize that they no longer represented anyone.[13]

Under these conditions the new Soviet state was in a position of relative weakness in the international arena, while it confronted newly formed independent states and often hostile governments on its borders. The Bolsheviks felt excluded from the peace process that decided the boundaries of Eastern Europe, and mistrusted the intentions of Western states towards Soviet Russia.[14] They did not want to lose Lithuania or Belorussia to "Polish imperialism," for example.[15] Meanwhile, Germany and Poland sought to contain their borders against Bolshevism, a phenomenon that, with the Hungarian Revolution of 1918, appeared to be in danger of spreading.[16] In 1919–20 the Russo-Polish War took place, in which Poles received French assistance, and as a result of the Treaty of Riga the Soviet Union lost parts of Belorussia and Ukraine.[17] Moreover, Soviet leaders feared that French-Polish co-operation in setting up the *cordon sanitaire* would encourage the political activity of émigré anti-Soviet groups on the borders.[18] The *cordon sanitaire* was complemented by the Polish-Romanian and Czech-Romanian alliance in 1921, and the Czech-French alliance of 1924.[19]

The uneasiness resulting from the support that the Western powers gave to these aspiring states and regimes contributed to the Bolsheviks' desire to seal off Soviet borders, which were, after all, borders with new significance: the Baltic states, Poland, Finland, and Bessarabia were no longer under Russian jurisdiction, and this created new borders that were more clearly defined, contentious, and insecure than before. The breakdown of Russian defence capabilities that preceded the 1917 Revolution meant that the country lost its ability to maintain control over peripheral parts of the country. This allowed the development of alternative sovereignties, ties, and allegiances with bordering countries and populations. Independent national governments were formed in Ukraine, the Caucasus, and the Baltic states, while other areas, such as Bessarabia, were conquered by other states.[20] The Soviet government would have to rebuild the state completely if it were to restore and control its former territorial borders.[21]

Along with the issue of contending territorial sovereignties there was also the fact that political oppositions tended to become concentrated in areas far from the regime's centre of power either because they were banished there or because they sought a small territorial base from which to build up power. During the Civil War the White opposition conceded Bolshevik authority in Russian centres but managed to develop strongholds in territories on the periphery – witness the Mensheviks in newly independent Georgia, the Socialist Revolutionaries in parts of Siberia, and various monarchist groups on the western border. In addition, the Bolsheviks had to deal with the incursions of bandit groups in remote parts of the country close to the border, such as those of Ataman Semenev in Manchuria and Boris Savinkov on the Polish border.[22] During the Civil War it was difficult to separate the border from the front.[23]

Lenin deemed it necessary to cut off the Whites' support from abroad in order to end the military threat to Bolshevik rule.[24] Baron von Wrangel, one of the anti- Bolshevik White leaders, had written in an appeal for support from the Allies in 1919 that the fragile governments in the borderlands could be safeguarded relatively easily, with minimal forces, from the encroachments of the Bolsheviks.[25] While the Bolsheviks tried to incorporate and set up their own border troops, using various competing organizations themselves, at least one of their opponents in the Civil War was trying to set up its own customs and other organs on the lines it controlled.[26] The Bolsheviks gained back an impressive amount of Russia's pre-war territory after fighting on various fronts.[27] The Soviet regime would conceive of its sovereignty as encompassing most of the jurisdiction of the territory of the former Russian Empire, and would define its borders accordingly.[28]

Even after the defeat of the Whites in the Civil War, the Bolsheviks felt weakest in the border areas of the country.[29] The remnants of White military formations, nationalist guerrilla organizations, and governments-in-exile continued to be significant actors outside of Soviet territory well beyond the post-revolutionary period, and some of those players engaged in overt military activity in Soviet border areas or tried to undermine the Soviet government by demanding legitimate representation at international conferences or organizations.[30] The new government also wanted to prevent anti-Soviet groups from having access to printing presses, paper, and other resources abroad, or from taking such printed materials out of the country, and to prevent anti-Bolshevik émigré printed materials from coming in.[31] After the First World War broke down intra-state networks of communication within the Russian Empire, populations in border areas began to communicate and trade more with populations in other countries. This led the Bolsheviks to seek control over such communications.[32]

The next problem of the border areas was the sum of mass population movements accompanying the end of the war and the Revolution. In his discussion of population changes in Europe during and between the world wars Eugene M. Kulischer argues that in Russia, revolution and mass migration, both within and outside the country, were products of the instability and destruction of the First World War.[33] The Bolsheviks faced the disorder caused by the mass movement of refugees on the Western border, which was straining local resources and disrupting transportation.[34] The problem was exacerbated by the state's monopoly on transportation, which effectively limited travel into and out of the country as the state requisitioned scarce transport resources for military purposes.[35] Many East European refugees were prevented from leaving the country because of the reluctance of the Revolutionary-Military Council (Revvoensovet) to let people cross the front lines. The hardships of stranded refugees vexed the local Soviet officials responsible for areas containing migrants or wounded combatants, who were now unable to return to their homes. Military authorities argued that strict restrictions on crossing the front lines were necessary for security reasons. In general, Revvoensovet was highly reluctant to allow population movements across the Western front because they would impede military operations.[36] So the refugees continued to gather.[37] Eventually, agreements were signed allowing the repatriation of refugees, and various exchanges of citizens and prisoners-of-war were conducted.[38]

The refugee problem during the Civil War was also in part a result of internal upheavals. Those who left Russia in the early years of the Revolution included political émigrés as well as people fleeing famine, and Jews, who fled outbreaks of ethnic violence during the Civil War.[39] By the most reliable estimate, 2 million refugees left Russia from 1914 to 1926.[40] Emigration consisted not just of masses of individuals but also of organizations and branches of organizations such as the Russian Orthodox Church and the Socialist Revolutionary, Menshevik, and Kadet parties; later, they would be joined by members of defeated White armies. They might go eastward, towards Manchuria from Siberia, or westward, like the many refugees who settled in Prague or Berlin.[41] Émigrés could be a threat to the Soviet regime in so far as they were opponents contending for power or claimed to be the legitimate representatives of internal resistance movements.[42] Iurii Felshtinskii claims that the flight to Finland of some one thousand participants in the 1921 Kronstadt uprising influenced future attitudes towards emigration.[43]

Lenin was also concerned with the possible links between emigrés and foreign powers.[44] Future border controls would try to limit the activity and influence of such opponents, neutralizing their contact with people inside the country; in 1921 laws were introduced to revoke the citizenship of people who had left Soviet Russia without permission, who had served in White armies, or who had been abroad more than five years without applying for Soviet citizenship.[45] Moreover, Iurii Felshtinskii argues, restrictions on the travel of military-age men in the 1920s were aimed at preventing them from joining foreign or émigré armies.[46] The White emigration was seen as a "new form of class struggle" wherein its members engaged in propaganda against the Bolshevik regime and formed alliances with capitalist powers.[47] Finally, many political immigrants and refugees came into the country in the early 1920s, causing a strain on the organs of social welfare.[48]

ECONOMIC CONCERNS AND REDISTRIBUTION

While the economic dimensions of border control will be discussed more thoroughly in the next chapter, the early economic crises the Soviets faced on the border were decisive. As a result of the economic collapse, shortages of basic foodstuffs and manufactured items led to a desire to ensure that they were not smuggled out of the country or smuggled in by profiteers. At least initially the Bolsheviks, in their professed goal to set up a government acting in the interests of the masses, sought to provide them with cheap goods and food. As prominent Bolshevik theorist Nikolai Bukharin wrote in 1918, the government took upon itself the responsibility to supply basic necessities in order to provide workers with food and eliminate speculation, which he saw as a form of capitalism in which entrepreneurs made profits from people's hardship.[49] Efforts were made to prevent "speculators" in food and goods from bringing their wares across the border illegally.[50] The reasoning was that as long as such profiteers existed, there would be challenges to Bolshevik rule. Eventually, the Soviet customs service and border troops would be agents of the campaign to eliminate private trade and consolidate the Soviet state's monopoly over the country's valuable resources – a political, not just an economic goal. Private property, which generated capital by exploiting labour to create profit, was in the Marxist view the distinguishing feature of capitalism and its greatest evil. The elimination of private property led to the state's expropriation of land, resources, and goods from companies and churches, and even the conspicuous possessions of bourgeois or aristocratic individuals. In fact, a number of early border-control measures were taken to prevent the possibility of capital flight; members of the aristocratic and bourgeois classes were trying to cut their losses by fleeing abroad with resources that now belonged to the state.

Immediately after the 1917 Revolution the Bolsheviks began to worry about the possibility that emigrants would take abroad wealth and possessions now deemed the rightful property of the workers' state. The nationalization of the banks soon after the October Revolution occurred in part to prevent the flight of gold abroad. As early as 11 November 1917 the *ad hoc* government, the Military-Revolutionary Committee, noted the need to prevent valuables from being taken out of the country.[51] In addition, various measures were passed to prevent the removal of gold and other valuables beyond Russia's borders: the removal of precious metals, large amounts of currency, or firearms from the country were all prohibited.[52] Though exact figures are unknown, there were considerable losses through capital flight during the revolutionary and Civil War periods.[53] During the particularly militant period of "war communism" the Soviet government tried, as of 25 July 1918, to take control of all gold and foreign-currency transactions, and the Commissariat of Finance was to regulate the exit of hard currency (*valiuta*) abroad.[54] The war-communism policy included seizure of precious metals and hard currency, to be turned over to the state; this went into effect through a decree issued 17 October 1921.[55] Other directives were passed to prevent the removal of musical instruments, paintings, and foodstuffs.[56] In 1922 the Council of People's Commissars passed a decree on customs control, which declared that the customs regimen was in place to implement previous decrees that had called for the requisition and confiscation of goods of individuals and societies; consequently, goods in excess of specified regulations could be confiscated.[57]

The Bolshevik decree establishing the state monopoly on foreign trade in April 1918 did not mention border or customs controls, although some such controls would be needed to enforce this monopoly.[58] In one author's estimation, the April 1918 decree formed the basis of Soviet customs administration.[59] In June 1918 the former Department of Customs Collection was renamed the Main Administration of Customs Control and made part of the People's Commissariat of Trade and Industry.[60] In 1919 contraband was defined as comprising all goods entering and leaving the country without permission.[61]

By mid-1918 economic imperatives and the nationalization of trade and industry had become a significant focus of the demand for a border guard. Early proponents of the creation of border-control organs argued that the post-revolutionary Soviet state would have a greater concern than the previous tsarist government for economic control of the border.[62] This new concern for customs represented more than a simple acknowledgment of the economic pressures on the Soviet state. It also assumed a crucial political function, in a situation in which smuggling over ill-defined borders had become easy, capital flight and the black market fueled the revolutionaries' will to control and maximize resources, and economic contraband was closely related to political opposition in borderland territories. As Krasin writes, instituting border controls was a corollary of the Soviet regime's need to re-establish control over peripheral territories and to rebuild state institutions. On the Soviet periphery, political opponents tended to seek sources of income and supply from abroad, while the state's denial of the right to trade privately with territories across the border in turn fueled political opposition.[63] The Soviet customs system was established in large part to prevent the loss of resources from the country.

EARLY SOVIET BORDER-CONTROL MEASURES

How did these structural dilemmas lead to the creation of new institutions? A number of writers on the establishment of Soviet government point to the early confusion of functions of state, party, and soviet (council) organs. A vacuum was created when some state institutions broke down, while conflict ensued when others persisted. New, *ad hoc* organizations, such as "extraordinary commissions," sprang up to fill the gaps.[64] Control of foreign trade and border points were seen by the Bolsheviks as one of the early measures necessary for consolidating power.[65] Stability and control on the borders was perceived as a necessary prerequisite for establishing and consolidating Soviet rule within the country; yet the difficulties of organizing effective border control were no less than the difficulties of establishing central government authority.[66] Despite the strategic and political importance of border-control structures, the extent of Soviet borders and their distance from the centre made policy difficult to implement, and there was a considerable time lag. In the Far Eastern Republic, for example, the organization of Soviet border control was only beginning in 1921.[67]

As early as 3 November 1917 the Military-Revolutionary Committee of the Petrograd Soviet passed a decision to close the state borders.[68] One of the first tasks of the Military-Revolutionary Committee was to establish control of foreign trade outlets and border points deemed to be of importance. It took responsibility for issuing exit visas.[69] On 12 November the Military-Revolutionary Committee released its first border regulations, which allowed border crossings (in the few areas where the Bolsheviks had control of border posts) only with its permission and restricted the removal of gold, currency, or firearms from the country.[70] On 17 December 1917 a general statute on entry and exit required a passport, with permission from the Commissariats of Internal Affairs and Foreign Affairs, for exit from the country, and required permission from the local Cheka and military authorities.[71] A circular was sent in January 1918 to Russian consulates, missions, and embassies asserting Soviet control over the granting of visas to enter the country, and stating that those desiring to immigrate as political sympathizers should be allowed in unconditionally.[72]

The Military-Revolutionary Committee's border-control functions were taken over by the Cheka, or All-Russian Extraordinary Commission for Combatting Counterrevolution, Speculation and Sabotage, often described as the forerunner of the Soviet secret police. The Cheka became an increasingly powerful institution. On 30 March 1918 the Main Administration for Border Control was formed, but it consisted largely of presumably unreliable personnel from the tsarist border corps.[73] Two organs were established: the Main Administration of Border Control (GUPO) and the Soviet of Border Control. These two organs were located in the People's Commissariat of Finance (Narkomfin), in conformity with the border guards' subordination to the Ministry of Finance before the Revolution. The Bolsheviks noted, however, that structural changes in administration would be required to make border-control functions serve the Revolution.[74] It was the need to unseat the previous Russian border-control authorities, such as they were, that contributed to the desire to establish new organs in this capacity: in June 1918 Lenin expressed alarm over an apparent outbreak of banditry and extortion by a border unit in the Kursk area, which was terrorizing the local population, and demanded that local authorities take action against them. Similar activity seems to have occurred along the former Western border.[75]

In order to combat the uncertainty and confusion regarding border activity, the Cheka publication *Ezhenedel'nik Vecheka* called for the creation of an effective border guard. It noted that smuggling and speculation were rife on the borders, creating thriving border towns where illicit trade was going on.[76] An article called for the establishment of well-trained border *chekas* to include recruits from the local population. In addition, the *chekas* would combat counter-revolutionary activity on the border and monitor the passage of people and goods.[77] One argument in favour of a separate border guard was the complaint that the Red Army in the areas of the front was committing abuses against citizens and could not be trusted to carry out its border-control functions. A separate customs apparatus was hence necessary to guard against the "hooliganism" of Red Army harassment at border stations.[78]

A decree on border control was adopted 28 May 1918; it established the tasks of border control and designated border zones (*polosy*) which were to be cleared of buildings or agricultural fields and reserved for the establishment of border posts. In addition, a special commission composed of representatives of various People's Commissariats met in late July and early August 1918 to discuss border issues and means of strengthening border controls.[79] The decree formally established a frontier guard (*Pogranichnaia Okhrana*) attached to a Frontier Guard Council under two commissars and a military director, within the administrative responsibility of Narkomfin. On 29 June 1918 the Main Administration of Border Protection was given over to the People's Commissariat of Trade and Industry (Narkomtorg). Later it would fall under the reorganized People's Commissariat of Foreign Trade (Narkomvneshtorg).[80] Local *chekas*, at the same time, were expected to observe people travelling across the border, monitor the activities of foreigners, and verify entry and exit documents.[81]

Under the conditions of the Civil War there were a great many problems in setting up a border guard. Border-troop leaders complained that their forces remained a very low priority in the regime's military considerations.[82] Initially, one of the main rationales advanced for the creation of a border guard was to free Red Army Troops from the mundane tasks of checking the documents of people crossing the border.[83] However, the Red Army had priority over troop allocations, and military authorities continually conflicted with the agencies that advocated a special border-control force, while agencies themselves battled over who should control this force. In peripheral territories the Red Army conflicted with the Cheka over who was responsible for what activities, since political and military, internal and external functions were blurred.[84] The General Staff of the Red Army wanted a controlling interest: they proposed dividing the border guard by functions, with its militarized part to go to the army. This was opposed by NKTIP (the People's Commissariat of Trade and Industry), which objected that any division or transfer of the border guard would weaken its ability to carry out its specialized functions. In November 1918, after a request from Revvoensovet, the border guards were subordinated into general military requirements. In July of the following year a number of border-guard divisions were transferred to the military commissariat.[85] However, some army leaders claimed that the border guards' dismemberment and integration into the army only confused the army.[86]

In addition, border guards conflicted with local governments and their *chekas*. Local leaders complained that border units were being formed without consultation with local Soviets.[87] The central Cheka, meanwhile, had formed its own political border organs. The Cheka had to fill in the gaps of the ineffective GUPO organization. At the first Cheka conference in July 1918 the frontier guard was criticized for its poor performance, and one of the military commissars in charge of it, Frolov, wrote to Dzerzhinskii on 31 July asking for Cheka aid to enforce order in the frontier zone. By 1 September there were thirty-four frontier *chekas*. A Cheka sub-department for frontiers was created, and frontier *chekas* were also administratively integrated into the system of local soviets. The responsibilities and procedures of frontier *chekas* (to help the customs service and frontier guard) were defined, including controlling documents, contraband, and apprehending spies.[88]

The border-control authorities were increasingly preoccupied with the political-security problems of refugees and immigrants. According to Iurii Felshtinskii, while the first Soviet immigration positions allowed for the entry of political refugees, in 1919 the Russian People's Commissariat of Internal Affairs (Narkomvnudel)[89] required the registration of foreigners in order to monitor their activities better, and required them to have visas to visit other Soviet republics.[90] Doubtless out of concern for border incursions, in 1921 Cheka border personnel were instructed to examine closely the class status of apprehended border violators, and those of higher class standing were to be either deported or arrested as spies.[91]

The Military-Revolutionary Council and the Cheka at times attempted, seemingly in vain, to clear the border *polosa* of refugees and send them back to the interior. The enterprising individuals who offered to smuggle refugees across the border for a price added to the confusion, while Jewish organizations charged that the Cheka was terrorizing the Jewish refugees who were attempting to flee Ukraine.[92] In 1921 thousands of Jews who wanted to flee Ukraine assembled on the Romanian border. The Soviet government tried to organize commissions in the border localities to deal with the problem and to ensure that those who were qualified to work would stay, as they were needed in the factories. It called upon the Ukrainian Communist Party's Jewish Department to conduct an agitation campaign against emigration abroad.[93] Even in this early period the Bolsheviks tried to prevent the emigration of Jews, particularly of able-bodied people deemed suitable for labour or military service, and had to be cajoled into allowing the departure of elderly Jews and women with husbands abroad.[94] In no uncertain terms the Soviet government tried to banish all would-be emigrants from the border zone, threatening the most severe punishment.[95] Officials were concerned that the refugees along the border were further disrupting the economic situation because they were selling their valuables in the border areas in order to raise money, while smugglers and speculators found in them an active market for foreign currency and assistance to cross the border illegally.[96] At the same time Soviet officials expressed concern for the refugees on the humanitarian grounds of lack of money and resources to travel and live abroad.

The official date of the founding of the Soviet border guard, which became celebrated as an annual holiday, is 15 February 1921. On this day a formal instruction was issued establishing a special department of the Cheka that was given sole responsibility for guarding the borders.[97] Gradually, border-control functions, long confined mostly to the Western border, were assigned to other parts of Soviet territory. In 1921 the Cheka and the Red Army divided responsibility for the border troops, and in September 1922 the Cheka's successor organization, OGPU, formed a separate frontier corps.[98] The new border troops were not yet a smoothly functioning organization. Located essentially in the middle of nowhere, border guards suffered from supply problems that would continue to plague them for years to come and complained of their lack of access to news: one wonders how well and how quickly they were informed of what was going on.[99] They would also spend some years adjusting to changes made in the border in response to various arrangements with other powers, and to the conversion and creation of border stations in new areas at least into 1922.[100] The political reliability of troops was also questionable and would also be an ongoing concern.[101]

None the less, with the end of the Civil War in 1921 there was an element of stability in that the Soviet state had essentially determined the borders of its territory. On 30 December 1920 the RSFSR and Soviet Ukraine signed a treaty that in effect created joint statehood, and were joined by the Republic of Belorussia, which signed a treaty with the RSFSR.[102] The RSFSR signed a treaty with Turkey regarding its borders on 2 July 1921, followed on 13 October by a similar treaty with Turkey and the trans-Caucasus republics. On 30 September 1921 a treaty between the RSFSR and Azerbaijan and Armenia gave control of the military, foreign commerce, finance, and international relations in those republics to Moscow.[103] Following the invasion of Georgia by the Red Army, the customs and border guards between the three Caucasian republics and Russia were removed.[104] But issues of sovereignty and border control were still in question: in 1921 Ukraine was granting its own passports and visas for travel across its borders.[105]

Only gradually were All-Union controls established on the borders of the republics. The USSR treaty of 1922 did not mention border control, nor customs, as a unified-state function.[106] Various republics signed treaties with neighbouring countries allowing for border crossings that were, at times, more liberal than those allowed by general policy.[107] The USSR constitution of 1923 (article 1) gave the Soviet Union the right to settle questions of the republics' frontiers, though theoretically each republic controlled its own frontiers.[108]

With the close of the Civil War the diplomatic recognition gradually extended by other countries would largely relieve the Soviet regime of fear of its borders being violated. Various treaties and foreign-relations efforts were made by Soviet authorities regarding the border.[109] In March 1922 the neighbouring countries attending the Genoa Conference resolved to facilitate free movement of citizens across the territory of those countries. A border commission had been set up with Poland, but various protests were made to Poland in 1922 about violations and incursions.[110] There were similar conflicts with other countries. Protests were made to Estonia in 1921 over the latter's alleged indifference to the volume of contraband on the Estonian-Russian border, for helping the activities of the "Committee for the Aid of Karelia," and also for harbouring illegally exported gold from RSFSR. Tense relations with bordering countries such as Romania and Poland contributed strongly to the desire to control Soviet borders tightly, as did the general uncertainty of intentions and allegiances during this period. As Kamenev said at the Tenth Party Congress in 1921, officially the war in Europe was over, but in fact interstate boundaries were still not decisively stabilized.[111]

The outcome of all these developments was a border-control policy that was an outgrowth of military and political exigencies; this process was influenced highly by the success of the secret police in gaining the upper hand in control over borders,[112] and by the influence of political-security concerns in shaping the institutions and policies governing border control. The Bolshevik state had managed under conditions of severe political conflict to survive and to carve out its borders as a territorial unit, as well as to establish the framework for its border-control structures. The increasing rigidity and restrictiveness of border-control measures in the Soviet system was conditioned by three factors: the Soviet state's economic and developmental strategies, the continuing state-building dilemmas of extending state authority into borderland territories, and the development of centralized bureaucratic and coercive institutions capable of enforcing these policies. The next three chapters will discuss these factors in depth.

4 The Politics of Autarky: Soviet Customs Institutions and the Post-revolutionary Economy in the 1920s

One function of any state's border controls is to maintain the economic order that the state's political leadership has chosen to protect. Controls over the movement of goods across a state's borders may be imposed to ensure that international economic transactions operate in a state's national interest, benefit its economic actors, and adhere to its laws. Customs institutions, tariffs, and state monopolies or restrictions on various imports and exports are examples of such controls. In the Soviet case border-control policies were a product of the particular set of economic and political strategies that the Soviet leadership adopted in order to achieve its developmental and redistributive goals. These policies evolved from particular decisions and struggles over how the post-revolutionary order should be constructed, considering the constraints of the Soviet Union's isolated international position.

In so far as economic factors played a role, border controls developed in the 1920s and 1930s under two sets of pressures. First, they were an indirect product of a number of the high-priority economic policies of the Bolsheviks, including state monopoly of foreign trade, centralized control over national labour resources, and collectivization of agriculture. Strict border controls served as an instrument of these policies because they helped to ensure that the state's authority over the economy and society was unchallenged. Secondly, there was a struggle of ideas between key Soviet leaders over the dilemma of creating "socialism in one country," a question in which the militantly autarkic, isolationist vision of the state advanced by Joseph Stalin ultimately prevailed over the desires of Leon Trotsky, Nikolai Bukharin, and others to keep the country somewhat more open to the outside world.[1] Intellectual debates over economic development in the 1920s led to the adoption of a strategy of "autarky of production."[2] Stephen D. Krasner defines autarky as a state strategy to "prevent movements across their borders," drawing a continuum between states' levels of autarky and openness.[3] New states may also often embark on isolationist strategies in an effort to bolster their self-sufficiency by resisting capitalist economic penetration from more established powers; closed societies can more easily resist such penetration.[4] Economic isolation thus became a strategy of survival for the post-revolutionary Soviet state. Border controls helped to make the Soviet economy self-sufficient and autonomous by preventing smuggling and by containing the fluctuations in labour that could result from mass migration.

In addition, the state-formation process itself requires decisions regarding foreign trade and the establishment of customs-control institutions. Emerging states often adopt protectionist strategies or economic monopolies in order to develop domestic economies and mobilize resources for the expansion of military power. Hence, state-building and the designation of new borders can "create" smuggling from what was previously quite legitimate economic activity.[5] In Western European state formation the development of capitalism meant that the ability to take "movable property" out of the country eventually tempered the state's ability or desire to suppress "exit," since the state promoted and benefited from capitalism.[6] Capitalism presumably thus requires relatively open borders for trade, whereas in the Soviet Union a conception of socialism based on an autarkic, state-planned internal economy was dependent on border controls to keep the economy self-contained. Since economic development was seen as essential to the achievement of socialism, border controls became a means of defending the Bolshevik Revolution from both military and economic threats from the capitalist West.

For the Bolsheviks of the 1920s, the period in which the most basic foundations of the border-control system were laid, political concerns were inseparable from economic concerns. The period of the New Economic Policy (NEP), initiated in 1921, is seen by many scholars as one of relative openness in the Soviet Union – a period of greater tolerance of private trade and free expression and of limited foreign-policy overtures to the West. Yet it was a period when contacts between citizens and the outside world were increasingly limited and controlled by the state, and the contacts which did occur were usually channelled through state organizations. Also, economic violations of the border were in Bolshevik eyes closely linked with continued political opposition to Soviet rule. Although there was debate within the Bolshevik party over opening up foreign trade under NEP, ultimately the state monopoly on foreign trade was seen as a matter of survival for the Soviet state.[7] Border control correspondingly was to be enhanced rather than weakened under NEP, as the new openings would make continued vigilance necessary.[8]

State economic agencies influenced the development of border controls, which were perceived as an aid to the government's desire to maximize key resources. The Civil War experience of an economy characterized by severe shortages, which was the formative experience of the Soviet state, created a scarcity mentality.[9] Amid this scarcity the Bolsheviks sought to monitor carefully the movement of goods, access to transportation, convertible currency, and even paper for passports. Human resources, particularly skilled labour and educated personnel, were in short supply. This stringency would eventually contribute to a system of closed borders. The more people who entered or left Soviet territory, the more this would tax Soviet transportation, labour, and currency resources, all of which were by the 1920s under the control of the state and which, with the development of the centrally planned industrial economy, were seen as scarce resources to be distributed strictly in accordance with the state's priority interests.[10] In fact, the state monopoly of transportation provided a *de facto* means of border control. This is not totally unique to the Soviet Union. For purposes of efficiency and economy, many states try to limit the number of points at which there are customs and border posts, and may even ban entry or exit except at designated border posts.[11] Evidence suggests that, in the USSR, restrictions on the sale of train tickets to destinations outside the country's international boundaries were useful devices for restricting movement beyond state borders.[12]

The Soviet economy's labour needs also fuelled the leadership's desire to prevent losses through emigration. Bukharin, a key Bolshevik theorist, saw emigration and immigration between states as results of the operation of the labour market under conditions of capitalism.[13] The assumption was that people emigrated from one country to another in order to escape hardship at home; they immigrated to seek employment provided by capitalist firms. Under the Soviet system this kind of exchange would not be necessary since, presumably, exploitation and competition would not exist. This helps to explain why mass immigration and emigration came to be seen as incongruous with a socialist state, which ostensibly controlled and provided for its own labour market.

In the early NEP period there were considerable numbers of people trying to enter the Soviet Union: foreign workers and investors, Russian former émigrés from the tsarist regime, and political sympathizers.

Measures were adopted to encourage such immigration: for instance, a 1925 resolution provided for worker and peasant immigrants to be given the same privileges and duties as colonists to new territories.[14] But the Bolsheviks also endeavoured to control and keep an eye on this influx; too much immigration, in a state already plagued by destabilizing mass refugee movements, added an extra source of confusion, a drain on social services, and a potential threat to political stability. In 1922 a permanent commission on immigration was established by the Council of Labour and Defence (STO), whose purpose was to regulate agricultural and industrial immigration: to help in admitting and transporting new arrivals, to see them through the border controls, to issue orders to local authorities, and to combat unauthorized immigration.[15] This commission prohibited entry into the country without its prior permission, in an attempt to contain the flow of potential immigrants to border points, and expressed some irritation that foreign shipping companies were advertising their sailings to Russia for this purpose.[16] Far from being welcomed with open arms, prospective immigrants were regarded as a potential problem. The STO's agricultural division also resolved in October 1923 to limit agricultural immigration to between 10,000 and 15,000 over a three-year period and to admit only "genuine" farmers.[17] The Cheka was instructed to keep an eye on immigrants, particularly Russian re-immigrants. In 1925 a standing commission on immigration and emigration was created to systematize rules of admission and exit from the country and to ensure that these rules were followed at border posts.[18] Increasing restrictions were imposed to limit both immigration and emigration.

Finally, border controls began to be instituted in part to prevent the flight of capital and property, now owned chiefly by the state, out of the country. Soviet customs institutions also reflected the leadership's redistributive goals. In order to prevent the capital flight that had accompanied their program of nationalization, the Bolshevik regime expanded the definition of contraband by drawing up a very detailed, spartan list of goods to constitute a maximum number of personal effects that individuals were allowed to take with them when leaving the country. These included, for example, three overcoats, six sets of underwear, one piece of soap, twenty-five photographs, and one-quarter pound of tobacco. (Other examples abound.) Permits and/or duties were required to take out additional goods, or they would be considered smuggled items.[19]

The Soviet customs system, however, originated largely from the imposition of a state monopoly over foreign trade, a political-economic system characterized by Jerry Hough as "protectionist" and inspired in part by the Bolsheviks' anti-Western nationalism. Protectionism was

furthermore the result of a debate over economic opening in which
Lenin and other advocates of state monopoly of foreign trade prevailed
over Bukharin, who wanted to expand the possibility of private firms'
participating in foreign trade, while still guaranteeing the protection of
the state's interests through a set of (presumably more flexible) customs
and border controls.[20] As the NEP came into effect, the Bolsheviks realized the need for customs-control bodies, and they passed a number of
laws and decrees regulating the goods that were allowed across the
border.[21]

Party and state leaders had differing opinions, however, on the state's
attitudes towards economic intercourse with the outside world. In the
early 1920s Lenin, Bukharin, and Krasin debated the importance of
border controls in the Soviet economy.[22] Bukharin advocated the tol-
eration of private foreign trade, to be bolstered by customs controls
and tariffs to ensure that the state's economic interests prevailed. To
Bukharin, the state's nationalization of foreign trade was a middle road
that avoided international economic isolation while preventing capitalists from spiriting goods abroad for a profit.[23] Like Bukharin, Leon
Trotsky did not favour the state's direct and exclusive control of foreign trade. In 1922 he wrote to Lenin supporting proposals that the
state give powers of foreign trade to authorized economic units or trading syndicates; although he supported the state's monopoly on foreign
trade, the state could conceivably delegate its export and import prerogatives to officially recognized bodies.[24] Lenin's position, which
eventually won out, was that a state monopoly over both foreign trade
and border controls was necessary to protect the country's indigenous
industries and resources against competition from capitalist countries.[25] Among those who advocated the continuing strict state monopoly of foreign trade was Joseph Stalin.[26] As Richard B. Day writes,
after Lenin's death a Stalinist consensus on economic isolation prevailed.[27]

The more isolated direction of the economy was evident in a resolution on foreign trade, adopted at the October 1925 plenum of the
Russian Communist Party, which specified which organizations could
engage in foreign trade and under what conditions.[28] The need for
strong border controls is implicit but obvious in the resolution's
expressed aim to strengthen the Soviet state's autarky. Two tasks were
identified: first, the containment of the productive forces and resources
of the country, by preventing them from escaping beyond Soviet borders; second, the defence of the economy from the economic blows of
the capitalist countries. Even a small rupture of the state monopoly of
foreign trade, the resolution claimed, could help the cause of capitalism and lead to bigger ruptures; worse, it could subordinate the Soviet

system to the technologically advanced international capitalist economy. This would allow hostile Western countries to undermine Soviet rule from without. Customs alone thus could not achieve the same goals as the state monopoly of foreign trade.[29]

The monopoly of foreign trade (and the border controls to enforce it) served a protectionist role, Krasin argued. During the Civil War these mechanisms served the interests of economic survival by increasing the economic independence of the Soviet republics, who would otherwise have been subordinated to other states, particularly when the value of the ruble fell so dramatically. Thus the foreign-trade monopoly allowed unprofitable industries a chance to break even.[30] Without such state controls, free trade with other countries would bring in cheap goods that would damage the progress of Soviet industries, particularly heavy industries. The capitalist countries would use the market as a weapon to turn the USSR into a colony, while putting up their own trade barriers to prevent Soviet gains in their countries.[31]

Strict customs controls would have to be a firm corollary of such a state policy. In 1926 the People's Commissariat of Trade issued customs regulations, strict, detailed guidelines of the means by which goods could leave the country and the restrictions to which they were subject. These guidelines were designed to ease the functioning of the several thousand, mostly inexperienced customs officials of the new Soviet government.[32] Engaging in contraband (broadly defined as carrying goods across the state border without permission of customs authorities) was entered as an offence in the All-Union and republican criminal codes as a socially dangerous crime. It was even a violation to bring contraband goods (those exceeding personal needs) into the border zones (*polosa*).[33] There were categories of simple and qualified contraband: the latter included the use of vehicles for smuggling, forgery of customs documents, the use of arms, participation in organizations expressly dealing in contraband, repeat offences, smuggling of military equipment and weapons, or engaging the participation of customs officials. The more serious offences could result in penalties from a year's imprisonment to execution.[34] The 1928 Customs Code detailed the rules concerning customs, specifying the permitted goods that one could take abroad, and established penalties for contraband violations of the state's monopoly of foreign trade.[35] A year later the first customs code was introduced.

THE STRUGGLE AGAINST CONTRABAND

The concern with customs controls notwithstanding, Soviet economic agencies were continually frustrated throughout the 1920s by the endemic smuggling of goods across Soviet borders, particularly in border localities. In general cross-border smuggling can be perceived as a form of resistance to state economic monopolies and taxes.[36] For example, in nineteenth-century England customs institutions became more centralized and aggressive in response to smugglers' attempts to evade the state wool monopoly and the payment of duties on various goods.[37] This shows the importance of border control to the development of a state-sponsored economy, to counter social resistance to the monopolies and protections involved.

Before the Russian Revolution, smuggling was mostly a matter of evasion of customs duties, or trade in the relatively limited categories of goods that were banned by the central authorities. In the Soviet period, with the state monopoly, the designation "contraband" was extended to all goods crossing the border without state permission; the customs authorities became responsible for controlling all goods across borders according to the state licensing system. Customs institutions were established through the Main Customs Administration under the People's Commissariat of Foreign Trade, which would have divisions in the Union republics and at individual border posts.[38] Meanwhile, consumer goods were scarce in Russia during the Civil War and NEP years, and this created a demand for smuggling across borders, particularly from the Baltic states and Poland, where officials were reportedly indifferent to such activity.[39]

Consequently, smuggling was rampant into the 1930s. An editorial in *Pravda* published late in 1922 argued that valuable resources were being lost from continued cross-border smuggling.[40] Contraband, border troops were told, "undermines our economy and does not allow the Russian proletariat and peasantry the possibility of taking rapid steps to walk out on the broad road of constructing a new and better life."[41] As of 1922 anyone who wanted to leave the country in order to engage in foreign trade required permission from the Commissariat of Foreign Trade.[42] Already in 1923 Ukraine was forbidding all trade in precious metals and stones within a fifteen-*verst* (approximately twelve-mile) border zone.[43] This marked the beginning of an effort to clear the border regions of unwanted economic and political activity. In addition, the Commissariat of Foreign Trade charged that foreign enterprises and speculators were carrying out business with the local population in Soviet border areas in exchange for gold and other valuables, and were bribing border officials in the process.[44] Hence, despite the monopoly of foreign trade, contraband assumed significant dimensions; economic scarcity contributed to the situation, as did the fact that in the early years of Soviet power border troops were generally more preoccupied with political opposition than with smuggling. Contraband was simply an extension of the black market that was pervasive in the country's war economy.[45]

Along the border zones of the USSR and in neighbouring countries, stores and co-operatives had emerged specifically for the purpose of supplying the Soviet black market, and the customs measures were designed to eliminate this activity on Soviet territory.[46] Concern arose regarding the illegal traffic of goods into the country – but also over those leaving, such as gold and precious metals.[47] While Soviet officials were justifiably concerned about smuggling of personal property out of the country, there seems to have been a much greater volume of smuggling occurring in foreign goods than in Russian ones, and a great deal was being smuggled *into* the country and sold.[48] Despite the Soviet regime's effort to take control of gold and foreign-currency supplies, people living in outlying areas still carried on operations in gold and hard currency, which, while not of much use within the country, were used on the borderland periphery for contraband and taken with them by emigrants.[49] In 1922, despite the state's efforts, gold money reportedly began to appear again in border areas, especially in parts of the Caucasus, the right bank of Ukraine, and the Far East, a development that was claimed to impede the state's efforts to unify the currency into the paper ruble.[50]

Cross-border smuggling was not merely a practice of bourgeois traders or rich aristocrats fleeing the country with their valuables; it was just as likely to be practised by peasants of border localities who were seeking to supplement their income by dealing in scarce goods. The rising prices of food and other goods in the country, including its western regions, caused hardship, while goods were apparently much cheaper across the border in Poland, for example. Under these circumstances markets in foreign goods cropped up in border villages, where smugglers conducted business in exchange for money.[51] In 1924 there were reports that contraband on the Far Eastern border had increased due to the difficulties of effective border control there, and the availability of cheap goods abroad. This traffic was a response to shortages of such goods as vodka, tobacco, and manufactured goods.[52] As a result, thriving border towns had sprung up wherever there were, just over the border, shops, goods, and settlements of Russian-speaking anti-Soviet émigrés.[53] By 1925 one contemporary scholar was writing that contraband had assumed epidemic proportions well beyond levels in the pre-revolutionary era, requiring more attention from the state. He noted that most contraband was apprehended on the Polish border; a significant part of all contraband passed across the border quickly, to be widely distributed throughout the republic.[54]

In Bolshevik eyes, particularly by the end of NEP, the participants in these economic activities were considered political enemies of the regime, either directly – as political opponents to the Bolshevik regime – or indirectly – as people who engaged in private, capitalist trade. The more smuggling flourished, the more serious a political and economic threat it was seen to be, particularly when it contributed to what was perceived as a climate of moral turpitude on the border: "If contraband constitutes an evil for every country, then so much the more it is a serious evil for the RSFSR under conditions when foreign trade is a state monopoly, serving as one of the fundamentals of our socialist construction."[55] The rhetoric against smuggling become more and more harsh, and more serious measures were taken to control it.

In the January 1924 Congress of Soviets, border economic issues were a matter of great concern, particularly in view of the state's inadequate hard-currency reserve and the subsequent need to export more goods abroad under the foreign-trade monopoly.[56] As one delegate pointed out, while the process of assuming state control over the economy was going well in the centre of the country, it was doing less well in the outlying regions, often populated by national minorities, where state control over the local economy was weak.[57] A 1924 resolution of the Presidium of the USSR Central Committee on contraband was to have temporary effect until the publication of the Customs Code. Simple (*obyknovennaia*) contraband was subject to administrative procedures and the levying of fines, while repeat offenders could be exiled beyond the fifty-kilometre border zone. Complex contraband was a matter for the judicial organs; among the offences included under this heading were the diversion of transport for contraband purposes, the use of false documents, and smuggling arms, telegraph, or radio equipment.[58]

At the 1927 Congress of Soviets, issues relating to border control were raised by a variety of representatives from the republics. One participant noted the existence of sites on the Caucasian-Turkish and western Polish borders that served as transfer points for businesses bringing contraband goods into the USSR and carrying on illegal transactions in hard currency, which in his view posed a threat to the struggle against private capital.[59] As of 1926, hard-currency (*valiuta*) transactions were allowed, for state organs or individuals, only with special permission from Narkomfin, and *valiuta* was not to be used for any transactions within the state.[60]

By the late 1920s the Soviet leadership desired to eliminate illicit trade completely and to prevent more effectively the loss of hard currency and valuables, which were now resources of the state domain. Documents of the 1930s show a concern with tightening border controls in order to maintain the state's strict trade balance and protect its hard-currency reserves.[61] A 1926 document notes that the Soviet government had few hard-currency reserves and, in order to improve its economic situation, needed to crack down on smuggling at the border, which disrupted its trade balance and drained valuable exports, such as furs, out of the country.[62]

The government also adopted measures to limit citizens' access to hard currency, which proved a further deterrent to travel outside the country, since it made it difficult for people to raise the money to go abroad. The inconvertibility of the ruble was a corollary of the state's monopoly of foreign trade and the centrally planned economy; it served to ensure that the state controlled hard currency and that citizens could not directly buy or sell goods from abroad.[63] The ruble's inconvertibility was a result in part of currency smuggling and the inability of Soviet border-control authorities to prevent it save through drastic measures. The 1924 Soviet currency reform created the newly stabilized *chervonets* ruble, which was floated at international exchanges. However, as Arthur Z. Arnold has described, the shortages of consumer goods in the Soviet Union encouraged smugglers and dealers in foreign goods to pay for their purchases abroad in *chervontsy*.[64] This, according to Arnold, threatened the stability of the *chervonets* and constituted a loss to the government, which badly needed foreign currency. On 9 July 1926 the removal of *chervontsy* from the country was made illegal; however, the smuggling continued. On 21 March 1928 the Soviet government made it illegal also to bring *chervontsy* into the country, thus making it an inconvertible, internal ruble.[65]

By the end of the 1920s the Soviet state completely controlled Soviet citizens' access to hard currency, which prevented travel abroad unless it was sanctioned by state authorities. In addition, it provided limits on the activity of foreigners coming into the country. In 1930 the USSR adopted strict regulations to govern currency coming into and out of the country; foreigners were permitted to bring currency in but had to record the amount with customs authorities when entering and departing. When leaving, the amount the authorities deemed necessary for their stay would be allowed, at the official rate of ten rubles a day. The rest would be confiscated, presumably, on the way out; this caused hardship for some travellers, according to British documents. Any undeclared currency would be confiscated.[66]

Like their commitment to rapid economic expansion, with an emphasis on autarky and heavy industrialization, the Soviets' preoccupation with developing their military power under conditions of capitalist encirclement was an important factor in the development of border controls, making them of strategic as well as economic significance. The Soviet military leader Mikhail Frunze at this time stressed the great military threat of other, capitalist states, including those bordering the USSR such as Poland and Romania, and argued that they were increasing their armaments against the USSR. Their combined might, strengthened by the presence of 1.5 million Russian émigrés, posed a formidable threat to the nascent Bolshevik state; Frunze noted the defence dilemma of capitalist encirclement and a long border.[67] Frunze's implication was that the Soviet Union required more armaments, which influenced the strengthening of border control in two ways: by developing the planned economy that stressed heavy industry, and by strengthening Soviet defences. The country increasingly steered in the direction of central planning.[68]

The relationship between the planned economy and border control was a synchronous rather than a subordinate relationship. The monopoly of foreign trade preceded and made possible the planned economy as well as being one of its chief instruments. According to Krasin, the Soviet Union would only be capable of creating a socialist state-planned economy because of, first, the successful struggle by the Red Army to secure Soviet borders in order to guarantee its integrity as a state; and secondly, the monopoly of foreign trade, both of which made the planned economy possible.[69] The state monopoly of foreign trade was even included in the Stalinist constitution (article 14.)[70] Stalin feared that the difficulties of controlling an economy that relied on foreign trade would make the economy vulnerable to external fluctuations, destabilize the economic plan, and make planning more complex.[71]

Stalin's bitter rival Leon Trotsky, whose view of political construction in the Soviet Union was more sophisticated than Stalin's, apparently lamented the isolationist direction the country was pursuing.[72] During the Civil War, when Trotsky was Commissar of the Army, he advocated sealing off the border to cut off Iudenich's army from Estonia.[73] However, what was necessary in war was not automatically desirable in peacetime: Trotsky's belief in the inevitability of the European revolution and his disdain for the excessive build-up of state bureaucratic structures disinclined him from a rigid system of closed borders. In 1926 he criticized the increasing self-imposed isolation of the USSR embodied in the phrase "socialism in one country." Trotsky felt this direction was excessively pessimistic about the future of the European revolution and implied a false belief that the Soviet Union could reach socialism independent of the international context. The success of the Soviet Revolution, he argued, depended on Europe and the rest of the world. It would be a mistake therefore to cut the USSR off from its neighbours because this would undermine the possibility of contact and involvement in the European revolutions. The result, according to Trotsky, would be the proliferation of an narrow, insular, and possibly chauvinistic self-absorption.[74] Later, in exile, Trotsky argued that "imperialist encirclement" had been one of the conditions that allowed Stalin's administrative elite to gain power.[75] He also acknowledged, however, that the trend towards autarky was a general European one that had accompanied the rise of fascism.[76]

CONCLUSION

Soviet border controls began in the Civil War rather than being imposed anew under Stalin, and were imposed for economic as much as geostrategic reasons. The limited contacts across borders that were allowed were a cause for concern on behalf of the security apparatus; they were seen as an opportunity for political penetration by anti-Soviet forces. Meanwhile, the pervasiveness of cross-border smuggling had a crucial effect on the development of a network of restrictive border-control policies. Smuggling constituted a loss of resources to the Soviet state and a challenge to its monopoly on the economy, as well as contributing to political instability in the border areas.

The next chapters discuss in greater detail the unwieldy political and institutional aspects of the various governmental organizations and agencies concerned with border control and how their interests combined to form a restrictive border-control policy. The emphasis of this chapter applies throughout, however: economic interests played a vital role in the development of Soviet border-control policy and were inseparable from the political conflicts and objectives of the Bolsheviks.

5 Border Control and Centre-Periphery Relations in the Soviet Union, 1921–1941

The implementation of Soviet border-control policy had several dimensions. The actual troops and structures on the border monitored cross-border movements and prevented unauthorized entry or exit. These forces had constantly to interact with local populations in border areas, and much of their attention was taken up with local border crossings. Central policies and institutions for border control also affected people living in the interior who wanted to leave the country legally. These central policies were from the beginning quite strict, but at the actual border it was possible to evade them. Chapter 6 describes how the Soviet government's border policies became increasingly centralized and bureaucratic as the system developed the capability to enforce them effectively. The current chapter, however, focuses on the interplay of central political concerns on the one hand and events on the Soviet periphery on the other, exploring the importance of that interplay to the development of border-control structures and the difficult struggle the Bolsheviks faced as they endeavoured to make their border impermeable. In order to understand Soviet border controls, we must consider the borderland areas, which were generally inhabited by rural populations. Border control became an instrument for the establishment of Soviet power over the country's periphery, which became particularly important with the violent process of the collectivization of agriculture in the late 1920s and early 1930s.

The concept of "centre-periphery relations" explores the state's penetration of areas that are far removed geographically and culturally from the centre of government power, which makes it difficult to establish state authority in rural areas.[1] The inhabitants of the periphery, who are often relatively poor peasants, may be among those who feel they have little to gain from the state's designs.[2] Centre-periphery relations often have an ethnic dimension when the periphery's inhabitants do not share the language or cultural origins of its dominant elite. Anthony Giddens argues that control of space and boundaries is an essential component of the modern state's efforts to extend central control outward to territories where the state's power is inherently weak.[3] Some scholars have applied the concept of centre-periphery relations to the Soviet Union. Alvin Gouldner, for example, describes Stalinism as a process of "internal colonialism."[4] It is important to note that while a state is trying to consolidate its rule over these peripheral localities, it is also, presumably, establishing its territorial integrity and military-defence capabilities at its borders. State power hence does not just extend outwards from the centre but inwards, from the border, and military authorities there can contribute to the state-building process. Peter Sahlins notes that the state-formation literature wrongly portrays the centre as extending out into the periphery and imposing its power; discussing the state-building experiences on the border between France and Spain, he argues that these two countries had to incorporate and compromise with local interests in the borderlands, who themselves played a role in determining national identity.[5] Sahlins is correct to take the border's role into consideration in state formation. But in the Soviet case this process of local co-optation and compromise did not take place. A better characterization is that central power in all its coercive force did not just push out from the interior; it also pushed inward from the border. Only this way could the state, in such a vast country, provide the medium not only for revolutionary survival but for revolutionary change.

The border is a highly charged area for new states because the border itself is a crucial locus of the centre's power – that is, it can become a site of contestation between the state and citizens. It is the point of the state's confrontation with other states, the ultimate interface between centre and periphery, the lightning rod of the dilemma of national security. In the Soviet post-revolutionary state, the successor to a former multi-ethnic empire, the border could not fail to be highly politicized. This politicization greatly contributed to the perceived need for restrictive borders, the surveillance at them, and their role as sites of social change.

Soviet border controls also literally tied a multinational state together, preventing territorial secession by putting a wall around the non-Russian republics. Many of the Soviet Union's border areas were located in territories in the non-Russian republics and were thus inhabited by ethnic groups other than Russians. Such a situation leads to an inherent security problem for the state, particularly when these populations are closely related ethnically to the citizens of the country on which they border.[6] From the perspective of Soviet nationalities, borders were drawn arbitrarily. International borders separated the Soviet Union from former parts of the Russian Empire, such as Poland, the Baltic states, and Bessarabia. After the First World War people suddenly had friends or relatives living in hostile states with whom they had been accustomed to visiting or trading;[7] such relationships now became politically suspect and evaded state economic monopolies. Geographic distance enhances the problem. In a state such as the Soviet Union the centre is a great distance from its borders; as Edward Shils notes, "the more territorially dispersed the institutional system, the less the likelihood of an intense affirmation of the value system."[8]

Paradoxically, border areas are those most vulnerable to other states and most likely to be directly controlled by the state; yet they are also most likely to be remote areas where state authority has not made inroads and where local economies are rural. Economic development is perhaps most needed in border areas because of their tendency to be backward and rural; yet, for strategic reasons, states are unlikely to want to develop them industrially. Furthermore, states tend to provide economic and cultural resources to developed rather than unsettled areas, which lack infrastructure.[9] For example, in the Soviet case a 1923 document called for the removal of all industry from the border areas of Ukraine as an appropriate security measure to prepare for the event of war.[10] The republics of Belorussia and Ukraine (and later Moldavia) were nearest to Western countries and thus could be targets in a war, a consideration in their relative lack of industrial development.[11] The Soviets avoided economic development in a radius near the border, thus keeping them peasant societies.[12]

THE MICROPOLITICS OF BORDER CONTROL

After the Civil War, Moscow made an increasing effort to gain control of the situation in border areas. In 1921 the central government demanded that local authorities report on their relations with bordering countries with regard to trade, border protection, and other issues.[13] Border posts were told to watch carefully for "speculators, emigrants, contrabandists, and criminal elements" who might try to steal across the border.[14] A Cheka leader, F. Fomin, who was sent by Feliks Dzerzhinskii to organize border-control work in Ukraine in 1921, claimed that Dzerzhinskii told him it was vitally important to "establish contact with the local population, so that they be direct and reliable helpers of border protection."[15] Fomin found that border-area residents often had close relatives in countries just on the other side of the border, and they wished to be able to visit them.[16]

Judging by newspaper accounts, Soviet border authorities were, to an extent, agents of Bolshevization in outlying areas of the country, where the border troops were called upon to suppress resistance, help to organize elections, and conduct anti-religious and literacy campaigns.[17] Meanwhile, local budgets were to pay for the housing and utility supply of border troops.[18] In the late 1920s and early 1930s party organizations, soviets, trade unions, Komsomol groups, factories, and *kolkhozy* would sponsor various border units and posts. Border guards in turn would help the party and Soviet organs in the border areas to construct *kolkhozy* and other local projects.[19] The troops were expected to enlist the assistance of poor peasants in the struggle against cross-border smuggling and to raise their awareness of how it would ultimately hurt them economically.[20]

Such activities stemmed from the realization that, to be effective, border control required the masses' support of the Soviet regime and the isolation of supposed "counter-revolutionaries" from the population. One document instructed that, in order to make border control effective on the Karelian border, the guards must be able to discredit anti-Soviet "White Finns" among the local population.[21] In 1926 a resolution of the Soviet government's Central Executive Committee demanded that more attention be paid to national-language education and the raising of Soviet consciousness in border areas, as the peasants there needed to have a better understanding of Soviet goals and officials needed to be more sensitive towards national minorities.[22]

There was an obvious gap between state intent and state capacity in the 1920s. Regardless of the supposed efficiency of secret-police organs relative to other organizations, the evidence suggests that, well into the 1920s, in some instances uninformed louts were defending the border.[23] Furthermore, among those crossing the border illegally were state employees or *pogranichniki* themselves.[24] Until the mid-1920s, it seems, few provisions were made to keep border personnel consistently informed of both central and local events or to provide them with tools for political organization.[25] They seem to have had a perennial problem in extracting funds from local government authorities, while central authorities, far away in Moscow, could be oblivious of their needs.[26] Dependent on local peasants for their lodging, border troops were in a vulnerable position, and they could be coerced to participate in villagers' illicit cross-border activities.[27] Sources claimed that in the early years of their formation, *pogranichniki* had inadequate living quarters, weapons, and supplies and often had to live with peasants in their homes; as a result, some turned a blind eye to the latter's contra-band activities. This lack of autonomy would impair the effectiveness of border authorities. Subsequently it was argued that border troops should be fully supported centrally and thus independent of the local population and party organization.[28]

Despite the wide variety of conditions on different borders, common patterns became obvious by the mid- to late 1920s; the Party paid a great deal of attention to the problems of the border areas, at one point declaring them to be of high priority. Special commissars and campaigns were set up to study the problem.[29] The concern was that the populations and institutions of border areas alike were not offering sufficient vigilance and security for such sensitive localities; local populations were considered all too often hostile or indifferent to Soviet power. Meanwhile, Party organizations were criticized as weak, consisting of resentful cadres who saw their border assignments as "exile."[30] Army and local Party authorities interfered with each other's activities;[31] smuggling in scarce goods flourished; local inhabitants' ties with populations in anti-Soviet bordering states were cause for concern; and such border-security measures as did exist were perceived as deep intrusions into the peasant way of life, which made it even harder to win over the local population.

The confrontation between state and society at the border took on an ethnic dimension, since the often non-Russian inhabitants saw the border authorities as "outsiders" (chuzhaki). The border populations often included various national minorities, such as Jews and Germans, who, owing to their particular grievances suffered since the 1917 Revolution, were inclined to seek emigration as a solution to their problems. This was seen by the Party as an indictment of local policy.[32] In Bolshevik eyes these groups had fallen under the spell of bourgeois movements and harmful foreign agents, whose influence had to be combated.

The result was a twofold policy whose inherent contradictions compromised its effectiveness. The first direction consisted of various positive measures and compromises designed to improve the border population's way of life and thereby ease friction with central authorities. These measures consisted of, for example, allowing partial exceptions to rural policy, such as easing the tax on grain, or urging local party organs in border areas to ensure that peasants had adequate supplies and seeds.[33] According to this reasoning, an influx of consumer goods and food products could potentially ease popular dissatisfaction and offset the demand for contraband goods: if people in remote border areas were better supplied with manufactured goods from the centre, then the need for smuggling would be eliminated.[34] As reinforcement,

emphasis was placed on greater education, books, and learning campaigns in the local population's native languages, so they would be
more accessible to Bolshevik ideas and information. Furthermore,
there was a policy of nativization in recruitment to promote greater
understanding between the locals and the Party, as well as demands
that central Party authorities and nationality policy-makers visit the
border localities more often. Finally, there was a partial easing of border-security regimes so as to afford citizens greater access to pastures,
national resources, water supplies, and other aspects of the peasants'
traditional livelihood – including, in some cases, the right to cross the
border into the neighbouring state as agreed by treaty.[35]

In addition, despite harsh penalties, the regime seemed to appreciate
that many "contrabandists" were not hard-core capitalists but small-
timers who were trying to improve their material situation. In 1924 a
reward of 30 per cent of confiscated contraband and fines collected
was offered as an incentive to those who apprehended smugglers, a
reward that applied to border guards as well.[36] Border troops in
Ukraine discussed in 1925 the sort of criminal penalties that should be
directed at smugglers and advocated that stiff fines rather than prison
sentences should await those found guilty of contraband offences, on
the grounds that they would provide a deterrent for poor peasants.[37]
Meanwhile, in the border areas of the republics of Central Asia and on
the Chinese border, local residents were allowed to bring agricultural
and forestry goods, fish, and livestock across the border for their livelihood, without duty.[38] Of course, such arrangements were also provided for by treaty with the neighbouring countries. This shows that in the
drawing of borders, at least prior to collectivization, accommodations
were sometimes made to respect the lives of ordinary rural populations, and that their needs were sometimes respected.

However, the main objective of policy was, of course, greater vigilance on the border; this was to be achieved through cultivating better-
motivated and -qualified border troops, drawing more dedicated Party
members into their ranks, who would more sternly enforce border
restrictions and conduct stringent campaigns against illicit cross-border smuggling, political contacts, and religious activity.[39] Further, there
were fears that if border troops or OGPU became too familiar with
locals, their political or military effectiveness could be compromised. It
could be argued that giving the border areas special treatment only prevented them from being integrated into Soviet rule, preserving their
ability to evade central authority.

Problems of the Ukrainian border played an exemplary role in the
development of Soviet border-control policy. The relative sovereignty
of the Ukrainian republic compared to other borderlands and the high-

ly strategic and sensitive nature of the Ukrainian border meant that developments there had important repercussions for the rest of the country.[40] In Ukraine the former military front of the First World War and Civil War became a border on the hostile states of Romania and Poland, with whom Ukraine had territorial disputes and whose potential access to Western influence and military assistance was feared. Some counter-revolutionary and émigré organizations were based on the western border, especially in Poland, from which they made incursions into Soviet territory throughout the 1920s. Although the military threat was perhaps exaggerated in Soviet eyes, the real danger was in the contacts and influence of the émigrés among the domestic Ukrainian border populations, whose allegiance to Soviet power was described throughout the 1920s as weak.[41]

To complicate matters, the national composition of the Ukrainian border population often separated them culturally and linguistically from local Soviet officials and contributed to a perception that border authorities were "outsiders." The rural, indigenous Ukrainian inhabitants of the border areas were often illiterate and inhospitable to Russian-speakers. In addition, Poles, Jews, and Germans were prominent among the other national minorities common to these border areas. The local population, documents claimed, did not trust the border authorities, particularly if they spoke only Russian; both border Party organizations and border-control authorities were urged in 1923 to recruit more Ukrainians and Ukrainian speakers.[42] The remoteness of the border from the country's cultural and publishing centres added to this problem.[43]

In addition, Ukraine experienced a variety of national migrations across its borders, which it sought to bring under control. These included the quest for emigration by many Jews, who, traumatized by persecution during the Civil War, sought to resettle in America or Palestine; disgruntled Germans and Mennonites, who sought mass exit to Germany; an influx of Russian immigrants fleeing Bessarabia's acquisition by Romania; and demands for repatriation in or out by groups who had ended up in one country or another as a result of the dislocations of the First World War. These political migrations continued until the late 1920s, when the Soviet government put an end to group movements. The Soviet authorities were concerned about the ideological implications of national minorities' demands to emigrate, for example, arguing that the desires of Jews and Germans to leave the country could be placated by improving the conditions and education of these nationality groups and scapegoating "bourgeois agitators" and "Zionist organizations," who were allegedly pressuring members of these groups to emigrate.[44]

In Central Asia problems of border control in the early years after the establishment of Soviet power centred around the Basmachi movement. This resistance movement to Soviet rule was linked with power bases in Afghanistan and Persia, where the British presence made Soviet leaders particularly nervous about the Turkmen opposition's dependence on cross-border contacts. The Central Asian Communist Party considered effective border control an indispensable part of its strategy to liquidate the Basmachi movement by cutting the communications between Basmachi supporters and their bases abroad.[45]

At the same time Soviet authorities displayed some concern to respect the way of life of the Turkic peoples and felt compelled to adopt various measures to allow local populations access to natural resources and pastures on the other side of the border, as well as to engage in limited cross-border trade (while resolving to send more Soviet goods to Central Asia and fighting organized smuggling.)[46] Meanwhile, the border troops and GPU stood quite apart from the population. Attempts to lure native Central Asians into their ranks were not very successful, and there was an obvious cultural and linguistic barrier between them and Soviet border authorities.[47] Central Asian borders had their share of mass population movements. According to Party sources, thousands of people emigrated and re-emigrated to and from Afghanistan and Soviet Central Asia, as refugees from the Civil War and the Basmachi movement respectively. This caused no small problem for the Soviet border authorities, who claimed their customs and other border structures were being disrupted, arguing that the refugees did not understand the nature of Soviet policies.[48]

By the mid- to late 1920s the border regions generally throughout the Soviet Union were considered by the Communist Party to be a security threat, owing to the attitudes of the domestic populations. As early as 1925 resettlement of the population away from the border zones was considered as an option by the Ukrainian Communist Party's commission to study border regions.[49] The party several times through the 1920s commissioned campaigns or groups to work on the serious problems of the border zones, in 1922–23, 1925, and 1927. In 1925 a report of conditions in the border regions of the Ukraine, Belorussia, and the Northwest Oblast of Russia concluded:

In almost all of the border zones, the political, economic and cultural position there, as well as the composition of the Party, soviet and professional *apparat,* is not fully satisfactory; and a number of *raiony* do not fulfil the promise of a screen against our enemies. In the best instance they do not in any way distinguish themselves from the average *okrug, uezd,* or *oblast* within their respective republics.[50]

The same report also concluded that many of the national minorities on those borders were either hostile to Soviet rule or had affiliations with another country, such as Palestine, Germany, or Finland.[51]

The Communist Party leadership periodically communicated with the border regions of the various Soviet republics on the situation in those areas.[52] But at least until the late 1920s they seem to have entrusted the border situation to the local Communist parties. This seems to have changed in a more centralist direction towards the end of the decade. In 1927 Lazar Kaganovich, first secretary of the Ukrainian Communist Party, took a keen interest in the security problems of Ukrainian border localities and brought them to the attention of the Party at its congress that year. Kaganovich said that he had visited Ukrainian border areas, and although they were well fortified, he thought that the people there (both peasants and workers) seemed politically indifferent. The Party thus needed to educate and prepare them.[53] Kaganovich repeatedly expressed alarm in 1927 and 1928 about the domestic political situation in border regions, telling local Party organizations to expand their educational work and military preparedness. He stressed that the local population did not sufficiently appreciate the danger of war and were susceptible to counter-revolutionary activity and influences. The Party should, by consequence, devote special attention to the border areas.[54] Similar points were made by Ukrainian GPU head V. Balitskii, who argued that because border areas tended to be remote, agricultural, and often multi-ethnic locations, they required more effective border-control structures.[55] These views suggest that the local population was considered to be a security threat.

In 1927 border policy took a more serious turn. To judge by documents from Pskov, border troop commanders were instructed to assemble detailed information on the enemy's border defences and to recruit from bordering territories agents who could inform on the border situation, including transborder smuggling, which, far from being a petty peasant crime, "assists the propagation of intelligence and is an essential subsidiary to the latter."[56] In 1929 there was a crackdown on the emigration of Germans; group emigrations were ended, and the Soviet government undertook to limit the issue of foreign passports. The OGPU was simultaneously instructed to root out *kulak* (the name used to describe a well-off peasant) pro-emigration agitators. German emigration was dramatically reduced.[57] By 1932 smugglers were considered among the supposedly hostile groups to be purged from the *kolkhoz*.[58] Later, smugglers would be depicted as spies. The 1927 border statute established, in border regions, four layers of border zones – at 4 metres, 500 metres, 7 1/2 kilometres, and 22 kilometres – entry to which required progressively stricter authorization.[59]

COLLECTIVIZATION

In the late 1920s the Bolsheviks made the fateful decision to collectivize agriculture by forcibly organizing peasants into collective farms (*kolkhozy*) and state farms (*sovkhozy*). Iurii Felshtinskii, in seeking to explain the degree and effectiveness of Soviet border control by the late 1920s, rightly draws the link between collectivization of the land and border control.[60] This policy was accompanied by the suppression of mass resistance among the peasantry. One form of this resistance was flight across the border. This was obviously not an option available to every peasant, but peasant flight from the *kolkhozy* did occur. Border control aimed in part to keep peasants on the *kolkhoz* – an element of the militarization of Soviet rural life. Border areas proved difficult to collectivize: construction of *kolkhozy* was slow; people were inhospitable to the idea of collectivization and were seen as, by definition, particularly receptive to anti-Soviet and bourgeois ideas.[61]

Inside the Soviet Union, in at least one *oblast* encompassing a border zone, the Soviet central government took intense interest in the question of national minorities living near the border and issued a set of regulations to ensure that Jews and other groups were incorporated into the *kolkhozy* and participated in industrialization plans.[62] An instruction to the OGPU of 1933 instructed officials to deal more judiciously with local peasants during collectivization, asking them not to detain peasants without trial for the less serious crimes. However, illicit border crossings and contraband were crimes where such detentions without trial, by the OGPU and militia, were allowed.[63] A tragic wave of attempted emigration occurred in 1932, when large numbers of Moldavian peasants are reported to have attempted to flee to Romania by crossing the frozen Dniestr River. Many of the would-be fugitives were caught by Soviet border troops; the Romanian government protested, which gained international attention. Similar events were reported on the Latvian and Polish borders.[64] In Kirgizia, resistance to collectivization among the population apparently sometimes led locals to flee abroad to avoid surrendering cattle.[65]

With the end of NEP, as the progress of collectivization accompanied increased Soviet militarization, border authorities were warned in the 1930s to take very seriously the threat of so-called *kulak* resistance and to be aware of the military threat from bordering capitalist countries such as Poland and Romania. The concurrence of these two realities was seen to require special care to ensure that the border regime was strictly enforced.[66] The party made *pogranichniki,* including demobilized ones, participate in collectivization; many graduates of border schools in the early 1930s were sent directly into agricultural work as heads of *kolkhozy*, accountants, and even tractor drivers.[67] The troops' participation in collectivization was portrayed as an essential part of guarding the front, and they were expected to help promote decisions of the party and government among the local peasantry. It was seen as a point of pride if border guards themselves were collectivized peasants.[68] Meanwhile, the local peasantry were expected to help in guarding the border and in the struggle against smuggling.[69] Localities were also encouraged to help the border guards materially. In the 1931 campaign fund to motorize border-guard units, border *kolkhozy* organized a campaign to solicit donations for the cost of this militarization.[70]

In 1931 the Communist Party Central Committee resolved to intensify border control in Ukraine and Belorussia, partly in order to prevent "*kulak* agitation" among the peasantry, who might be incited to cross the border illegally during the collectivization of agriculture. The authorities were concerned about the poor state of collective farms in border areas, where local officials were admonished for inadequate performance, and resolved to send some of the country's best collective farmers to these areas to improve the order in the countryside.[71]

At the Seventeenth Party Congress in 1934, in euphemistic language, delegates expressed concern about the political system in border areas. According to a delegate from Belorussia, the party needed to be more active in border localities there, where nationalities policy had not been as successful as in Ukraine and where counter-revolutionary elements with links abroad in Poland and Germany still existed.[72] One person in attendance from the East Siberian *krai*, was also deeply concerned about the Manchurian border and the alleged activity of Cossacks and White forces on either side of the border with the Japanese.[73]

To stabilize population movements and prevent flight to the cities following collectivization, internal passports were introduced in 1932. The passport system created categories of places for which people had to have permission to live. The primary "special" category was the border strip, followed by the first category, the city of Moscow. In 1935 a secret resolution of the Council of People's Commissars forbade those guilty of various crimes from living in the border zone. These crimes included armed robbery, banditry, burglary, currency forgery, speculation, prostitution, drug trafficking, begging, and embezzlement.[74] Most border sectors had control-*propusk* points where official border crossings took place (such as Shepetovka and Pogranichnaia).[75] Subsequently, through the late 1930s, Soviet border zones and restrictions upon them were expanded. By 1932–33 already, and again in 1935, under the influence of Tukhachevsky the USSR began a program of increasing frontier military defences and installations.[76] The increasing uncertainty of the frontier up to 1941 contributed to the increased emphasis on political education and organization of the border troops, according to Soviet sources.[77] A resolution of 5 October 1936 established one to three years in prison as the penalty for crossing the border without permission.[78]

By the 1930s the border could be permeated only with difficulty. The increasing demarcation of border zones, the extension of the border-control system across the country, and the militarization of the system made it increasingly difficult for an individual to cross the state border. The border-control system was closely linked to the Soviet policies that are identified with Stalinism. Collectivization of the land led to a great deal of peasant resistance; border controls were considered a fundamentally important means of stabilizing the agricultural situation and of preventing peasant flight. In addition, the fear of peasant unrest in border areas contributed to the military presence there and to the role of the border troops in local political life. The Soviet system was not just being extended to the border; the border itself was growing, extending farther and farther into the heartland, putting greater and greater parts of the country under a security regime. Meanwhile, in the border-control system there was an element of colonization; although it is difficult to find conclusive evidence, according to émigré sources, by the Second World War border guards were generally Russians, and from districts very far away from where they served.[79] State authority, strong at the border, was creeping inwards to meet the centre's restrictive institutions, whose role in policy will be explored in the next chapter.

6 State-Sponsored Isolation and Institutional Politics

By the late 1930s the Soviet border-control system was tight and highly militarized, following new allocations of military resources and methods of police surveillance. Soviet authorities saw border controls as a means of sealing off the population's contacts with "the enemy" and of protecting the state's economic monopoly. It preserved a maximum supply of labour and military personnel and enforced the state's monopoly of foreign trade.[1] A further feature of the system's development was the increased involvement of Soviet bureaucracies in border control, which created administrative barriers to cross-border travel in addition to the more obvious coercive mechanisms. Such bureaucratization was becoming a general feature of the Soviet system. Leon Trotsky wrote in 1930 that the growth of an oppressive bureaucracy in the Stalinist state was crippling the country's political activity and progress.[2]

The border-control network, like other aspects of the Soviet system, developed over a long period of time and had many dimensions, but it fits the pattern of the Soviet bureaucracy described by scholars. Merle Fainsod, for example, depicts a governmental organization that was chaotic and unwieldy, whose restrictive features were caused as much by bureaucratic buck-passing and bottlenecks as by overt design.[3] Seweryn Bialer writes that the Stalinist bureaucracy had widely overlapping responsibilities, with duplication of functions and changing patterns of control and responsibility; the whole structure was held together by force.[4]

With the Stalinist repressions of the 1930s the Soviet system of border control became one means to impose the state's will on a beleaguered population in a situation where eventually even the desire to emigrate became tantamount to treason. But it was also used as a means of stabilization in the face of the dislocations and upheavals of Stalinism. Border controls helped to ensure, by force, that the population participated in the radical socio-economic construction of Stalinism. The idea that the Soviet Union was a totalitarian state, in which citizens were completely subordinate to an all-powerful state, has some validity here. In the climate of spy mania that prevailed during the purges, it became extremely dangerous for citizens to have any correspondence with foreigners, to have travelled abroad, or to be a member of a national minority identified by Stalin as a fifth column for espionage. Personnel of the border-control organs themselves were subjected to intense pressure and terror by the late 1930s, which would eventually deter their personnel from permitting any travel or emigration by citizens, who in turn would become more and more afraid to show any desire to leave the country. The severity of Soviet border-control policy can be attributed in part to this psychological factor, which was a highly effective means of coercion.

The importance of the growth of state institutions as a factor in explaining the restrictive nature of the Soviet system has been less frequently examined than the role of the Communist Party. In fact, the bureaucratic scope and growth of state institutions were important factors in the development of the Soviet system.[5] Thus, the structural and institutional motivations for political outcomes are closely linked. When a country faces extreme circumstances during the process of state-building, it is likely to form correspondingly extreme institutions. Once such institutions are formed, they become difficult to change.[6] It is significant that the official responsibilities for Soviet border control have historically been diffused throughout many different state organizations rather than concentrated in clearly defined, co-ordinated government bodies. These various organizations, with unclear and overlapping sets of duties, created enough red tape among them to add to the restrictiveness of the border-control process, since there were many government agencies involved in the implementation process, each of which had the right to interfere at some stage. The Communist Party also took a proactive role in ensuring that there were various levels of tripwires and hoops, guaranteeing the party's involvement in the process.

SOVIET INSTITUTIONS AND BORDER CONTROL

In some respects Soviet border control was something of an afterthought, at lest in part determined by practical concerns and by the requirements of fulfilling other policies. From the beginning border control was a product of the interaction of many different branches of government. Leaders such as Khristian Rakovskii (of the Soviet Ukrainian government), Lazar Kaganovich, and Feliks Dzerzhinskii (of the Cheka) were clearly interested in border control and played significant roles in determining policy, but wrote relatively little about it.[7] When they did, it was usually to portray border control as a necessary response to a counter-revolutionary threat.[8] Border control was not considered a sphere of policy that was very interesting, as Leonid Krasin, commissar for Foreign Trade, admitted for all intents and purposes in his discussion of the customs bureaucracy. It was a routine function of government that key Soviet leaders preferred to delegate.[9] Published sources are scarce on the Communist Party's attitude towards emigration, immigration, and border controls, though in general the Party seemed to take a firmly negative line against emigration of any kind.[10] To be sure, the Party considered border control a politically sensitive subject.

One legacy of the Civil War was the proliferation of border-control bodies. With the army, the Cheka, and various ministries all sharing some responsibility for border control, one hand did not necessarily know what the other was doing. Duplicate bodies often executed the same function; the old and the new, central and local bodies all exercised some control over borders. As a result, in the 1920s the question of exactly which agency controlled what function in the sphere of emigration, immigration, and travel seems to have been a matter of confusion, particularly in the localities; nor was it always clear in the central commissariats what the division of responsibilities was amid the changing procedures for immigration, emigration, entry, and exit.[11] As the decade wore on there were greater efforts to define what the various responsibilities were, but there was still little expressed desire to streamline or rationalize the process to ensure that state border controls did not become overly restrictive or prohibitive.

Archival documents detail the involvement of a number of government bodies in border control. The OGPU (political security apparatus) had control over actual border crossings and the right to take all necessary security measures and approve documents, according to a 1923 statute.[12] The Central Executive Committee (TsIK) of the Council of People's Commissars had the power to grant citizenship to immigrants and to intervene in the emigration process in exceptional cases. The Commissariat of Foreign Affairs had the formal power to grant passports and visas to individuals; it decided all questions of the rights and obligations of Soviet citizens abroad, as well as ruling on the entry of foreigners into the country.[13] Meanwhile, the Narkomvnudely (Commissariats of Internal Affairs, or NKVDs) in the republics handled the actual passport-application procedure and the payment of passport fees. Finally, the Main Customs Administration of the Commissariat of Foreign Trade handled the customs-control service. The OGPU administered the border troops, which had close relations with the Red Army. The OGPU in effect had to give a type of political security clearance to anyone who left the country legally. The Party, meanwhile, had its own bodies to recommend or deny travel to its own members, and checked up on the GPU.

Hence, many state political and economic agencies insisted on some form of veto power on the people and goods permitted to enter the country. Moreover, they often worked in co-operation on matters of general policy of emigration, immigration, passports, and repatriation, as on, for example, the STO Permanent Commission on Immigration and Emigration.[14] Representatives from various state bodies had a say not only in general policy but even in approving the names of individuals permitted to enter and leave the country.[15] The co-operative nature of the commission and the relative absence of conflict over policy was striking.[16]

The state authorities concerned with the labour supply had a strong voice in emigration and immigration policy. In particular, documents from the Commissariat of Labour reveal that government bodies were reluctant to allow the departure abroad of people whose labour was considered valuable to the state, in the belief that permitting such emigration to capitalist countries would amount to sanctioning the economic exploitation of Soviet citizens who did not know any better.[17] The paternalism inherent in these views – the assumption that Soviet citizens needed to be enlightened in order to realize the folly of leaving the country – is obvious and demonstrates how Marxist ideology coloured these institutions' assessments of whether or not to allow emigration; Soviet workers needed to be protected from the operation of an international labour market, which could only work to their disadvantage. The emigration of able-bodied individuals was also seen as economically disadvantageous for the Bolshevik state, which needed labour resources to construct its new economic order (even if there was hunger and unemployment in the interim). Furthermore, peoples' motives for emigration were suspect, on the presumption that they might have been duped by foreign passenger-shipping companies, anti-Soviet leaders, and the like. Soviet and Party agencies would at times conduct campaigns to discourage emigration among groups seen as prone to such negative influences, such as Mennonites and Jews (who were seeking to emigrate on the grounds of religious and ethnic persecution). The NKVD and OGPU were at times told to seek out and punish individuals or agencies that were advocating emigration.[18]

Meanwhile, in the early 1920s immigration, particularly of skilled workers, was to some extent encouraged, although carefully controlled. A 1921 RSFSR law required that foreign students who received a state stipend were obliged to stay after graduation and perform service for a set period in their area of specialization.[19] Measures were taken to allow for the absorption and colonization of immigrants, albeit in an orderly fashion, in order to reflect well on the image of Bolshevik society.[20] But by 1928 the policy of mass immigration was abandoned, in part because of the large expenditures involved and the dilemmas of absorbing the immigrants.[21] Dzerzhinskii wrote in 1924 that, given the unsatisfactory results of the influx of arrivals, immigration would henceforth generally be limited to individual cases.[22] This decision presumably created greater pressures for the state to limit exit from the country in order to guarantee the labour supply. The Commissariat of Labour issued special regulations to regulate the conduct of *komandirovki* (work-related trips abroad.) If one was applying for permission to travel abroad on a *komandirovka*, then designated personnel at one's place of work would fill out the required forms.[23] Generally, *komandirovki* could not exceed two months in Europe or three months elsewhere except in special cases.[24] In addition, unless one went abroad for a very long time (three to four years), one was not allowed to take one's family.[25] The currency situation provided an additional means of control. The perpetual dilemma of the prospective Soviet emigrant in the non-convertible ruble economy was to obtain the money to go abroad, since, as of the currency reform of the late 1920s, only the state dispensed hard currency legally. Significantly, the Commissariat of Labour would decide how much currency one would be allowed to take abroad.[26]

Furthermore, travel abroad could be financially prohibitive given the high fees charged for passports. The regular passport fee, 200 rubles for workers, 300 for others, was very high for the average citizen, although in some cases the fees could be reduced or even waived.[27] One could pay a reduced fee only if one persuaded the NKVD's Central Administrative Division that one was going abroad for valid reasons, a procedure that required documentation from one's workplace and, often, from other government organizations intervening on one's behalf. One would also have to fill out a form attesting to one's political reliability.[28] Finally, the military high command had input into the process as well. Anyone in the military or eligible for military service had to have permission of the military authorities to travel, and had to submit a report stating why it was necessary.[29]

In the mid- to late 1920s a steady accumulation of cumbersome bureaucratic restrictions incrementally imposed limits on individuals' abilities to travel abroad. Archival documents suggest that although there was certainly a centrally co-ordinated border-control policy, a progression of separate instructions from various official bodies added considerable barriers to cross-border movement. The evidence suggests that a somewhat haphazard output of regulations contributed in the long run to boundaries that were increasingly difficult to penetrate. In this period, border controls resulted in part from a creeping progression of red tape rather than a purely planned, deliberate determination involving all the institutions concerned.

For example, the bureaucratic obstacles inherent in official Soviet practices for granting travel privileges developed in a manner that surely must have been confusing to all concerned. In 1926 the foreign passports that would permit Soviet citizens to travel abroad (as opposed to the internal passports later used for identification purposes) were recalled and invalidated.[30] A set of NKVD regulations established the practice whereby a foreign passport would be valid only for a single trip abroad within three months of its issue. Soviet citizens were required to supply additional paperwork in order to obtain a foreign passport and exit visa. For example, an applicant seeking permission for a foreign *komandirovka* was compelled to submit documents from his/her employer; artists and even athletes had to receive permission from the state bodies respectively in charge of culture and sport. Would-be travellers also had to secure statements from their workplaces, local soviets, or educational institutions affirming that there were no reasons to object to the individual's travel abroad.[31] When applying for a passport, a citizen might be required to supply an official confirmation that he or she owed no back taxes.[32] Meanwhile, the NKVD could refuse permission for an individual to leave the country on the vague grounds of "inexpediency."[33] If planning to leave the USSR permanently, prospective emigrants were required to supply proof that they were planning to join relatives abroad.[34] Bureaucratic control extended to foreigners entering the USSR, who were required to register their legal entry into the country with local authorities in the place where they would reside. Foreign travellers would be permitted to visit localities outside their place of registration only with official permission.[35]

Two institutions (whose functions eventually merged into one) came to have a dominant role in deciding policy. First, the Narkomvnudely of the individual republics had very broad functions in the 1920s, from police functions and the maintenance of prisons to responsibility for local housing and agricultural organization, roads, local administration and registration, as well as the granting of visas and foreign pass-ports.[36] The control of the local passport bureaucracy and their local administrative powers, the ability to investigate individuals, plus the ability to determine the passport fee seem to have vested the republi-can Narkomvnudely with a fair degree of power. While the Commis-sariat of Foreign Affairs (NKID) technically had the power to grant passports and visas, it seems to have delegated much of the decision-making minutiae to the Narkomvnudely, and even government com-missariats and delegations had to appeal to it for passports. Moreover, the NKID at times wrote to the Narkomvnudely asking for clarification of the procedures that were supposedly its own responsibility.[37]

Secondly, the OGPU (descendent of the Cheka, the political-security apparatus), seems to have had a power of total veto gained through its monopoly of security and secrecy. The NKVD and OGPU had, of course, a co-operative relationship, and with the abolition of the republican NKVDs and the creation of a new USSR central NKVD in 1934, the func-tions of these two organizations were later merged. The GPU was told that, in considering who to permit to leave the country, they were to prioritize political-security concerns.[38] At times people were simply refused passports "for political reasons" by the OGPU, who felt little need to explain such refusals.[39] This refusal could take place, for instance, if one had relatives who had fled abroad with the Whites in the Civil War.[40]

There was increasing concern with the political-security implications of *komandirovki*. Feliks Dzerzhinskii demanded that prospective trav-ellers on Soviet business be screened for their political maturity and invulnerability to the lures of capitalism.[41] The OGPU advised the Party Central Committee on which Party members should and should not be allowed to go abroad on Party business.[42] Meanwhile, prominent lead-ers such as Dzerzhinskii and Stalin, even while embarking on policies to make travel abroad more difficult, were not above demanding from the passport bureaucracy that application procedures be simplified, or intervening in favour of individuals who had experienced difficulties or refusals.[43] The Commissariat of Foreign Affairs was known to com-plain to the Party about interference from the party and the GPU con-cerning those it allowed to travel abroad, as such interventions dis-rupted its own diplomatic work.[44] Meanwhile, the Communist Party itself kept tabs on the OGPU's activities and held it responsible for any erroneous or undesirable exit permissions granted to individuals.[45] The Party had its own Commission on Exit that parallelled that of the GPU.[46] Finally, there was some concern over the import of subversive ideas across borders.[47] The OGPU's political-control authorities were responsible for the struggle against political literature not allowed by the censorship authorities of Glavlit (Committee for the Protection of State Secrecy in Publishing), and imposed controls at customs and border points against forbidden literature.[48]

Despite the bureaucratic hurdles involved, the process of granting permission operated rather arbitrarily. Procedures were juggled at will; who decided what might depend on who meddled, and there was a lack of accountability to citizens. The border-control policies adopted were evidently not popular. Many citizens thought they had the "right" to travel and were frustrated by the red tape involved; they were eventually drawn into the bureaucrats' mentality. Many sought the assistance of state patrons, pleaded, or made elaborate justifications for their need for a passport or visa. Clearly travel abroad was by the late 1920s an act that entailed close contact with many different central and local government organs, which would know almost everything about the prospective traveller.

By the late 1920s there were efforts to establish elaborate legislation and procedures for the implementation of border control. The 1924 criminal code made illegal crossing of the border a criminal offence against the state subject to six months of forced labour or a 500-ruble fine. Engaging in contraband was also a crime, with stricter penalties for repeat offenders.[49] The state's border policy, defining the functions and operation of border control, appeared in 1927.[50] The 1927 statute, while it does not seem to have introduced new restrictions, systematized the border regime's division of functions and clearly elaborated border restrictions, organizing a formerly haphazard series of measures and decrees into a single legal authority. In addition, it established border control as an All-Union prerogative, minimizing the authority that the Soviet republics could have over this function. It clearly entrusted the control of state borders to the Main Administration of Border Control of the OGPU.[51]

The various layers and restrictions surrounding border control created a system of various tiers. If one was a state employee, one used one system; an artist, another; a high official a third; a Party member yet another; and a private citizen another. Depending on one's social identity, one might need permission from the military, the workplace, financial authorities, or one's family. If one were a citizen of a border area, or belonged to a certain nationality, one might have special permissions or restrictions. This complex process finally reached a point where the rules guiding entry and exit were quite indecipherable and, as a tangled web, difficult to change without great effort. The ability to travel, to have access to hard currency and transport, and to bring goods into and out of the country became extremely hierarchical. Party and government higher-ups, leaders, and economic officials could travel abroad under different sets of rules, receiving diplomatic or service passports. But increasingly they had to demonstrate their political loyalty in order to do so.

Finally, the success of Soviet border-control institutions depended on the capacities the state developed in order to implement its policies. Here we must look at the extent to which Soviet border control represented a new development in the modern state. At the border there was a complex network of Soviet technologies of border surveillance. Border troops had dual subordination to the secret police and military, and they were better equipped and fed than the army. There were frontier strips, varying in scale depending on the border, with layers of restricted zones that no one could enter without special permission. These ploughed strips were equipped with barriers, alarms, traps, and mines as well as sentries, observation posts, patrols, and passport-control posts. Border guards organized support groups, volunteer patrols, and agents from among the local population.[52] Hence the Soviet border-control system consisted not just of laws but of new methods of demarcating and enclosing space. This was made possible by the extension of Soviet bureaucracy and power into the localities and by techniques of surveillance. It was thus an extension of a new will and capacity of power characteristic of the totalitarian regime.

A new discourse linking the heightened threat of the enemies of socialism with the border accompanied the intensified militarization of the border-control system.[53] This discourse constrained the Party's view of the border and eliminated the possibility of recognizing that a citizen might wish to cross the border independent of state sanction for benign or politically neutral reasons. It channelled any desire to do so directly to the institution of state surveillance, the GPU. As high Party politics broke into overt struggle at the end of NEP in the late 1920s, a resolution of the Communist Party Congress against the Bukharinist "right deviation" called for further preparedness on the border and was publicized in border newspapers.[54] In the midst of the Shakhty trials (where alleged "wreckers" were accused of trying to sabotage the Soviet economy in 1928), border troops were urged to tighten up border defences and, implicitly, to watch out for any potential Shakhty escapees, who were said to have ties with Poland.[55] Through the 1930s border violators were portrayed as spies for foreign powers and supporters of Bukharinite or Trotskyite gangs. The need to uphold state secrecy against foreign espionage became a prominent theme of border control,[56] and thus an argument for the further build-up of border defences.[57] The border guards were instructed to prevent *nepmen* and *kulaks* from escaping from the country with their wealth, as they were to prevent "wreckers" and saboteurs from escaping punishment.[58]

The Stalinist campaign against the "enemies of the people," including Stalin's vanquished party rivals Bukharin and Trotsky, was linked with the theme of closed borders and expounded on the supposed danger of opening up the country to the foreign enemy and allowing free movement of spies. Trotsky's presence abroad as a threat to Stalinist rule was presented as one justification for closed borders.[59] In the high Stalinist period a frequent theme in the Soviet press was the danger of the violation of the border by spies and diversionists. In keeping with the spirit of the great purges, Stalin's *History of the CPSU* (the "Short Course") showed a preoccupation with border transgressors, foreign agents, émigré "White-guard bandits," and renegades, who according to this text were all seeking to sabotage the Soviet economy and subvert the government.

As the evidence above demonstrates, any compromises or concessions to social groups in border-control policies were effectively obliterated by the Stalinist terror of the 1930s. Drastic policies were instituted to eliminate and deter cross-border movement and communication and to neutralize people who were seen as a potential fifth column. Already in 1928 the "Zinovievite" and "Trotskyite" oppositions were deemed to have too many links abroad and to have potentially dangerous access to the foreign media.[60] By 1935, with the political repressions that followed the murder of Stalin's rival and fellow Communist the popular leader Sergei Kirov, among those targets of political repression were people who had crossed the border in the past or had too many personal links with foreign countries.

The campaign against espionage was decidedly xenophobic and appears often to have affected members of national minorities living on the border. Reports show that the label "spy" was attached indiscriminately to people who had been abroad in the past, were once refugees, had some acquaintances or relatives abroad, or had visited a foreign embassy or consulate. Anyone who had crossed the border at any time – even in the early 1920s – was liable to be arrested as an agent of a foreign intelligence service. It was often mentioned that they had crossed the border illegally, regardless of the meaninglessness of this charge; it was alleged that, while abroad, they had been recruited as intelligence agents. There is evidence that border national minorities numbered prominently among the accused spies – Jews, Germans, Karelian Finns, Bessarabian Russians, and particularly Poles.[61] These arrests were carried out on all parts of the border, accompanied by accusations of espionage for various countries' intelligence agencies. There were separate, even more nebulous categories for those suspected of spy activity or of having contact with spies. Those who had immigrated to the USSR as political sympathizers were considered to be possible spies, as were refugees of any sort or those who associated with refugees.[62]

According to figures for the last half of 1935, 326 spies were arrested. The largest numbers were from Ukraine and Belorussia. However, the progress of Central Asia, Caucasus, and the Far East in rooting out spies was deemed unsatisfactory.[63] Border NKVD authorities were expected to root out spies. In 1935, 740 border or internal NKVD troops were expelled from the party and arrested, some of them for espionage. There were claims that the effectiveness of border troops had increased, effectiveness being measured by the number of apprehensions of border violators.[64] Deportations to clear people from the 500-metre border zone and to forbid entry into them had already begun.[65]

Furthermore, even the most benign reasons for wanting to travel outside Soviet borders became grounds for suspicion; spies and diversionists were depicted as using innocent motives such as visiting family members abroad, as a cover for their illegal activities as foreign agents. Moreover, the word "contrabandist" could be mentioned in the same breath as the word "traitor."[66] The terror against smugglers and spies deterred citizens from trying to leave the country, since the border-control bureaucracy was controlled by the NKVD, the country's most feared institution in the 1930s, responsible for the arrests of millions, usually as spies or foreign saboteurs. Given that many innocent people were shot for alleged espionage, merely expressing the wish to go abroad would automatically have made one suspect in the eyes of the police. As Iurii Felshtinskii argues, in the atmosphere of fear of the 1930s people simply became afraid even to try to leave the country.[67]

The terror reached its peak in 1937 and 1938. At the Central Committee plenum in March 1937 Stalin railed against the danger of foreign spies and diversionists, linking the internal and foreign threat of the Zinoviev-Trotsky bloc, implying that the permeability of borders had allowed the diffusion of spy and enemy activity inside the country. The Party had concentrated on great economic achievements but had neglected the implications of the USSR's international position; Trotskyism, Stalin argued, was a greater threat with the rise of fascism.[68] In 1937 there were efforts to improve agricultural and industrial conditions in border areas, and this was portrayed as a key to strengthening the country's security against spies and diversionists.[69]

The importance of border control in the Soviet system is revealed by the cult of border troops that emerged in the 1930s. The image of the border as the "dividing line between Good and Evil" was a prominent one.[70] Katerina Clark has written about the popularization of border-guard content and imagery in the Stalinist literature of the 1930s. She notes that in the 1930s the border guards acquired a popular, indeed glorified image in popular culture:

One of the obsessions of thirties rhetoric was the nation's "enemies" ... in public life a special place was given to the Soviet border guards ... When the Soviet leaders warned of danger from enemies both within and without, it was in part to provide a mandate for the extraordinary degree of social cohesion they demanded and the extreme means they were using against "unmasked enemies." [71]

The Stalinist regime mythologized its border controls by depicting the relationship between its border troops and the Soviet population as a harmonious one. Border guards were represented as a dedicated elite who would protect the people but would also discourage politically unsophisticated citizens from succumbing to the border's admitted temptations. The border guards also engaged in surveillance: by casting a vigilant eye on supposed internal and external foes of the Soviet regime, they advanced the regime's capacity to educate the masses in an unchallenged socialist ideology. [72]

In the late 1930s, the border was sealed even more tightly. In 1935 new measures extending the border zone expanded it to include new districts. In Leningrad it was reported that Finnish, Estonian, and Lettish peasants were being deported from a 20-kilometre frontier zone to Saratov, Samara, and other parts of Russia. [73] In 1936 there seems to have been an observable increase in the scale of such deportations, judging from the Soviet-Finnish border, where ethnic Finns were being deported. [74] A 1935 decree provided for even stricter rules for entry into and residence in border areas, and created a no-man's land where entry into the immediate proximity of the border was forbidden. [75]

In 1940 the Soviet border itself changed following the annexations of territory agreed upon in the Molotov-Ribbentrop agreement of 1939, and Soviet policies in those areas reflected earlier developments in the country's border zones. The journal *Pogranichnik* was established in September 1939; in its inaugural issue editor S. Presman expressly linked its formation to the Nazi-Soviet treaty and the need to strengthen the armed forces and improve their political indoctrination. [76] This happened to coincide with the period of intense change and activity among the border troops brought about by the Soviet advance into western Ukraine, Belorussia, the Baltic states, and Finland. Border troops participated as "liberators" and set up new border lines and installations. They were exhorted to repeat the same kind of political activity they had earlier: to conduct mass political work among the residents of the new border areas, to bring them into elections, and in

other ways to include them in life in the USSR.[77] Incidentally, in striking contrast to the coverage of the western Ukraine and Belorussian
annexation, the Baltic occupation is barely mentioned in the journal,
save in small articles for "the propagandist and agitator" and one article that reports that the peoples of the Baltic states voted to join the
Soviet Union but says nothing about the military's role, save that the
Red Army "met" the masses.[78]

In western Ukraine and the Baltics the borders were quickly closed
and strict controls set up.[79] In western Ukraine and Belorussia, Soviet
border troops were active in the invasion and quickly set up a new border zone, a process that involved displacing villages and deporting the
people who lived there, in addition to the deportations of purportedly
suspect people (such as former government officials, small farmers, and
families of arrested people). Jails were set up along the border where
many were imprisoned for trying to flee (either into the new border
area from the German zone, as had many Jews, or across into the German zone, as had some Ukrainians.)[80]

With the military forces occupying western Belorussia (eastern
Poland), the Belorussian NKVD were instructed as one of their first
tasks to seize existing border-control instruments, police, and army
documents from occupied police buildings and to prevent cross-border
movement of the population. A division of the *pogranichniki* entered
with the Red Army. The NKVD established new border controls there,
both to combat the emergent smuggling and flight and as a precondi-
tion of the integration of these areas into the Soviet order.[81] In 1939,
during the Soviet occupations, a secret NKVD order allowed for the
introduction of the internal-passport system in the western Ukraine
and Belorussia, and in 1940 the Baltic states and Bessarabia. The
"third passportization" made these areas themselves plus a hundred-
metre border zone "categories under regime." Unauthorized exit and
entry into and out of the regime zone were to be considered tantamount to espionage. This also applied to the old border zones as they
had been prior to the incorporation of these areas, even though they
were no longer on an international border.[82]

By the late 1930s a highly restrictive Soviet border-control system
was in place, held together by strong coercive physical barriers, a
daunting bureaucracy, and an atmosphere of severe psychological
intimidation. Ironically, the system was all about to unravel in the
chaos of the Second World War, a trauma that would force the Soviet
Union to repeat its state-building experience in many border areas and
would produce a border-control system that was tighter than ever.

7 The Reconstruction and Maintenance of Border Controls, 1941-1985

In the history of Soviet border-control policy, the period 1945 to 1985 was static, in that the basic goals and assumptions of the border-control regime changed very little. The very existence of the system was treated with secrecy and ideological obfuscation.[1] Despite the country's apparent domestic stability, border controls were not seriously re-examined or modified. The system was, in fact, extended to cover the new openings for outside contacts and influences that had been created by forces outside the country, new forms of travel, communication, and weaponry. These advances created new difficulties in maintaining Soviet isolation. International forces and technological developments changed the meaning and relevance of border-control structures, which became increasingly irrelevant as modern communications and outside influences penetrated Soviet society despite the state's efforts to counteract them.[2]

Initially, however, border controls after the Second World War responded to state-building prerogatives and structural pressures similar to those of the Civil War and the 1920s; in effect the country underwent a repeated state-building experience in borderland areas, which was coloured by bitterness over the severity of the German invasion and a desire to prevent the recurrence of such a devastating attack. The Second World War upset Soviet border-control policy as well as temporarily reversing the inroads Soviet authorities had made in establishing control over border territories, particularly in the west. The borders of the Soviet Union, of course, changed after the war; Soviet territory was extended to trans-Carpathian Ukraine, the Kurile Islands, and East Prussia (which became Kaliningrad Oblast).[3] Meanwhile, Soviet rule over the Baltic states (Latvia, Lithuania, and Estonia) and the western part of Ukraine had been interrupted. This meant that Soviet authorities would have to reimpose border controls as part of the state-rebuilding process, as during the Civil War. In addition, the war would see the revival and flourishing of anti-Soviet nationalist guerrilla movements in the Baltic and western parts of the country; for many years to come Soviet border guards would again find themselves fighting the challenge to authority in these regions, which, along with the refugee movements, would contribute to the drive to seal borders once again.[4]

The Vlasov movement and the revival of the Ukrainian resistance organization OUN[5] were living examples that domestic political oppositions could be strengthened by support from sympathetic movements abroad. In the post-war years the Cold War and the division of Europe into Soviet and Western "spheres of influence" exacerbated the Soviets' increasing preoccupation with securing the inviolability of their territorial borders. In the immediate post-war period the friendly ties between the Soviet Union and the Western Allies came to an end, and contact with citizens of Western countries ceased to be considered desirable. The Soviet press denounced the allegedly sinister motives of foreigners in the Soviet Union; tourists, missionaries, and others on business in the USSR were depicted as agents of hostile spy organizations. Despite the fact that the country's borders were quite closed, Soviet writings claimed that their borders were being constantly violated.[6]

Soviet border controls were also intended to restore order amid the great displacement of population that the war had produced. Many refugees had left the USSR when it was possible to do so; fearing Stalin's repressions, they took advantage of the chaotic situation at the end of the war to flee to the West or, having found themselves outside Soviet borders, chose to stay there.[7] It is one of the fundamental paradoxes, and revealing features, of Soviet border-control policy that, as Soviet law specialist George Ginsburgs declared, "The Soviet Union, since its inception in 1917, has been the world's largest source of refugees and displaced persons."[8] The numbers prove both that border controls were indeed a response to a destabilizing mass outflow of population, but also that the Soviet Union's repressive policies had in turn created the outflow. The exodus was a source of great concern to Stalin's government. In 1946 Soviet representative A.Y. Vyshinskii, in a speech to the United Nations on refugees, noted that a great many Soviet refugees had "found themselves" outside Soviet borders after the war and expressed doubts about whether they would return; he meanwhile accused Western countries of deterring them from coming back to the Soviet Union and pressed strongly for the return of these "traitors" to their country of origin.

The difficult position of these people is aggravated by the fact that they are subjected to constant political pressure on the part of fascist elements who seek to set the refugees and displaced persons against their countries of nationality, to prevent in every way their return home and to make use of them as instruments in aggressive designs and plans in regard to the states whose nationals these refugees and displaced persons are.[9]

Subsequently, the Soviet Union did negotiate various agreements with other states for exchanges of population and for the repatriation of various national minorities.[10] Hence, it became possible for limited numbers of some national minorities and displaced persons to enter or leave the country, either voluntarily or forcibly, depending on the agreement.

The Cold War and the division of Europe into "spheres of influence" had a profound effect on the USSR's border controls. The hostility between the USSR and the West reinforced the desire of the Communist leadership to seal off the Soviet Union from outside influences, to prevent military invasions, and to extend border controls to Eastern Europe, which fell under Soviet control. Border controls similar to the Soviet model were imposed throughout Eastern Europe, particularly in East Germany, where rigid barriers – and eventually the Berlin Wall – served to sever the flow of migrants to the West.[11] Soviet border controls, through this entire period, were again ideologically justified on the basis of the existence of "capitalist encirclement" and the intrigues of bourgeois states against the USSR.[12]

However, the fear of espionage and foreign aggression used by the Soviets as justification for continued border controls is incongruous in light of the Soviet "liberation" of the states of Eastern Europe. The Soviet Union was no longer in a situation of "capitalist encirclement," nor facing the lonely task of creating "socialism in one country"; rather, with the creation of buffer satellite states in Eastern Europe it faced fellow socialist countries on its formerly onerous western border.[13] Cross-border trade between the USSR and the East European countries was facilitated, and a number of border economic and military-co-operation arrangements were established.[14] Theoretically, borders between socialist states were to be of a different, more friendly nature than those with and between capitalist countries, as a joint defence against the capitalist bloc. None the less, the individual states of Eastern Europe would retain their sovereignty and their own state border controls. This was not seen by Soviet theoreticians as inconsistent with the eventual "withering away of the state" and the disappearance of state borders.[15]

Soviet border-control institutions changed to reflect post-war changes in the international system and in technology. With the advent of long-range nuclear weapons in the 1950s the military justifications of the border regime became less relevant. Despite this innovation, the border-control regime does not seem to have been significantly scaled down until the Gorbachev era. The military nature of the border itself changed, and the creation of the Air Defence Division (PVO) in part added to the country's border defences.[16]

The border-troop system also endured a number of administrative changes. Upon Stalin's death in 1953 the troops were transferred briefly to the Ministry of Defence (from the Ministry of Internal Affairs, which was suffering internal problems after the discrediting of brutal NKVD head Lavrentii Beria) and then to the newly formed KGB (Committee for State Security), which was in turn separated from the Ministry of Internal Affairs.[17] Therefore, border troops remained under the control of the internal political-security apparatus. In 1960 a new regulation on border control was passed that took into account the changes in the post-war system. There were two main innovations. The first was to establish the PVO's control over air defence and airspace violations, giving this new branch of the military more border-defence responsibilities. The law also kept abreast of technological innovations that affected Soviet sovereignty, mentioning that communications links and oil and other pipelines that crossed Soviet borders were to observe the laws and agreements of the USSR.[18]

In truth, under Khrushchev and Brezhnev the "Iron Curtain" did lift somewhat. Foreign travel and academic exchanges were resumed; the country was opened to tourism; and there were increasing cultural contacts and co-operation between the USSR and foreign countries. In addition, the country attracted a large influx of students and travellers from Eastern Europe and Third World countries.[19] It was easier for Soviet citizens to travel on *komandirovki* to visit these countries than Western countries, and travel fees and regulations were somewhat less prohibitive. This amounted to an increase in border *traffic*, but without a lifting of border *controls*, which were if anything increased. The traffic was still carefully monitored and channelled by the state, and took place through state-sponsored organizations.[20]

In addition, while substantial Jewish emigration was allowed in the early 1970s and 1980s, it was, as Seweryn Bialer argues, an exception to general policy.[21] Laurie P. Salitan convincingly argues that the mass Soviet Jewish, Armenian, and German emigration of the 1970s and

1980s was a carefully controlled development that resulted from those groups' special position in Soviet nationality policy. Members of other groups who had family ties abroad, such as Ukrainians, Russians, and Balts, were rarely permitted to leave the country.[22] The state still did not permit mass travel; emigration and travel both were subject to administrative restrictions rather than guaranteed by law.[23] Applicants who sought to emigrate were frequently harassed and persecuted by the police. In addition, emigrants required permission from their workplace, and their employer had to produce a character reference on their behalf, which constituted a further deterrent. Constantly changing application procedures added further insecurity to any attempt to leave the country legally.[24]

During the Brezhnev period, various published legal regulations on border control, some of them the first of their kind since the 1920s, were issued; despite the vast differences in the structural conditions of the two periods, there was relatively little change. The 1970 statute on entry and exit reaffirmed the responsibility of the organs of the Ministry of Internal Affairs (under its division of visas and registration, OVIR) for granting foreign passports and exit visas to citizens.[25] As for the conditions under which people were entitled to leave the USSR for personal reasons, the statute stated only that passports and visas would be granted "following the established order."[26] The 1970 statute publicly affirmed and elaborated the existence of a privilege system with respect to rights to travel abroad. Diplomats and ranking officials who wished to travel fell under a separate system of diplomatic and official passports handled by the Ministry of Foreign Affairs.[27]

This state of affairs was, of course, not unique to the Soviet Union. Other countries also issue diplomatic passports, presumably to confirm the special status of diplomats working at embassies abroad and to expedite the conduct of official business by state leaders. In the Soviet Union the list of people eligible for diplomatic passports was very large, going well beyond the ranks of diplomats and state leaders into what was basically a *nomenklatura* of people allowed to apply to the Ministry of Foreign Affairs. It provided for travel for upper levels of the Party hierarchy.[28]

Ultimately, three major factors operated in this period to propel the country towards changing its closed-border regime. The first problem was that the Soviet Union's border-control regime hurt the country's image and position in the international community. The restrictiveness of Soviet border controls remained a major sticking-point of East-West relations in general and received a great deal of international publicity in the 1970s.[29] The Soviets attracted attention both domestically and abroad to their restrictive emigration policy by signing various agreements that supported free emigration and travel as basic human rights. These included the 1948 United Nations International Declaration on Human Rights, which reads, "Everyone has the right to leave any country, including his own, and to return to his country" – although the USSR tried to have a clause included in the agreement to add "in accordance with the procedure laid down by the laws of the country."[30]

In discussions about the pan-European security conference that would eventually become the Conference on Security and Co-operation in Europe (CSCE, or the Helsinki Process) in 1970, the NATO bloc proposed the extension of the conference to include human-rights issues, including the freedom of ideas and movement across borders. While the USSR opposed making this part of the agenda, eventually freedom-of-movement issues were placed in the realm of Basket Three of the conference's agenda.[31] Various freedom-of-movement issues, including family reunification, greater cultural co-operation, and the like, were discussed. The concluding document (the Helsinki Final Act) included four pages on human contacts, including the right of "wider travel by all citizens."[32]

Among the dissident groups that arose in the USSR in the 1970s, and in the content of much of the *samizdat* of unofficial opposition groups, the demand for the right to emigrate as a human right was a prominent theme. These groups, absorbing the norms of the outside world, demanded that the USSR adhere to international law in this regard and conform to the agreements it had signed.[33] In addition, dissident groups of other nationalities, such as Ukrainians, demanded the same rights to emigrate as Jews,[34] evidence that many Soviets wanted to use the "exit option" that had been historically denied to them and already saw the Soviet border-control regime as a cause for grievance. That dissident groups were able to muster resources and support from, and keep up communications with the outside world was itself a source of consternation to the Soviet authorities. In the Soviet press pro-emigration activists were often painted as spies and conspirators. None the less, their existence was evidence of the failure of Soviet border controls to keep out all unwanted influences and ideas. The Soviets were put on the defensive with regard to this issue, since to Western observers the restrictiveness of the Soviet emigration policy did not match any existing internal-security threat.

The second major factor in impelling changes in the border-control regime was that controls were not totally effective: despite increased efforts and resources devoted to controls, the country still remained permeable to anti-Soviet influences, illegal smuggling of goods, and unauthorized movements and defections. The achievement of what had originally been merely been border "control" – the restriction of the movement of people, ideas, and goods into and out of the country – became much more difficult and complex. First, border controls had to be established at airports through which international travel took place, not just the actual border. Second, the activity of foreigners, who were increasingly entering and leaving the country, had to be monitored, a difficult task. Third, foreign radio stations broadcasting to the USSR, such as Voice of America and Radio Liberty, would be jammed, with great effort.[35] All these tasks required an enormous expenditure of resources. But the pursuit of these measures demonstrates that, until Mikhail Gorbachev came to power in 1985, the Soviet leadership and its institutional apparatuses did not seriously revise the goals that had caused the border-control system to be created. Thus, ironically, just when the USSR had finally honed its abilities to close its borders on land, new border-control mechanisms were necessary to fulfil the same goals, such as the jamming of radio broadcasts.[36] The state apparatus was unable completely to counteract the influence of anti-Soviet émigrés, who by listening to Radio Liberty were able to keep contact with their compatriots.[37]

The effort was also made to control tourism strictly and prevent it from violating the USSR's internal-security goals. Yet particularly with the growth of tourism into the Soviet Union of the 1970s, this goal proved impossible to achieve. Westerners, accustomed to more liberal values and less afraid of the Soviet state's sanctions, smuggled unknown but obviously considerable quantities of goods into and out of the country.[38] Soviet smugglers also carried on illicit cross-border economic activities. The most commonly smuggled goods, according to a 1987 official publication, included jeans, footwear, radios, tricotage, umbrellas, sunglasses, and pornography, which were all in short supply in the Soviet Union. The authorities argued that increases in travel and tourism increased the smuggling problem.[39] Soviet writers on the subject also noted that in the contemporary period there was a close relationship between the black market and smuggling; goods smuggled into the country later ended up in the second economy.[40]

So border controls were aimed in part at combating illegal trade that satisfied the thirst for Western goods, a situation not so different from that of the 1920s, when the demand for consumer goods had given rise to such a serious smuggling problem. The organs of the Bureau to Combat Economic Speculation and Sabotage (BKhSS) were created by the Ministry of Internal Affairs in the 1960s in part to prevent the smuggling of foreign currency across Soviet borders.[41] According to Soviet figures, from 1959 to 1968 the number of Soviets crossing the border increased 250 per cent, while the number of foreigners increased 500 per cent.[42] Smuggling was seen as a threat; particularly in the 1980s there was a concern that, in addition to the jeans and sneakers coming from foreigners, and the scholarly materials and Bibles brought by Western academics and members of organizations, Soviet citizens would be "sold" the non-Soviet ideas and values that came with them. Thus the Soviet border-control regime was violated; the influx of foreigners provided a limited but real means of exposure to alternative political ideas and values.[43] The presence of foreigners in the USSR provided to Soviet citizens evidence that people in other countries enjoyed rights to travel that they did not; this would later cause resentment.

The final major problem that made changes in the border-control regime inevitable was hat its benefits were outweighed by its costs.[44] In the immediate post-revolutionary period and into the 1940s border control was presented as having concrete, positive goals, to defend the state from security threats. But in the post-war period the USSR was at odds with the norms, economic practices, and political trends of the advanced industrial states with which it claimed to be on a par, and in the long run this affected its ability to participate in the new global community. This shows the long-term inadaptability of the Soviet leadership, and that leaders can pursue policies that are obsolete or out of step with reality.[45]

In the important work *Change in Communist Systems* Chalmers Johnson and Richard Lowenthal, among others, argued in 1970 that the pressures produced by modernization would eventually impel the Soviet Union towards a more open and democratic political society, although leaders would try to suppress these pressures out of fear of political and national instability.[46] The obsolescence of Soviet border-control policy and its rigidity despite the compelling forces against it demonstrates the existence both of these pressures and of resistance to them. Many scholars argue the importance of the pressures of international economic co-operation and global technological advances in producing pressure for Soviet domestic political reform.[47] Participation in these new global trends, however, would have meant opening up the entrenched border-control institutions that had served to keep out positive aspects of transnational contact as well as negative. Strict border controls seemed obsolete in an era of jet travel, satellite communications, and computer networks, and the Soviet government's preoccupation with security was impeding the country's ability to take part in the world communications revolution.[48] Stephen D. Krasner has argued that technological advantages affect power relations between states; states that pioneer important new technologies – in this case the United States and Japan – are able to set the terms internationally, deciding to what use the technology will be put and with what values in mind.[49] For the USSR in the late 1980s, this meant opening its entire political system in order to participate in new economic and informational gains.

By 1985, when Mikhail Sergeevich Gorbachev came to power as General Secretary of the CPSU, a number of European states were preparing virtually to eliminate their mutual state border controls through the increasing integration of the European Economic Community (which later became the European Union), a development heralded as a means of pooling their resources and maximizing their cooperation. Perhaps, at least regionally, borders and border controls were becoming less necessary in the new transnational order. But in the Soviet Union border-control barriers had never been stronger. In the 1980s there was a last, desperate push. Soviet propaganda and the press depicted vigilance as more necessary than ever to combat the ideological and economic sabotage of erstwhile foreign agents. In 1982 a law on the USSR state border (the first such complete law since 1927) was passed. In his speech to the Supreme Soviet on the occasion of its discussion of this law KGB chief V.V. Fedorchuk accused the West of systematically violating the Soviet border and conducting illegal trade:

cynically trampling on norms of international law, Western spy organizations and centres of ideological diversion are trying to send into our country their agents and emissaries, illegally bring into the USSR weapons and explosives, drugs, radio and reprographic equipment, printed materials of a subversive nature. All possible tricks are encountered by border troops and customs agents, who must foil and counteract their enemy activities.[50]

The 1982 law was the first true Soviet law on the state border.[51] It ruled that anybody who attempted to leave or enter the country without permission was violating the border. Politically, there were two distinguishing features of the law. It gave border troops a wide sphere of powers over traffic coming across the border, including the right to detain, for up to three days, people suspected of violating the rules of border crossings (including customs violations) or who crossed it illegally. It also paid great attention to listing the various media that border guards were allowed to scrutinize: documents, videocassettes, recordings, and other printed material, again showing concern over the passage of ideas between Soviet citizens and the West.[52] Supplementing this law, a series of measures restricting the contact between Soviet citizens and foreigners was enacted in 1984.[53]

In 1985 Mikhail Gorbachev succeeded Konstantin Chernenko as

head of the Communist Party of the Soviet Union. In 1986 a new series of amendments on emigration was passed that was widely seen as legalizing and codifying previously existing restrictive administrative procedures and practices. The law was a rationalization and clarification of exit/entry policy and constituted an open expression of emigration policy.[54] It also introduced some innovations: the principle that citizens could leave and enter the country regardless of nationality, social standing, religion, and other social categories; and that refused people must be told of the reasons for refusal and given the right to reapply after six months.[55] The main new feature spelled out in the amendments was their specification of the reasons for which citizens could be refused permission to leave the country on private business.[56] These included the provisos that the right to travel could be refused "in the interests of safeguarding public order or the population's health or morality ... If during a previous trip abroad [the applicants had] acted in violation of state interests or if it is established that they violated customs or foreign exchange legislation; [or] If they provide false information when applying to leave."[57]

Interestingly, however, the regulations attempted to correct past abuses by allowing citizens to reapply if refused and by granting them the right to have a prompt answer to their application to go abroad (within a month.)[58] It also declared that people "may enter or leave the USSR irrespective of their provenance, social standing, property status, race, nationality, sex, education, language, or religious beliefs."[59] At this time OVIR still granted permission to enter and leave the country. The Ministry of Internal Affairs had been shaken by a scandal revealed upon Iurii Andropov's accession to power in 1983, and there were rumours that visas had been bought and sold.[60] Notorious for their rudeness, OVIR officials were reportedly ordered to be more polite and businesslike soon after the 1986 emigration law was passed.[61]

Despite the sweeping nature of this law, however, emigration and visa policy began to be drastically relaxed not long after its passage, as the Gorbachev reforms were instituted. Just as border-control policy became publicly elaborated in its most stringent form, it began to open up. The next chapter will explore the liberalization of Soviet border-control policy, which began in 1987.

8 *Perestroika* and the Iron Curtain: The Dilemmas of Changing Institutions, 1986–1991

The process of economic and political transformation initiated under Mikhail Sergeevich Gorbachev in 1986 led to an opening up of the Soviet system. The reforms of *glasnost* and *perestroika*, as they were envisaged, were incongruous with restrictive border controls, and the pressures to change the border-control system came from many different directions.[1] Comprehensive legislative efforts, beginning in 1989, were undertaken to co-ordinate the various institutional interests involved in the border-control process and to develop a consensus in favour of liberalized borders among newly elected Soviet legislators. But by the time these laws were finally passed, reform of the Soviet system of border control was undermined by two related developments: first, the state's excessive use of coercion on its borders to suppress nationality unrest and economic destabilization contradicted the overall reform effort; and second, the republics' demands for their own border controls led to the creation of new barriers while the old ones lost their legitimacy. Meanwhile, a new, economic "Iron Curtain" emerged; as transport and communications companies began to operate on profit and loss, they began to demand hard currency and high ruble prices, which left citizens unable to afford to travel abroad. Consequently, the central reform initiatives heralded by Soviet liberals became irrelevant by 1991. At the same time the republics were setting up border-control systems of their own as they began to assert their sovereignty.

Fairly early in Gorbachev's tenure as Communist Party General Secretary he acknowledged that the Soviet Union should adjust to the greater economic and technological interdependence of the world system. His "new political thinking" in foreign policy introduced the concept of mutual security between the Soviet Union and the West and, along with it, modified the question of borders.[2] Increasingly, liberalizing borders was seen as compatible with the state's economic interests in facilitating foreign trade and the exchange of information and communication. The goals of economic reform included increased trade with foreign countries, expanded rights of enterprises to engage in trade, and the permission to undertake joint ventures with foreign companies. These objectives in turn would necessitate increased travel and communications for business trips to and from the USSR for both Soviet citizens and foreigners.[3] Economic co-operation and improved foreign relations between the USSR and other countries became not just officially permissible but desirable.[4] The new Soviet goals included expanding participation in the international market system and exploring a new-found interest in international institutions such as the General Agreement on Tariffs and Trade (GATT). These new goals created an impetus for reforming customs controls and tariffs.[5]

The second source of reform was the Soviet Union's conciliatory foreign-policy initiatives towards the West. With the 1987 inauguration of *novoe myshlenie* – the "new political thinking" in foreign policy – the Soviet leadership began to advocate a more co-operative attitude towards the outside world, one that favoured greater integration in the international economy. As a result the USSR ceased to be necessarily in a hostile relationship with the non-socialist world. This eventually allowed Soviet borders to be thought of as less politically charged, to be regarded as potential conduits of beneficial trade and inter-societal communication rather than walls to keep out alien influences. Gorbachev's attitude of conciliation in the context of foreign policy had an immediate impact on border-control reform. In his speech to the United Nations in December 1988 he referred to the development of growing international independence and unity, especially in Europe; he vowed that the emigration process would be "resolved in a humane way" and the problem of *refuseniks* eliminated.[6] Gorbachev argued that opening up the system to international contact was a crucial part of Soviet reform. He called for the abandonment of a system developed under "extreme conditions" and its replacement with one that was more in line with the concept of participation in an interdependent world system: "The process of *perestroika* in the Soviet Union holds out fresh opportunities for international co-operation. Unbiased observers predict growth in the Soviet Union's share of the world economy and invigoration of foreign economic, scientific, and technological ties, including those maintained through international organizations."[7]

The third source of reform in border-control structures was the thrust of political reforms, which put questions of democratization, human rights, and rule of law on the agenda. In 1987 Gorbachev initiated the policy of *glasnost*, which allowed a greater range of free expression in the media. This produced ever-greater calls for democracy. As *glasnost* expanded after Gorbachev's accession to power, intellectuals and economists began to express vaguely the need for more open borders as part of Soviet strategies for change.[8] In contrast to the secrecy with which the reality of Soviet emigration had been treated in the pre-reform era, the Soviet press began to publish statistics of those travelling and leaving the country permanently. For example, one pair of reporters presented the fact that 100,000 Soviets had emigrated in 1988 as a sign of a more open society and "the humanization of Soviet laws."[9] *Glasnost* also allowed citizens to voice grievances. Freedom of movement to citizens was, as some argued, a necessary part of the process of democratization.[10]

By 1988 tentative steps towards the liberalization of border-control policy had begun. The issue was considered sufficiently important for the Soviet Communist Party Central Committee to consider ways of facilitating business travel abroad, particularly for purposes of economic, scientific, and technical co-operation. Institutes, ministries, and enterprises were encouraged to increase significantly the number of foreign trips for purposes of economic collaboration. Soviet embassies and missions were called upon to facilitate this process, and central visa-granting agencies were to grant more powers to their branches in the localities.[11] The ensuing changes made travel, particularly from Moscow, much easier. While individuals would still require invitations from relatives abroad to travel, and those travelling on business needed some kind of sponsorship from abroad or from their Soviet institution, many more such permissions were granted than previously. For travel to socialist countries, one could apply to one's *raion* organs and receive the visa the same day; the application process became simpler and faster; and multiple-entry/exit visas were granted under some circumstances.[12]

The regulations on goods allowed to cross the border were also modified to reflect the changed political atmosphere. V. Boiarov, director of the Main Administration of State Customs Control, declared the implementation of "a new concept – the principle of trusting everyone who crosses the USSR state border." On 1 August 1989 "New Rules for the Import into and Export out of the USSR of Items, Currency and Valuables by Citizens" were introduced. These rules allowed some increases in the amount of goods that citizens could bring with them upon entering or leaving the country. Restrictions on printed matter (political contraband) were eased so as to cover only those materials that advocated the violent overthrow of the Soviet state or its territorial integrity.[13]

At roughly the same time the activity of the state border troops was also called into question, allegedly at the KGB's own initiative. Border-troop chiefs had announced that, in light of democratization, the policy of closed border zones was being re-examined because the crisis conditions that had engendered the closed-border regime no longer existed and, like other branches of the state bureaucracy, the border troops should appropriately scale down their administrative apparatus appropriately. Plans were drawn up for border zones to be dismantled, beginning in the northwest.[14] In the fall of 1988 imminent changes in the border security system to simplify the actual crossing of borders were announced by Chebrikov.[15] The chief of the KGB in 1990 declared that his organization was dedicated to the goal of eliminating the border zones on the boundary with "socialist countries" and significantly reducing them on other borders. Moreover, there was an expressed drive to make the border zones more harmonious with the local population's way of life by excluding rivers, populated areas, and religious sites from border zones.[16]

The opening of the Soviet system reached its second stage with the initiation of legislation on border-control issues. Reform-minded leaders in the Soviet state and in the reconstituted legislature (the Supreme Soviet) sought to give the new openings in the Soviet system a legal basis. In March 1991 a new All-Union customs law was passed after two years of effort. The law allowed individuals, enterprises, and organizations to take goods across the border (with the exception of certain forbidden categories of goods, such as drugs, regulations concerning which which were left open-ended). It created a new institution, the central Customs Committee, and, in a separate law, a new customs tariff.[17] The customs law was followed two months later by a new law on emigration. The proposed draft law on exit from and entry into the USSR was first raised for discussion by the Supreme Soviet in 1989. The draft law was apparently favoured by Gorbachev himself and found many avid supporters in its first reading. Even though it was eventually defeated in the Council of Nationalities chamber of the legislature, at the 1989 first reading many deputies criticized the draft for not going far enough.[18] The draft was intended to facilitate and clarify the process of emigration and travel. It was to provide for a single five-year passport for travel to all countries.[19] Still, negative attitudes towards freer emigration were common, and the draft took over a year and a half to reach the Supreme Soviet. Until May 1991 it was deliberately left off the Soviet's agenda by the Presidium because of what its chief advocate, Fedor Mikhailovich Burlatskii, called "doubts within the government."[20] Yet some observers noted that, while the negative effects of the proposed law were continually emphasized, there would be positive effects as well: the possibility of fostering more specialists and technical experts, the development of more international business contacts, the potential of bringing in more foreign investment, and the economic benefits of remittances from Soviet citizens working abroad.[21]

In the debate on the emigration law, moral imperatives battled reflex responses. Ironically, even though the Soviet system was more democratic, the fears of open borders obviously did not evaporate overnight. In the May 1991 Supreme Soviet debate on the emigration law, some deputies voiced objections about the expenses that would be incurred in the development of new border posts and staff, the printing of passports, and other potential financial burdens; they also expressed concern about a possible brain drain. The State Foreign Economic Commission released a statement that the law would require 11.8 billion hard rubles to print passports, cover the cost of additional border-control and passport staff, and increase the number of flights outside of the country. This figure was hotly debated by the law's proponents, who deemed the figures exaggerated and noted that in any case many of these costs would be borne by the prospective travellers themselves.[22] The bill was sent back to committee for "discussions"; one of its disappointed proponents, Vladimir I. Kirillov, claimed the financial argument was an excuse for those who feared emigration. Soviet institutions, by preventing the passage of this law, were preventing the country from being granted most-favoured-nation status by the United States and from receiving credits from the Export-Import Bank.[23] A Labour Ministry official expressed concern that principles of "orderly labour migration" be adopted prior to the passage of the law to prevent Soviet citizens from facing unemployment and other social hardships abroad.[24] Again, the assumption was that Soviet citizens needed to be protected from harmful foreign influences.

Burlatskii reminded the delegates that these expenditures were largely to be paid for by the collection of passport fees (to be raised to one thousand rubles a person). He also argued that, although perhaps many would leave the country, at least temporarily, many would return to the Soviet Union, bringing back new skills and ideas. Moreover, Soviet citizens who went abroad as guest workers might send back financial remittances to the USSR, a practice that had led to great financial benefit in Yugoslavia. Ivan Laptev reminded delegates that facilitated entry and exit were already being observed *de facto*, and that many of the discussed expenditures would be required regardless of whether the law was actually passed.[25]

The advocates of the law tended to draw on normative arguments in favour of freedom of movement, while its opponents were nervous about potentially disruptive effects. Those in favour of the law tended to phrase their support in terms of the following arguments. First, the law would enable the USSR to conform to its international agreements on human rights. Second, the law would end the arbitrary administrative practices of the Ministry of Internal Affairs and the political-security authorities in matters of applications for passports; it would thus constitute a victory for the rule of law over bureaucratic interference. Third, it would produce the positive economic benefits associated with free international movement and facilitate the USSR's entry into the world market economy. Finally, it would provide an egalitarian basis for the right to emigrate and travel, so that travel would no longer be a privilege enjoyed only by the elite.[26]

Those opposed to the law were not necessarily against it in principle but rather were preoccupied with a number of short-term objections. First, they protested its appearance on the legislature's agenda, perceiving it as a frivolous issue compared to more urgent reform initiatives amidst the country's deepening economic crisis. A related argument was that Russia had to rely on its own resources to solve its own problems and should not bow to the dictates of foreigners' human-rights standards.[27] Second, there were again the fears that the law would be far too expensive in its implementation to justify. Third, deputies feared the country was too poor and unstable at present to have a positive experience with free emigration; the talented would leave, draining capital along with them. Finally, there was an uneasy feeling that the law would in fact benefit sectors of society (namely, "*mafias*") who already had unfair advantages over the majority of simple workers, who would never have the opportunity to travel. Thus, in the law's second reading, the discourse took the combative nature of a split between "workers" and "intelligentsia."[28]

It was a source of frustration to the law's advocates that, after almost two years of conciliatory work on the draft by deputies, members of interested bureaucracies, and academics, the law would suddenly find such heated opposition in the Supreme Soviet. The law was subject to detailed discussion of its financial and budgetary implications and fared poorly in the initial voting in May; this time, as A. Lukianov ironically noted, it was rejected by the Council of the Union. rather than the Council of Nationalities, as in 1989.[29] Particularly contentious was the law's accompanying resolution, which discussed the implementation of the law. Finally, the law was passed on 20 May 1991; after the resolution was rewritten, the date of implementation was delayed to 1 January 1993, and the law subjected to line-by-line voting and further changes.[30]

The All-Union law, far from the sweeping reform heralded in 1989, contained some key limitations. For instance, it paid far more attention than the original draft to ensuring that passports could be refused, and contained a broader range of instances where this could happen.[31] Furthermore, the law was not to go into effect until 1993. Finally, both the original draft and the final law contained some important problems: they left the passport process in the hands of the applicant's local MVD office rather than transferring it to the Ministry of Foreign Affairs.[32]

The struggle to pass the emigration law revealed not only the difficulty of achieving consensus through the many government institutions involved in the emigration process (an institutional configuration that, although it was criticized, remained virtually untouched by the new law). It also showed the deep-seated resistance and persistence of old attitudes towards opening up the country. Many Supreme Soviet deputies persisted in seeing emigration as an issue that should be subordinated to what they perceived as political and economic situational factors, presenting a negative view of travellers as speculators and profiteers. They showed little understanding of the principle of free emigration as an abstract moral issue and remained preoccupied by the perception that freedom of movement could only produce a net loss of resources from the country. This was in part a result of Burlatskii's attempt in 1989 to link the budgetary issue of modernization and expansion of the travel apparatus to the law, sending out the message that free emigration and travel would require large expenditures difficult to justify while the country was in a severe economic crisis.

As in the 1920s, the issue in 1991 was the question of priorities rather than the moral or long-term consequences of refusing to change the closed-border system. Meanwhile, the deputies' participation in the debates showed limited awareness of the emigration and immigration standards of other countries. To some extent the law was the brainchild of Gorbachev and his supporters in the late 1980s. Its difficulties reflect the fall of his star; Ivan Laptev, who led the conciliatory commission to redraft the law after its difficulties in the 1989 first reading, argues that some deputies saw opposition to the law as an opportunity to discredit Gorbachev in the international community.[33]

However, the law did contain various important positive changes. It allowed for a guarantee of free entry and exit without the need for an invitation or exit visa. It instituted a single five-year passport for cross-border travel, prompt processing of passport applications, and strictly defined limitations of the instances in which passports could be refused temporarily. In such instances, moreover, citizens would have the right to appeal to the Cabinet of Ministers, which would have the final authority on such matters.[34] These changes, aiming for greater legality of the system, an easier process of application, and less power to refuse passports, are significant.

In spite of – or perhaps because of – reform of the All-Union system, there were disquieting signs of border conflict as the repercussions of *perestroika* created new political problems. The individual republics increasingly wanted not a centrally determined reform of Soviet borders but the right to control their own borders. Gregory Gleason has argued that the Soviet version of centralized federalism attached great importance to the boundaries of republics, which would ultimately sow the seeds of irredentism and separatism among Soviet nationalities under *perestroika*.[35] Legislative efforts to reform the border-control system had one crucial flaw: they assumed the Soviet Union's territorial integrity as a single state. The disruptions of *perestroika* thus put new pressures on Soviet borders, leading to new pressures for border controls even as the old ones became obsolete.

The upsurge of nationality unrest and the Soviet republics' demands for sovereignty served to reinforce the status quo of the Soviet border regime. Just when Soviet international borders seemed about to become more open and manageable, the republics threatened to make theirs more closed and unruly. In the Baltic states, where demands for sovereignty reached a high pitch, the Soviet military and security spheres became targets for social protest. In December 1989 the Estonian Supreme Soviet passed a law that, among other measures calling for an Estonian-only military in the republic, would create border guards from the republic's population[36] – a development that would have profound consequences for the republic's sovereignty.

In January 1990 angry residents of Nakhichevan, Azerbaijan, destroyed border posts and crossed the border en masse into Iran, where they had relatives. This demonstrated that some Soviet citizens resented the restricted border zones. Items in the Soviet press praised the actions of the Soviet border troops and condemned the Azerbaijanis' violation of the "sacred" Law on State Borders of 1982.[37] Events seemed to justify the need for strict border security. However, the events in Nakhichevan not only brought into the open criticism of the state's restrictive border-control policy but also revealed potential weaknesses in the capacity of the border troops. Nakhichevan provided an opportunity for the closed-border system to be called into question, and further examples of resistance to state border-control policies were to follow, along with isolated outbreaks of terrorism and vio-

lence.[38] In Tajikistan, following February 1990 riots in Dushanbe, border-troop representatives declared there was a threat of incursions by
Afghan rebels, who were reportedly preparing to cross the Soviet border and in the previous year had been targets of complaints of drug-
running into the country.[39] It was acknowledged, on Border Guard
Day 1990, that "relations between the local population and the Border
Guards have changed, and they have not changed for the better."[40]

The struggle over the attempt to revise the Union treaty reflected the
fact that border control had become a contentious issue in the struggle
for power between the centre and the republics, as well as the fact that
their relationship had become antagonistic: unlike the 1922 treaty, the
draft Union treaty delegated to the centre the powers over border *protection*, and also gave it control over customs, which again was not in
the 1922 treaty.[41] However, since most of the republics refused to sign
the new treaty, they did not accept this attempt by Gorbachev and the
centre to appropriate new powers when the purported attempt of the
treaty was to make the Union more decentralized.

The problems of opening up border institutions were most pro-
nounced in the Baltic states. Following the Lithuanian Supreme Council's declaration of sovereignty in March 1990, the Soviet leadership
hastened to seal off the republic. In invoking his new presidential powers granted in the decree of 21 March 1990, Gorbachev, among other
measures, called on the KGB border troops to step up the security
regime on the Lithuanian border; he also entreated the Soviet Foreign
Ministry and MVD to guard against violations of Soviet visa provisions
and entry and exit regulations.[42] The central government was incensed
and claimed that the Lithuanian government was enlisting volunteers
for future border forces and planning to erect posts and markers on its
borders with the RSFSR and Belorussia.[43] In August 1990 the Lithuanian Supreme Council made a statement asserting Lithuanian control
over its own borders.[44] Meanwhile, Latvia and Belorussia jointly set up
fifty posts on their mutual border.[45] Estonia tried to set up twenty-eight
customs posts. Roads were closed to ensure that traffic passed through
the new border posts. This, however, led to clashes with central border
authorities, since the Estonian posts served to prevent scarce food and
goods from leaving the republic. Men of draft age sought to enlist in
the new customs police forces in lieu of military service – a situation
tolerated by Moscow up until the Black Beret crackdown of 1991.[46]
Into 1991 republican border posts in the Baltic were a source of con-
tinual attack by central forces. The Black Beret forces of the MVD
destroyed and burned border posts set up by the republics on the
Lithuanian-Latvian and Lithuanian-Belorussian borders.[47]

The republics' border-control initiatives should also be seen in the context of increasing economic scarcity in the USSR. After the wave of sovereignty declarations of 1990, republics, *oblasts*, and cities (including Moscow) began to try to limit the removal of consumer goods from their territory and to prevent non-residents from buying up available stocks of goods. The new USSR customs code passed in the spring of 1991 (replacing the earlier 1964 code) asserted the Soviet government's sole control over customs administration.[48] The republics would have only an indirect role in making customs policy.[49] The law was passed easily in the Supreme Soviet, in a debate that dwelt on its importance for reform of the foreign-trade system rather than on its nationality repercussions.[50] However, several of the republics rejected the new code altogether, affirming their sovereignty over customs.[51] Meanwhile, the proposed radical new law liberalizing emigration was also anticlimactic. Some of the republics had claimed the right to grant their own passports and visas, although they were not able to exercise it until after the August 1991 attempted coup by Soviet hardliners and security forces.[52] In the wake of the coup attempt, the republics began to take over central border-control structures, up to the formal end of the Soviet Union on 1 January 1992. The Russian Federation and the other republics inherited Soviet border-control structures.

Thus ends the discussion of the Soviet experience. How did it affect the governments of the former Soviet republics, which were faced with the task of building their own border-control institutions as independent states? At least initially, republican state leaders generally saw opening up the system to the outside world as of key importance to the state's economic interest. The integrationist trends in the new republics, the desire to draw closer to the West and become part of the international capitalist system, were the most important pressures for them to open rather than close their borders. However, once the republics were scrambling for sovereignty, among the foremost tasks in their leaders' minds was securing control over their own boundaries. This ultimately meant the ability to limit their economic and political transactions with Moscow and to put up safeguards against Russian domination. Further, under conditions of economic crisis, tendencies towards economic protectionism and resource maximization continued in the customs limits on the amount of consumer goods and food allowed to leave the country. Shortages led many of the republics to impose such controls. This, plus the nationalist-inspired desire of some republics to limit Russian immigration, was an ominous sign. Meanwhile, continued bureaucratic resistance and red tape still operated in some respects, since the republics inherited the old Soviet OVIR and customs structures. It was to be hoped that in their respective transitions to greater sovereignty, the post-Soviet states would not put up new walls against each other, since they were united in their hatred of the Soviet legacy. Yet aspects of the Iron Curtain would outlive the Soviet Union: as the early post-Soviet period proved, only an active commitment on the part of the post-Soviet republics would bring it to an end.

9 Ending Isolation: Border Control in the Soviet Successor States

With the collapse of the USSR the Soviet successor states are embarking on a unique phase of development that combines state-building, since these states have for the most part never experienced sustained independence, and post-Communist political reconstruction. As Sarah Meiklejohn Terry argues, the challenges of democratization and market reform render the post-Communist political-development process unique.[1] From 1991 until the present, new states in the region have struggled to defend their independence and to define their sovereign interests while trying to re-establish authority over society. The republics have varied greatly in their inclination and ability to achieve these tasks, and their leaders have often been divided internally over priorities and strategies. Even where there is a serious commitment to ending all manifestations of the old Communist system, the republics have found that economic-reform goals on the one hand and state-building pressures on the other can contradict each other. This bears out Adam Przeworski's claim that economic reform and political stability in post-Communist states are difficult to balance.[2] These diverse pressures are manifest in the difficulties of transforming post-Soviet state institutions.

The case of border and customs controls reveals an inherent tension between state-building and reform. The break-up of the Soviet Union created fundamental changes in Soviet borders, which meant not only that republics would now have sovereignty over their own customs policies but that they would now have to create customs posts anew on what had formerly been purely administrative borders within the republics. The question of responsibility for international borders in the wake of the collapse of the USSR has been raised by both Russian and Western analysts as one of the important security problems to emerge in the former Soviet Union and has usually been approached from a strictly military perspective. The break-up of the Soviet Union caused a change in the existing security arrangements on the borders of that country; since the Soviet Union's republics had each had an international boundary, this meant that these borders now came under the control of those newly independent states, while Russia's borders with the those states, formerly merely administrative boundaries within the USSR, now became a site of uncertainty and possible instability. This, according to some scholars, contributed to Russia's increasing impulse after 1992 to reassert its national security interest over the territory of the former Soviet Union, since the international borders of the Soviet Union became volatile (in areas such as Tajikistan), while the republics were unable to defend or police them adequately.[3] Other scholars argue that the breakdown in state authority that accompanied the collapse of the Soviet Union triggered instability and conflict, particularly in regions such as the Caucasus and Central Asia, where political institutions were weak and where conflicts between old and new elites quickly assumed nationalist or regional dimensions.[4]

The issue of border controls also reveals some of the conflicts of institutional change in the region: on one level, there was a tug-of-war between economic integration and political sovereignty within the states of the former Soviet Union.[5] The arguments for and against opening up border controls that permeated the debates on that topic of the Soviet legislature in its last year of existence found echoes in the Soviet successor states as they struggled to balance the benefits of freer international contact with the protection of a border regime. As noted in the previous chapter, economic concerns in the republics are the key to explaining why individual republics began to set up border controls of their own that rivalled the central government's monopoly on this state function. In 1991 economic pressures and the relative retrenchment of the central government from republican redistribution influenced the rise of local protectionisms and controls on consumer goods.[6] Border controls formed in the Soviet republics stemmed from the desire to protect the domestic market; moreover, as the struggle between the USSR and the republics for sovereignty escalated, border controls became an issue of conflict and sometimes violence. This politicization of the issue of border control would ensure that the post-Soviet states would continue to value their sovereignty over this issue, despite the costs involved. At the same time, the common desire among the republics to expand their participation in international trade would require a substantial departure from the restrictive Soviet-style customs policy associated with the command economy.

Another reason for examining customs controls lies precisely in their mundane nature. At some point even grandiose plans for state-building must descend to the level of details, and if "routine" sectors of government are neglected by leaders, they may interfere with the implementation of more urgent priorities. Even change in "routine" government functions can provoke minor controversies in post-Communist politics. Eventually, some republics introduced a greater rationalization of state customs policy, demonstrating that there has been a learning process within post-Soviet governments. Such measures have responded to concerns about the flight of goods and raw materials abroad, particularly from Russia; smuggling, corruption, and political unrest in border areas; and Western pressure to introduce more precisely defined customs and tariff systems. None the less, serious difficulties remain in this and other state sectors.

We can identify three phases in the institutional transition of border control: first, the development of republican border controls in the late Soviet period in 1991, discussed in the previous chapter; secondly, the 1992 reactive expansion of restrictive border controls in the region; and finally, attempts by 1993 to harmonize the goals of state security and economic integration so that border controls would effectively promote trade while regulating it according to the state's interests.

THE CIS AND THE PROLIFERATION OF BORDER CONTROLS, 1992

When the Soviet Union broke up in 1991, the fate of former Soviet border controls was only one of a host of issues to be resolved. Among the most difficult choices facing the successor states, including the Russian Federation, and among the decisions that would have the most important consequences for them, was the nature of their economic and political relations with each other. At the beginning of the reform process few questioned the importance of Soviet openness to the international environment or of economic integration within the Soviet republics. Leaders such as Eduard Shevardnadze urged that republics maintain their open borders and resist the wave of autarky in the region.[7] With the fall of the USSR, there was discussion of the possibility that the new Commonwealth of Independent States would include a customs union along the lines of the European Economic Community (EEC, now European Union). Indeed, the Soviet Customs Committee was one of the last All-Union institutions to be abolished, reflecting some faith that it would continue to operate as a CIS instrument.[8] Article 7 of the CIS agreement called for "co-operation in the formation and development of a common economic space, of all-European and Eurasian markets, and in the sphere of customs policy."[9]

At the time of its formation the CIS was expected to maintain some common functions; one of its intents was to preserve a "transparent border" (*prozrachnaia granitsa*) between member states. Article 5 read:

The High Contracting Parties recognize and respect each other's territorial integrity and the inviolability of existing frontiers within the framework of the commonwealth.

They guarantee the openness of frontiers and freedom of movement of citizens and the transfer of information within the framework of the commonwealth.[10]

The assumption was that the republics would not erect customs barriers against each other. The question of institutions is paramount here: should the republics build customs institutions to safeguard their own sovereignty and realize short-term economic goals, or should they strive to create an integrated customs union on a more equitable and voluntary basis than the centralized Soviet Union? These two goals are by no means mutually exclusive; yet at times they seemed to be so in the all-or-nothing environment of post-Soviet politics.

The inherent conflict within the CIS between sovereign borders and open borders became quickly obvious. In March 1992 a CIS customs agreement was signed by Armenia, Belarus, Kazakhstan, Kyrgyzstan, Moldova, Russia, Tajikistan, and Turkmenistan (with some individual stipulations). In the interest of promoting economic development, the agreement was to provide for a common economic space, with free movement of goods across the borders of member states. Those who signed the document agreed to establish a joint customs policy, a single tariff, and a co-ordinating institution, the Customs Council. There were to be no customs barriers or duties, and the parties vowed not to pass measures that violated the agreement.[11] Yet subsequent to the agreement, the republics continued to develop their own individual customs policies and border controls.

By the spring of 1992 most of the republics had declared their intent to set up their own customs controls; indeed, many had earlier established very strict limits on the quantities of consumer goods and food leaving their territory. The Baltic states took the lead (they were never CIS members), but were followed by a basic sequence of Georgia, Ukraine, Russia, Central Asia, and Azerbaijan.[12] By June 1992 Boris Yeltsin stated that Russia would soon intensify its border controls with the republics of the CIS, citing the need to keep out criminal and "bandit" activity.[13] In September, Russia decided to put up new customs controls along the borders of the states that had refused to join the customs agreement – Azerbaijan, Georgia, Ukraine, and the Baltic states.[14] The State Customs Committee of Russia announced that, as of 1 October, it would have sixty-four customs posts operating on its borders with the Baltic states, Ukraine, Azerbaijan, and Georgia.[15] Even holdouts like Belarus and Kazakhstan eventually joined the customs trend, as did the renegade regions of Chechnia and the Trans-Dniestr Republic within the Russian Federation and Moldova. By September, Russia was putting controls in place to close its border with Chechnia, to prevent the flow of weapons and goods there.[16] In addition, Russia established tariffs and duties for CIS states, although in a simplified and preferential form.[17] It should be borne in mind, however, that these measures constituted declarations of intent, and that in some of these republics customs measures existed mainly on paper.

Political and institutional factors help to explain this development. The poorly defined and vague mandate of the CIS, and the republics' wariness of any centralized binding authority, has been noted by many observers as contributing to its ineffectualness.[18] Marshal Evgenii Shaposhnikov, the former head of the CIS armed forces, recalls in his memoirs trying in vain to convince the heads of the Soviet republics to agree to maintain a common central command over the military and to keep an open economic space, which he believed was essential to maintain security in the former Soviet Union: Shaposhnikov claims that Ukrainian leaders, for example, told him that Ukraine wanted its own armed forces simply because an indigenous military was one of the defining attributes of a sovereign state.[19] According to Teresa Rakowska-Harmstone, the weakness of the republics and the lack of resolve to act jointly through the CIS encouraged Russia to use the pretext of intervention in order to reassert its influence and involvement over CIS territory and to satisfy at the same time nationalist demands at home for the resurgence of Russia's "great power" status over the "near abroad."[20]

THE RUSSIAN FEDERATION AND
BORDER CONTROLS

The situation on the borders of the former Soviet Union put Russia in a curious and pivotal position. The newly sovereign Russian Federation had an extremely long border, due to the country's size; the Russian Republic, or RSFSR, had been the Soviet Union's largest republic, and its borders with foreign countries (including Finland, China, Poland, and Mongolia) had composed much of the length of the Soviet Union's foreign boundary. However, the collapse of the Soviet Union meant that Russia suddenly also had international boundaries with ten former Soviet republics. This meant that Russia now had a new set of borders that, strictly speaking, had not previously been controlled, policed, or defended. As Pavel K. Baev has argued, for Russia to firmly establish its own borders within the Russian Federation would cut that country off from the many Russians now left in other newly independent states of the "near abroad."[21] At the same time, the other republics found themselves facing the choice of what to do about the Soviet border-control institutions they had inherited, which variously meant assuming indigenous control over them, negotiating with Russia for conditions of Russian control over border forces, or scaling down the border forces.[22]

Russia became one of the countries most urgently concerned about border controls, for a number of reasons. Russia has by far the longest borders, and the collapse of the Soviet Union left Russia bordering ten of the newly independent states, proximate to some of the most conflict-prone areas of the Eurasian region. Secondly, accompanying the uncertainty and conflict in the republics of the Soviet Union, there has been an upsurge of migration and refugee movements – for example, of migrants to the Russian interior from Central Asia and the Caucasus, a development that the Russian government has viewed with trepidation, given the dislocation and strain on resources that this causes.[23] Thirdly, Russia has the most natural resources and economic wealth, and therefore a common perception within Russia is that it has the most to lose from open borders.

Adding to the problem was the uncertainty that characterized the defence capacities and border troops on the former international borders of the Soviet Union. Initially, the CIS planned to maintain continuity by keeping former Soviet border forces under the CIS rubric. However, the delays in reaching agreement on the CIS led to inaction and subsequently confused and demoralized the border troops. Moreover, various republics, such as Ukraine and Georgia (not then a CIS member), elected to "nationalize" the border troops on their soil, and republics created their own border troops. Meanwhile, Russia took responsibility for CIS border troops in Tajikistan, where there was a high degree of conflict, and also in the Baltic states, purportedly to facilitate the question of troop withdrawal. This led to an ambiguous situation, and often a volatile one, as non-Russian populations tended to resent "foreign" border troops as a reminder of the Soviet regime. As one article in *Krasnaia zvezda* expressed it, "Exactly whose borders are we protecting? This has hardly been a rhetorical question, which we have been asked more than once by Russian border guards carrying out service in the Caucasus."[24] The head of the Russian border troops, Colonel Alexander Baranov, described the situation on the borders as in flux; while CIS/Russian border troops were being removed from certain areas to be replaced by republican border troops, the latter were described as being far less effective in preventing unwanted border crossings.[25] Indeed, at the 10 December 1992 Congress of People's Deputies session, Russian security minister V.P. Barannikov (later notorious for his involvement with Aleksandr Rutskoi and Ruslan Khasbulatov) used a metaphor of the type common to Russian political "hard-liners" when he deemed the border a very serious problem: "Why am I raising this issue so sharply? The lack of legal regulation of Russia's state border in essence paralyses the activity of law-enforcement bodies in the struggle with such dangerous crimes as smuggling and creates, to use a vivid phrase, the situation of a vacuum cleaner sucking the lifeblood out of our country."[26] It should surprise no one that representatives of the border troops should want to publicize the border's shortcomings in order to defend their vested interests. Yet the confusion over the military border contributed to the vulnerability of customs forces.

Meanwhile, Russia became involved in regions on the borders between former Soviet republics, the "hot spots" (*goriachie tochki*) such as Trans-Dniestr (on the border between Ukraine and Moldova) and Abkhazia (between Georgia and Russia), on the grounds that since the CIS had not achieved conflict-resolution mechanisms of its own, only Russia had the resources to contain these potentially dangerous conflicts and that it was in Russia's interest to prevent them from spreading.[27] These actions in turn risked provoking defensive responses from the countries of the former Soviet Union. Border controls, after all, are by definition aimed at protecting one state from the influences of another; once one country starts to establish border controls, it is easy to trigger a chain reaction. Russian officials, for example, sometimes argue that their border controls are reactive, set up in response to the initiatives of other post-Soviet republics to set up border checkpoints on their boundary with Russia.[28]

INTERNAL VERSUS INTERNATIONAL BORDERS

An argument that focuses on geopolitical constraints is useful to help explain the evolution of border-control arrangements in the former Soviet Union, which have tended to grow in response to conflicts and tensions in border areas. But geopolitics alone does not explain the development of border control institutions. The Soviet Union's borders were established arbitrarily rather than organically, and changed with the aid of military force and territorial expansion, thereby creating the possibility that border and territorial disputes would emerge in the wake of the collapse of the Soviet Union.[29] An example of how the Soviet legacy of contradictory territorial boundary claims influenced the volatility of a disputed territory on the Russian border is the conflict that broke out between North Ossetia and Ingushetia; in addition, demands of secessionist minorities for control over territory also triggered conflict in various parts of the former Soviet Union.[30]

Second, the dynamic of secessionist tendencies spread to border territories such as Crimea, Trans-Dniestr, and Chechnia, where proximity to another newly independent state or to an international border might hold the promise of outside resources for the independence movements. Disputes over territorial borders and issues relating to internal borders within the state are beyond the scope of this study, which deals with border controls on international boundaries. However, the collapse of the Soviet Union blurred the distinction between internal boundaries and international boundaries. The previously internal borders between the Soviet republics became the controlled borders between independent states. For those territories that were contemplating secession of their own, borders were quickly recognized as a priority for any self-proclaimed state that wished to assert its autonomy, and border controls became an issue of competing claims for sovereignty in areas such as Crimea, where a separatist movement attempted to press the issue of leaving Ukraine, and Chechnia, where the Russian government initiated a brutal invasion in 1994 that became a long-term commitment to put down rebels who asserted the republic's independence from the Russian Federation. Among the annoyances that the separatist Dudaev regime caused the Russian government by attempting to declare independence was the Chechens' bid to regulate their own borders and issue their own visas.[31] In the summer of 1994, the Russian government set up control posts on the administrative border between Chechnia and Stavropol *krai* in order to prevent the spread of instability and the exit of arms and terrorists from Chechnia to other parts of Russia.[32] As Russia's campaign against Chechnia intensified, so did the desire to try to seal off the Chechen border.

The attempt to set up controls on both sides of the Chechen border reveals the extent to which border controls had become a political lightning-rod in the competition for sovereignty, and the attachment to physical demarcation of territory as a means to isolate and protect certain territories from "harmful" influences. Significantly, areas such as Crimea and Chechnia became politicized regions partly because they became border territories with uncertain political loyalties in a way they were not during the life of the USSR. The fact that they are border areas doubtless accelerates their cause and complicates the response, and likely has much to do with why these two areas have been of particular concern to the Ukrainian and Russian governments respectively.

However, not all regional conflicts occurring in the former Soviet Union take place in border areas, and there are many complicated reasons for the prevalence of regions' disputes with their central government. As Philip Hanson has argued, the republics' tendencies to date to set up their own customs and export controls should not be seen merely as emerging inter-state barriers. Rather, they form part of a broader phenomenon of local protectionisms, which has been equally visible in regions within republics as a result of the chronic shortages of goods.[33] Localities within Russia, for example, have been attempting to protect their outflow of goods and to control their resources.

The political geography of the Soviet Union, and the history of its administrative boundaries, is still an underresearched subject. For our purposes, what is important is that border controls have been a crucial prop in the ongoing drama of the struggle for sovereignty in the former Soviet Union, a symbol with particular resonance in the often theatrical discourse of the Eurasian political arena. A cynic might proffer the wisdom that, if a region within the former Soviet Union wants to be taken seriously by its central government, if it wants to provoke an immediate response, then it need only declare its intention to establish its own border or customs controls.

BORDER CONTROLS AND INTEGRATION

Border controls have revealed the Janus-faced attitude of the former Soviet republics towards striving for international co-operation and European-style open borders on the one hand and secure territorial defences and protectionism in the interests of state security on the other. As discussed in the previous chapter, economic factors have encouraged the growth of border controls, yet the post-Soviet republics have also demonstrated strong interest in the expansion of trade and the benefits of international co-operation. Border-control measures resemble, even if only to a minor degree, the Soviet principle of the state preventing the removal of goods from the country, which is rather at odds with the market-based notion of promoting exports. The implications of this problem have been noted by a number of Western scholars, particularly economists.[34] Some Western economists see regional integration and open borders to be in the interest of the economic recovery and eventual market reform of the former Soviet Union (FSU).

This approach suggests that some form of customs union within the FSU should be encouraged without export barriers; ideally, eventual currency convertibility would ensure that the republics would not try to buy up all of each other's goods. This, in the view of its proponents, would contribute to more sound international trade and economic development.[35]

According to these views, the republics' comprehensive erection of customs barriers, export duties, and export controls are a cause for concern. Havrylyshyn and Williamson (1991) argue that the republics' "autarkic" erection of trade barriers in the form of customs duties could be economically damaging; the ensuing trade wars between republics could create interruptions for these very interdependent republics.[36] Similarly, a 1992 report published by the International Monetary Fund notes that the trend to declining trade between the republics, caused in part by export restrictions, has hurt the cause of reform and threatened the establishment of market relations in the region.[37] As one expert laments, "Unlike the rest of the world, trade wars in the former Soviet Union have surfaced, not over attempts to restrict imports or to broaden access to foreign markets, but over export ceilings."[38]

What caused this wave of enthusiasm for customs controls among post-Soviet leaders? There are both political and economic reasons. First, the political obstacles to securing agreement on a customs union are great.[39] Border controls have become a prominent motif in the discourse and imagery of sovereignty as the actions of the republics have demonstrated the symbolic connection between statehood and border controls. Political fears have been a significant cause: as well as the fear of Russian domination, emerging border disputes and tensions have contributed to the use of border controls in the republics to strengthen their own defensive positions. It has been argued that maintaining existing open economic borders would have meant preserving elements of the centralized Soviet economic structures that governed economic relations between the republics.[40]

The second, equally important impetus was economic contingency; the first customs measures were established as shortages became acute amidst the disintegration of the Soviet economy. Republics attempted to protect their supplies of consumer goods and food with the express intention of preventing resources from being drained from one country to another. This motive has been enhanced by the inequities of inter-republican trade in the post-Soviet era. Among these constraints, Russia's large economy means that it has a sizeable trade surplus with other republics; the lack of convertible currencies or other resources, and Russia's low prices for raw materials, mean that Russia is in effect "subsidizing" the other economies of the republics.[41] The problem of the ruble and a common monetary policy are extremely important here and have influenced Russian concerns.[42] According to economists, the export restrictions are also a manifestation of the monetary situation in the former Soviet Union, since demand for goods is so high relative to supply; a sound monetary supply, currency convertibility, and price reform would remedy this.[43] Beverly Crawford points to structural problems in the international environment as another contributing factor. Western countries might be pressuring the FSU countries to integrate with the world market but have not encouragedg them to trade with each other and with Eastern Europe.[44]

The difficulties of creating post-Soviet customs institutions must be seen in the larger political and economic context. Yet we must also consider the institutional dimension: border controls suffer from the organizational deficiencies endemic to these transitional polities. State institutions were not adequately harmonized with the goals of leaders and across state bureaucracies; comprehensive legal frameworks to guide state activity have not yet been implemented; and the state has not managed to keep its own personnel either obedient to higher authority or autonomous from society. Beverly Crawford, in noting the difficulties of transition to institutions reflecting market economies and democratic structures, posits weak states as an important part of the problem.[45]

The first problem in customs-control structures is one of chaotic and contradictory state organization. The restrictive and defensive nature of border controls seems to undermine earlier, half-implemented Soviet reforms and has spread quickly across the region, while unravelling the CIS's efforts to create a customs union. This has created tensions among CIS member states, as well as bureaucratic confusion. Moreover, export controls are often arbitrarily applied.[46]

The second, related institutional problem is the weakness of border controls. In countries that are newly setting up customs administration, smuggling problems are to be expected.[47] Ironically, if the former Soviet Union's republics seriously want to end all manifestations of the Iron Curtain and enter fully into international trade, then customs functions will need to be expanded in order to meet new needs. As the chairman of Russia's State Customs Committee, Anatolii Kruglov, notes, under Soviet rule the main purpose of customs officers was to examine passenger luggage and baggage; but in the aftermath of the Soviet collapse the application of customs controls to freight, imports, and exports expanded Russia's customs volume and functions before the country had sufficient capacity to cope with them. Moreover, customs have a new role to work with state agencies because they will now have to supervise military freight.[48] This raises the question of illicit smuggling and theft coming from within the state itself. Previously, there was little question of subjecting the state sector to customs surveillance. In Russia, much of the recent concern with introducing customs controls between CIS member states has been provoked by the desire to prevent the loss of strategic raw materials and military equipment through porous borders,[49] traffic that has concerned foreign governments as well as Russian leaders.

Customs officials in the Russian Federation admit to difficulties in adjustment. One regional customs chief claims, for example, that customs posts are poorly staffed and trained and that personnel face personal danger, as evidenced by a presidential *ukaz* to allow them to use weapons. He blames the lack of a customs law, which would limit their accountability to the supervision of any legal organs, and admits that in some instances customs officials have been fulfilling instructions overzealously, even while ignoring others.[50] In Ukraine it has also been reported that illegal smuggling is increasing, and that customs administration lacks a comprehensive legal basis for its activities.[51] Even though the predecessor of these republican institutions, the Soviet customs system, was not known for its high standards of professional and ethical conduct, corruption seems to remain a problem.

This points to a potentially arbitrary and chaotic customs organization. The disorder of the break-up of the USSR has certainly added to the problem. The newspaper *Ekonomika i zhizn'* reported in 1993 that instances of commercial smuggling had greatly expanded in Russia in the previous two years and that contraband was continuing to increase in scale; it cited incidents of armed violence and blackmail against customs officers, as well as corruption and bribery within the customs service.[52] Low-paid and often isolated, Russian customs officials may submit to the pressure of threats or bribes.

Thus, we might summarize institutional developments in border controls during 1992 in terms of three conflicting trends: (1) the expression of genuine intentions to create open borders, including the conclusion of bilateral and inter-CIS agreements; (2) individual countries' erection of border controls, customs barriers, tariffs, and other restrictions; and (3) gaps in state capacity, which impeded the implementation of already contradictory policy. Therefore, on the symbolic level, there was a strong normative commitment to the idea of the customs union and the *prozrachnaia granitsa*, but without the institutions to back it up. Meanwhile, the non-Russian republics seemed to possess a strong attachment to the idea of border controls as a visible image of their sovereignty, which demonstrates a desire to create the state on a symbolic level.[53]

PRESSURES FOR RATIONALIZATION AND
INSTITUTIONAL CHANGE, 1993

By 1993 there were attempts to rectify some of these problems. Four trends can be observed. First, there has been recognition of the need to reinforce the goal of more open borders with institutional mechanisms, albeit on the basis of the republics as fully sovereign states. Second, there is a commitment to improving state organization, on the assumption that this requires greater systematization of previously spasmodic policies. Third, Russia has made an effort to entrench reformist changes in customs law. Finally, there is an increasing differentiation between republics as the republics introduce more sophisticated customs administrations, tariffs, and export controls.

External influences have been one source of change for customs institutions. Here it is important to consider the role of international institutions and regimes, such as the International Monetary Fund/World Bank and the General Agreement on Tariffs and Trade (GATT, which has been succeeded by the World Trade Organization, WTO). The IMF/World Bank provides loans, while the GATT/WTO is an agreement that grants most-favoured nation (MFN) status to its members and hence desirable for a country that wants to break into world trade on an equal advantage. As institutions oriented towards market reform, each takes a potentially dim view of export controls and trade barriers such as were observed in the successor states after 1991. The WTO favours the replacement of non-tariff trade barriers, such as export quotas, licences, and discriminatory trade practices, with tariffs, and a commitment to reducing those as well. A country applying for membership in the WTO normally has to demonstrate progress towards these goals; a country without a market economy is on shaky ground to begin with.[54] Moreover, the successor states' progress towards the WTO depends on whether reformers are able to prevail over conservatives, who tend to oppose the full implications of market reform.[55] The post-Soviet republics value the benefits of membership in these institutions; in Russia specifically, market- and export-oriented reform was an early goal of Boris Yeltsin's administration. Hence the removal of trade barriers, state controls over exports, and other inhibiting mechanisms, to be replaced in the short term with customs duties, would be a desirable goal for Russia wishing to join the WTO. Accordingly, the Russian government formally applied for GATT membership shortly after its new law on the customs tariff passed in the legislature in the spring of 1993.[56] Russia applied formally in December 1994 to join the World Trade Organization, and entered into negotiations to allow it to participate in the international trade regime, which would require it to reduce its customs and tariffs barriers.[57] Ironically enough, that was the same month that Russia invaded Chechnia, demonstrating the ambivalence that the Russian government has towards border issues.

Although evidence is scarce, the customs law may have been part of conflicts over Yeltsin's policies within the Russian parliament – a minor sideshow in the struggle, maybe, but still an issue. *Commersant* reported that Yeltsin and the Russian Supreme Soviet (which Yeltsin attempted later to dissolve, in September of 1993) had issued contradictory instructions about foreign trade when the parliament rejected Yeltsin's actions to reduce existing privileges in foreign trade.[58] Moreover, Russian conservatives often see trade as a net loss. Certainly, in the pages of conservative newspapers such as *Pravda* and *Sovetskaia Rossiia* one can find expressions of the view that trade is a disadvantage for a weakened Russia, which allegedly needs protection against the foreigners and criminal elements who would seek to drain resources out of the country. In such quarters there is a conviction that exports constitute, in the words of one article, a "black hole" where funds escape that could have been used for state benefits such as social welfare or agriculture.[59] Logically following from this view, customs should serve to limit rather than promote this drain of resources. In the larger context, uneasiness over the role of trade in the post-Soviet state can be situated in the controversy in Russia between advocates of "shock therapy" and the more conservative or gradual approach to economic reform. Of course, this is no less sharp a controversy for Western scholars than it is in Russia.[60]

In Russia the law on the customs tariff was passed in the Supreme Soviet in May 1993, to be brought into effect that summer.[61] The law followed, and was intended to replace, Yeltsin's earlier decrees and customs instructions.[62] The new tariff was to eliminate previous privileges except in limited cases with respect to the payment of export and import duties, and to bring export duties fully into effect, while calling for gradual reductions of import duties. (Export duties were intended to replace export quotas, licences, and unequal privileges. Western economists and institutions have criticized republics' tendencies to impose high tariffs and export controls, but it is fair to say that there is some recognition that they are preferable to licences and quotas).[63] The law also called for gradual steps, by 1996, to limit export duties and quotas, thereby demonstrating a concern for a law that would satisfy Western countries and international organizations, and the text of the law paid great attention to the need to bring Russia into an integrated world economy. Shortly afterward, in June 1993, Russia officially applied for membership in the GATT.[64] This expression of intent was in fact somewhat diluted by the law's commitment to "protection of the Russian Federation economy from the unfavourable effect of foreign competition."[65]

In order to strengthen customs institutions, a May 1993 resolution of the Russian Council of Ministers authorized the allocation of funds to expand customs institutions, create infrastructure, improve customs communications and social facilities, and better co-ordinate customs-administration needs with other ministries and localities.[66] Subsequently, the customs code, as distinguished from the customs tariff, was passed in the Supreme Soviet in July 1993. It constituted a legal departure for the operation of customs institutions and personnel, with clearly denoted procedures for customs collection, registration, and function. It expounded at length on the definition and punishments for smuggling, which included undeclared removal of drugs, weaponry, "strategically important raw materials," and addressed the issue of smuggling by state officials. It also established lengthy rules for the correct procedures for customs operations, including rules forbidding customs officials from engaging in politics or in profiting from their customs activities, thereby tackling the issue of corruption by customs officials. It also laid out proscriptions against attempts to influence, extort, or evade customs officials.[67]

The new rules were intended to ensure that all imported goods came into contact with customs organs rather than getting around them.[68] It was also asserted that the new code expanded the status of customs officers as law-enforcement officers.[69] The customs laws followed a series of new state measures to regulate foreign trade. David Dyker has expressed scepticism about the government's foreign trade laws, arguing that what was being presented as liberalization could actually be conceived as a recentralization of state control over foreign trade; he cites customs controls among his evidence.[70] Yet regulation and expansion of customs administration is not in itself necessarily a sign of a renewed state monopoly. A state's attempt to gain control over trade problems related to the breakdown of the Soviet system in general may not mean a restriction of trade.[71] Regulation and restriction of trade are two different things.

The interesting feature about border controls by 1994 was that, notwithstanding the ideological break with the Soviet past, border controls in the Soviet successor states seemed to reproduce many features of the former Soviet system and to draw on the same justifications for imposing these controls. It is true that some of the most objectionable aspects of Communist border controls have been repudiated or modified, while there has also been an effort to introduce new principles (such as the notion of the subordination of border guards to the rule of law) to demonstrate, at least for declaratory principles, that these are not the repressive, arbitrary border controls of the past. Important features from the past none the less find echoes in some of the new laws and regimes, although we must keep in mind that the laws and declarations that exist on paper by no means necessarily correspond to the situation prevailing in the border zone.

Russia's new law on the border was passed in 1993 (it was subsequently amended slightly in 1994). When the draft law was introduced in the Russian parliament, it was clear that the Russian border situation was still volatile, which influenced the discussion of the law. This uncertainty and ambivalence was reflected in remarks by Sergei Stepashin, who was at that time chair of the Supreme Soviet's Defence and Security Committee. Stepashin argued that, although it was imperative to have a new border law to reflect the new goals and realities of Russia following the collapse of the USSR, Russia's relationships and border-control arrangements with its neighbouring states were yet to be completely resolved and the law would have to take this into account. He argued that the law would, on the one hand, institutionalize a more open, co-operative, and less militarized border, based on the dictates of strict law and order and international obligations, but on the other aimed to protect state security against the proliferation of threats on the border amidst the instability of the collapse of the Soviet system.[72]

One of the areas of concern in the parliament's discussion of the law was apparently the question of whether or not border controls would be set up all along the Russian border; the law allows for open border arrangements in some unspecified instances, and affirms that the border zone will be considerably narrower (five kilometres) than that of the former Soviet Union and that it will not be permitted to cut through residential areas or displace public buildings.[73] The law has a number of important innovations that seem intended to establish border controls strictly on the framework of the rule of law and to prevent the abuse of power by border authorities; it devotes a great deal of attention to establishing the competence, scope, and limits of powers, and subordination of the various border authorities. The law also defines the responsibilities of the various government ministries and organs that are involved in border protection, which seems an obvious attempt to prevent confusion, or stepping on another's toes. Finally, the law asserts that border control is a central government function in which regions are expected to co-operate. It affirms the Russian state's general commitments to international co-operation, state security, law and order, and peaceful resolution of disputes.[74]

There are, however, some troubling features in the law. The security mandate concerning the border is very broadly and vaguely defined.

The powers of the border troops to protect against security threats in border areas seem very broad. There is little discussion of human rights or of the facilitation of cross-border movement. Border controls seem intended in part to police the border localities and maintain surveillance over them, while border-area residents are expected to participate directly in border security. There is no reference to border troops outside the borders of the Russian Federation nor to CIS borders.

Regardless of border-control restrictions in the republics, they should not necessarily be seen as new Iron Curtains. Increasingly they appear to represent the normal border-regulatory mechanisms of sovereign states and to act as levers of state economic goals. Border controls also represent a cost to these states that one might argue they can ill afford. But the new controls, at least in Russia, Ukraine, and Kazakhstan, reflect some efforts, however ambivalent, to ensure that the restrictive, isolationist border-control mechanisms of the Soviet Union become a thing of the past. Ukraine and Kazakhstan have introduced changes in their customs systems to reduce export controls and replace them with duties, with the ultimate goal of lowering these duties. They have also declared their intention to have customs institutions reflect a greater commitment to foreign trade, though they have not yet tackled customs institutions as comprehensively as Russia has.[75] Other republics have held the line in customs policy, seemingly stuck in the protective mode rather than promoting open borders. Some have changed relatively little in their customs policies and capacities since 1991. For example, information on Uzbek customs is scarce, but available evidence suggests a greater concern to protect the internal market and prevent the removal of raw materials abroad than to pursue economic reform.[76] Moldova seems to have done the same with its customs regime, set up December 1992, restricting the removal of food and consumer goods from the country.[77]

Since 1992, border-control policy in the Soviet successor states has exhibited a number of contradictory trends. On the one hand, ongoing discussion and debate about bolstering the CIS economic union points to the possibility of closer relations among the republics. With respect to the macro-environment of the Soviet successor states, some would argue that the CIS has slowly but surely made progress in achieving common goals, even if the extent of Russian influence remains controversial; among those goals are institutions of customs co-ordination.[78] On 14 May 1993 CIS members (excluding Turkmenistan) passed a declaration of intent to increase integration, supposedly representing a more serious attempt to implement and back up the customs union and other CIS economic agreements.[79] A customs union among the successor states would by necessity involve reducing the trade and customs barriers within them.[80] Havrylyshyn and Williamson have argued that an early stage of autarkic policy was likely to last during the transition, but inevitably the republics would see the advantages of a closer economic union.[81]

The establishment of border controls between the various countries of the former Soviet Union has taken a mixed path. In July 1994 an accord on joint defence of the CIS southern border was signed by Russia, Uzbekistan, Tajikistan, and Turkmenistan in Tashkent.[82] In February 1994 Russia and Georgia signed an agreement of joint co-operation with respect to border controls and defences.[83] Russia's agreement with Belarus that year included a commitment to eliminate customs controls between the two countries.[84] In the Baltic republics there was, not surprisingly, total disinterest in participating in any common border security arrangements with the other former Soviet republics. Latvia, Lithuania and Estonia all had a border with Russia, and they proceeded to establish their own border controls and policies.[85] A complicating factor is that Estonia is demanding restoration of its pre–Second World War boundary with Russia, claiming that Estonian territory was transferred by the Soviet Union to Russia, a demand to which Russia has thus far been unwilling to accede.[86]

As a case-study of a particularly strategic Soviet institution, the history of border controls demonstrates that when Soviet state structures broke down, the resulting uncertainty created gaps in the post-Soviet republics, since state functions could not be exercised uniformly or consistently. Officials did not have the means or the mandate to respond to changed conditions, even though they were often the first to realize the need for change. Yet political struggles and priorities have meant that comprehensive state-building changes have been delayed, even while interim measures are taken to rectify the chaos resulting from the gaps in state authority. These interim measures to secure authority have at times contradicted the long-term goals of reform. The lesson is that state-building needs to be harmonized both with a consensus on reform and with realistic expectations and goals of building state capacities; however, many factors combine to prevent this from happening.

Border-control authorities must recognize that, as during the Civil War, the presence of border controls dividing communities that were formerly part of a single Soviet state is not necessarily legitimate to the residents of border areas and may be seen as intrusive or threatening. The reality of imposing border controls where none existed before is daunting in both the military and human dimensions; given that border controls became sites of grievances under *perestroika*, the imposition of new border-control checkpoints runs the risk of provoking social alienation. This is why, for example, the Russian law established that border zones could not disrupt or displace local communities or buildings, whereas the Soviet Union had never been particularly sensitive to this concern. Finally, as was the situation under NEP, the establishment of newly significant border divisions has influenced economic developments in border communities.

Yet aspects of the previous Soviet system still exist. Border authorities have become more militarized in the expectation that they will be dealing with violent situations, and they have many powers. As during the Soviet period, border controls are used to seal off potentially dangerous linkages and contacts. For example, in 1992 Russia set up border controls to close the border with Abkhazia.[87] The border is still seen as a symbol of the state's struggle to assure its presence and a manifestation of its power over the territory. The rituals and symbols of the border presence seem far more important than the actual functions they perform and their goals. For the Baltic countries, for instance, border controls with Russia likely serve a nationalist agenda for domestic consumption as much as they serve the interests of the state. The rise of nationalist and expansionist politics only exacerbates the attachment to territory that the border represents.

Does this case-study reveal any lessons about post-Soviet state-building? It is difficult to generalize for the state as a whole from the narrow sector of customs administration, yet the conclusions of this study may provide hypotheses for other institutions. It is not surprising that in this early transition period the initial state-building process in the former Soviet republics contains inconsistencies. Over time, leaders can resolve some of the ambivalence in inter-state activities, allowing them a period to "catch up" to the state. Yet there are deeper problems in the state. Given an economic crisis in a region such as the former Soviet Union, the ability of the state to muster the resources for effective organization is in question; this in turn creates spaces for arbitrary behaviour. Even routine, mundane issues of government can be problematic. Issues that initially no one could disagree with – such as opening up the USSR's restrictive border-control mechanisms to allow greater foreign contact and foreign trade – can become surprisingly contentious. Admittedly, any case-study can only scratch the surface of the post-Soviet institutional dilemma. One commonly hears the argument that theories of political development do not take into account the many unique features of the post-Soviet transition. Yet Western theories may have been right about one thing: state-building and economic modernization are fraught with many "crises," and the path to stable and effective statehood may take decades – even centuries – to achieve.[88]

Conclusion

In the past century, borders in the former Soviet Union have been repeatedly subject to revolutionary volatility. The maintenance and strengthening of border controls in the Eurasian region today is occurring under the pretext that it prevents the spread of conflict and instability – interestingly enough, these are the same justifications that the Bolsheviks invoked earlier this century when they set up their own border controls. The symbolic existence of border controls in countries such as Ukraine seems far more important to those countries than the actual purpose and mandate of the controls. Both cases are responses to a simple truth: that border controls continue to represent a powerful image of statehood.

This study has outlined the history of one small piece of the state in the Soviet Union and its successor states. As such, the study has its limitations. First, Soviet border controls remain a politically sensitive topic in Russia, still identified with state security, which means that much archival material may exist to which scholars have not yet been granted access. Secondly, this topic is intrinsically difficult to research, given the relative paucity of research materials. Some scholars find that they are overwhelmed by the materials available. This study does not fall into that category. Rather, it is the product of much "detective work," poking in archives, looking for clues, waiting to stumble upon the evidence that ultimately proved worth waiting for. Border control in itself is, of course, a relatively narrow topic. There are a number of promising directions for future research in related areas of interest. Among the rich topics of investigation for future scholarly research are the cultural themes of isolation in Soviet propaganda and literature, the social and ethnic relations of various borderland populations, and the creation of Soviet internal administrative boundaries. These areas are not explored in depth in this particular study, which treats international border controls as a case-study of the state.

Yet the research in this study offers a number of conclusions that are relevant to our understanding both of the nature of the Soviet state and of its contemporary prospects for change. First of all, the case of border controls leads to a number of generalizations about Soviet state institutions. It confirms that the Communist authorities devoted considerable planning and resources to creating a society that was isolated as much as possible from the outside world. Border controls were considered a necessary and worthwhile investment in maintaining a loyal population, protecting it from "harmful" influences, limiting the access of the regime's enemies to Soviet territory, and controlling the domestic economy as fully as possible. The evidence also suggests that this was one of the Soviet regime's priorities, from the Bolshevik Revolution until Gorbachev initiated the reforms of *perestroika*, and that autarky was an indispensable component of what was later known as the "command-administrative system." This study confirms that the bureaucracies in the Soviet state were hierarchical, multi-layered, and elaborate, but that they sometimes contradicted and worked at cross-purposes with each other. Finally, it suggests that no matter how much the post-Soviet leaders pay lip service to the importance of reforming the state, they remain constrained by labyrinthine, dispersed bureaucracies that work through a complex machinery that cannot be changed until it is fully understood; furthermore, unwittingly or not, post-Soviet leaders' reactions to political turmoil sometimes echo the responses and policies of their Bolshevik prececessors.

This study does not intend to advance the deterministic argument that Russian political culture enslaves and entraps any would-be reformer. Rather, it suggests that certain ongoing factors in history, such as territorial expanse and multi-ethnic borderlands, are structural factors that have influenced the decision-making of Russian, Soviet, and post-Soviet leaders. The case of border controls shows that decisions about the state are notably realist, even Machiavellian; they are often phrased in the language of political necessity and stability of rule rather than of ideological principle and moral values. Although leaders may be committed in principle to openness, human rights, and international communication, the nuts-and-bolts discussion of border-control institutions reflects a hard-nosed attitude towards the imperative of security.

Finally, this study offers a modest contribution towards the continu-

ing scholarly debate on the collapse of the Soviet state. The fall of the
Soviet political system came as a great surprise to many observers, and
many scholars have written essays seeking to "explain" the downfall
of the Soviet state.[1] Some explanations have focused on the immorali-
ty of the Communist system, the rise of nationalism, or the severity of
the economic crisis. Yet, as Alexander Dallin has argued, there is no
pat answer to the question of the Soviet collapse: the fall of the USSR
was the result of complex, interactive causes stemming from a particular configuration of events.[2] In the 1970s and 1980s expert assessments
often presented the Communist regime as relatively stable and responsible for modest successes in economic development, even while suggesting that the regime would have difficulty sustaining its achievements.[3] This is why the rapid turn of events in the USSR under the five
years of *perestroika* is of such interest.

Scholars advance various explanations for the collapse of the Soviet
Union. As Reinhard Bendix argued decades before the collapse, states
that do not achieve an inclusive "nation-building" phase of development can have problems of legitimacy.[4] Some Sovietologists have portrayed the role of society as a critical variable, pointing to the rise of
nationalist and democratic opposition to Soviet rule and the initiative
of newly elected republican governments in the independence process.
This approach stresses the Soviet regime's loss of legitimacy among the
population it sought to control and the progressive empowerment of
opposition movements and elites under *perestroika*.[5] Revelations of
Stalinist repression and coercion under *glasnost* had already undermined the legitimacy of the Soviet government.[6] As Guiseppe di Palma
has noted of the collapse of Communist regimes in Eastern Europe, the
lack of popular legitimacy was a crucial factor in those regimes'
demise.[7]

A second factor to consider is the decline of the Soviet state. For
example, the state's ability to deploy coercive power effectively was
seriously compromised and overextended under *perestroika* because of
the decline of the armed forces.[8] Some political scientists have explored
a geopolitical approach to state collapse, which attempts to explain
loss of territorial control over areas in the periphery, particularly in
"empires." States may decline seriously when they overcommit themselves and spread themselves too thinly across a large territory. If a
state has too many territorial obligations relative to its capacity, this
will eventually cause political and fiscal strain, especially when imperial rule has been imposed over recalcitrant, ethnically diverse populations.[9] Powerful states that become overambitious in their territorial
commitments and overconfident on their economic might eventually
deplete their resources in trying to maintain their position unless, as

Jack Snyder argues, their leaders learn to retrench to a smaller scale.[10] Similarly, Alexander J. Motyl has argued that the expanse of the Soviet Union's "imperial" territory, combined with its totalitarian state organization, proved difficult to rule, and these difficulties contributed to the country's inability to withstand the social pressures that *perestroika* unleashed. The Soviet state, whose size and bureaucratic scale made it very difficult to rule, had already been weakened by the complications of the reform process and the rise of ethnic demands.[11] One could argue that Gorbachev's country fell when it was strained by the emergence of parallel governments on its territorial peripheries. In effect, the Soviet Union was faced with several regional conflicts at a time when it had already destabilized itself. If a state is shaped by its state-building process, then elements created in that process could eventually lead to its undoing. An intriguing possibility emerges: the Soviet Union's rise was in some way related to its dramatic decline. Its coercive and dictatorial tendencies, although useful in the early state-building process of the 1920s to 1950s, eventually proved its undoing.[12]

If we explore the structural factors influencing Soviet state-building, we find that strategies of rule that seem illogical in 1991 were successful, albeit brutal methods of state-building in 1924. Border controls, for example, performed a certain function, however unpalatable, in the early decades of the Bolshevik state but seemed more of a liability by the 1980s, when although the international environment surrounding the Soviet state had dramatically changed, they came to symbolize an internal structure that had not. The system had protected itself from the disadvantages of open communication, but it had also cut itself off from the benefits. Even when the Gorbachev leadership became committed to opening up the system, the complexity of the bureaucracy and the complications of reforming Soviet political structures ensured that border controls could not be liberalized overnight. Ironically enough, by the time the Soviet legislature passed laws institutionalizing more open borders in 1991, republics had already seized the initiative to establish and protect their own borders, having learned well the lesson that controlling borders is key to forming a sovereign state.

Border controls show that it would be erroneous to see Soviet decline as an across-the-board collapse in the state's capacities. In Max Weber's influential conception of the modern political system, a state must monopolize coercive power within its territory: it must have final authority over government functions within its jurisdiction.[13] The fall of the Soviet Union, significantly, was accompanied by multiple sites of small-scale violence and the spread of secessionism.[14] The issue was not that Soviet state organizations themselves stopped functioning but that they were unsuccessful in maintaining their supremacy on the territory of the republics: in short, the monopoly on coercion was eroded. Meanwhile, citizens rejected the Soviet state's monopoly of state power. The attempt to destroy rival sovereignties through coercive means failed, most notably in the coup attempt of August 1991. We might use Hirschman's terminology of "exit" and "voice" to describe the actions of the Soviet republics. These republics did not simply "exit" unequivocally from the USSR through outright secession. Rather, they eroded central state authority by "exiting" selectively from certain aspects of the established Soviet power structure instead of using voice to participate in the reconstruction of the Soviet political system.[15] Even at its demise in December 1991 the Soviet state still retained sectors of significant institutional and coercive power. Once republics established institutions such as border controls and militias, they challenged the Soviet state's claims to control a single system of authority across its entire territory. The multiplication of claims to sovereignty, the rivalry for control of the state, and the unravelling of Soviet power at the periphery all contributed to the collapse, in combination with the decline in legitimacy and political effectiveness of Soviet authority.

Still, Communism alone was not responsible for all of the problems the Soviet Union. My research confirms that many of the problems of the Soviet state have outlived Communism and continue to plague its successor states. If the post-Soviet republics, wittingly or not, replicate Soviet patterns of behaviour, then we should re-examine our assumption of the finality of the USSR's demise. At this writing, analysts are already beginning to speak of the renewed possibility of a new Russian imperial power claiming domination over the economically weakened former Soviet republics.[16] In addition, the prominence of communists and neo-communists in a number of the former Soviet republics since 1991 – Russia's parliamentary elections of December 1995 are a case in point – raises the question of whether some form of renewed neo-Soviet association might possibly be formed in the future.

The Soviet state's extreme reliance on coercion ultimately came back to haunt it. Moreover, it taught the republics the valuable lesson that the key to state independence is the ability to construct effective instruments of power, such as border controls. The case of border controls shows that the collapse of the Communist system did not automatically usher the new states into a reformist era. The historical ambivalence of border-control policy reflects a deep fear that liberalized borders will allow human and material resources to be drained from the country in excess of the benefits that open communication will bring. Unless this knee-jerk attitude is re-evaluated, borders will continue to be restricted. We can only hope that post-Soviet leaders choose to break with the coercive methods of their predecessors by seeking more consensual, co-operative ways to accommodate their ethnic minorities and resolve their economic crises.

Does this suggest that the countries of the former Soviet Union are prisoners of their history, doomed to repeat their past mistakes? Again, the answer is no. We cannot underestimate the desire of many post-Soviet individuals, groups, and influential leaders to make a decisive break with the most oppressive features of the Soviet Union. Anyone who travelled to the Soviet Union before *perestroika* and has travelled there since knows very well that border controls are on the whole much more relaxed and less intrusive than they used to be. Few indeed are the individuals who want to restore the system to Stalinist totalitarianism. None the less, when it comes to border controls, the government institutions of the former Soviet Union seem to suffer from "Stockholm Syndrome" – the curious predilection of hostages to identify with the captor who imprisons and mistreats them.[17] The countries of the Soviet Union seem to cling to authoritarian institutions, such as border controls, as "the devil they know," which is perhaps less threatening than taking the risk to move to a new system based on openness, trust, and co-operation. Only a conscious, co-ordinated effort by determined individuals is likely to reverse this pattern. However, barring the reimposition of the Communist system, sealing the international border outright is no longer an option; the post-Communist governments all have to deal with the consequences and trade-offs of a more open border.

Notes

CHAPTER ONE

1 "Agreement on the Creation of a Commonwealth of Independent States" (8 Dec. 1991), in Black, ed., *Into the Dustbin of History*, 312.
2 See Mosely, "Aspects of Russian Expansion," 197–213; Yaney, "War and the Evolution," 291–306.
3 Hirschman, "Exit, Voice, and the State," 90–107.
4 Bahry, "The Union Republics and Contradictions," 215–55.
5 Roeder, *Red Sunset*.
6 Lewin, *Making of the Soviet System*; Siegelbaum, *Soviet State and Society*.
7 Snyder, "International Leverage," 1–30.
8 The argument that the USSR would be unable to achieve full modernization due to its state-centred neglect of societal initiative is made by Chalmers Johnson, "Comparing Communist Nations," in Johnson, ed., *Change in Communist Systems*, 12. In 1986 Seweryn Bialer had already expressed doubts on the inclination of the Soviet leadership to reform despite the increasing ineffectiveness of the system; see *The Soviet Paradox*. The severe problems that Gorbachev had in trying to reform in response to social modernization, and the long-term inadequacies of the existing command-authoritarian system, are discussed in Lewin, *The Gorbachev Phenomenon*, expanded ed., 1991. Another recent analysis is Thomas F. Remington, "Regime Transition in Communist Systems: The Soviet Case," in Fleron and Hoffman, ed., *Post-Communist Studies and Political Science*, 265–98.

9 This follows the approach of Theda Skocpol, who argues that "structural factors" and the international environment influenced the creation of strong post-revolutionary states. See Skocpol, *States and Social Revolutions.*

10 Alfred G. Meyer persuasively argues that political expediency was the core of Leninism, in his book *Leninism.* Meyer also criticizes the tendency in Sovietology to rely on ideological determinism as diminishing the importance of ideological compromise and improvization in determining Soviet policy; at the same time, he argues that the importance of ideology as a world-view determining Soviet leaders' perception of politics should not be underestimated. Meyer, "Functions of Ideology," 275–7. Similarly, Stephen F. Cohen disputes the idea that Stalinism was the inevitable outcome of Marxist-Leninist ideology, in his essay "Bolshevism and Stalinism," in *Rethinking the Soviet Experience,* 38–70.

11 Joseph Schull argues that ideology in the Soviet Union was a "discourse," a pattern of language and thinking, rather than a system of deeply held values and faith. However, Schull has been criticized by some scholars for de-emphasizing belief. See Schull, "What is Ideology?" 728; Robinson, "What Was Soviet Ideology?" 325–32; Walker, "Thinking about Ideology and Method," 333–42.

12 For example, Archie Brown, "Ideology and Political Culture," in Bialer, ed., *Inside Gorbachev's Russia,* 2–3, 11. Malcolm B. Hamilton sees ideology as a set of common beliefs and goals favouring a certain order of social relations; see "Elements of the Concept," 38.

13 See Elazar, "International and Comparative Federalism," 190–5; Rakowska-Harmstone, "The Dialectics of Nationalism," 1–22.

14 Ian Bremmer, "Reassessing Soviet Nationalities Theory," in Bremmer and Taras, eds., *Nations and Politics,* 3–26; Slezkine, "USSR as Communal Apartment," 427–30.

15 Gleason and Buck, "De-colonization in Former Soviet Borderlands," 522–3. Teresa Rakowska-Harmstone argues that the creation of the USSR as a system with a federal type of organization, divided into national-based republics, tended to expand nationalist tendencies and the political resources of elites within the republics; see Rakowska-Harmstone, "The Dialectics of Nationalism," 1–22.

16 See, for example, Subtelny, *Ukraine,* 413–15.

17 Gleason, *Federalism and Nationalism,* 11–12.

18 The debate is: are states in the contemporary world coming together through international integration, thereby losing some of their significance as nation-states, or does nationalism indicate the strength of the nation-state? A variation on this theme asks whether the wave of secessionism and ethnic conflict in recent years points to "fragmentation" of the nation-state rather than its integration. See, for example, Kratochwil,

"Of Systems, Boundaries, and Territoriality," 27; Motyl, "Modernity of Nationalism," 307–23; John W. Meyer, "The World Polity and the Authority of the Nation-State," in Thomas, Meyer, Ramirez, and Boli, eds., *Institutional Structure*, 41–70; L.J. Sharpe, "Fragmentation and Territoriality," 223–38; Mann, "Nation-States in Europe," 115–40.

CHAPTER TWO

1 Much of the literature on the state has focused either on advanced industrial welfare states or on the problems of states in the Third World (variously, in responding to the dilemmas of dependency for the state or to the creation of post-colonial states). See Krasner, "Approaches to the State," 223–46; Stepan, *State and Society*; Nordlinger, *On the Autonomy*; Skocpol, *States and Social Revolutions*; Evans, Rueschemeyer, and Skocpol, eds., *Bringing the State Back In*. The study of Soviet and Leninist regimes experienced a certain isolation from the rest of comparative politics, although there are exceptions, including Skocpol's work. Some works that have applied concepts of the state to the Soviet Union include Harding, ed., *State in Socialist Society*, which largely deals with theoretical issues surrounding the state, rather than assessing the Soviet state comparatively and empirically; Motyl, who explores the question of ethnic stability in the Soviet state in *Will the Non-Russians Rebel?*; and Easter, "Personal Networks."

2 See Arendt, *Origins of Totalitarianism*; Brzezinski and Friedrich, *Totalitarian Dictatorship and Autocracy*.

3 Knight, KGB, 243; Tillett, "National Minorities Factor," 241–2; Reitz, "Soviet Security Troops," 285.

4 S. Frederick Starr posits that Soviet restriction of international communications was one dimension of an authoritarian, hierarchical political system that traditionally did not permit the existence of a private "civil society." See S. Frederick Starr, "New Communications Technologies and Civil Society," in Graham, ed., *Science and the Soviet Social Order*, 19-50.

5 He particularly argues the importance of border controls in cutting off communications between domestic populations and anti-state émigrés. Alexander J. Motyl, *Will the Non-Russians Rebel?* 148–51.

6 Jerry Hough refers to the USSR as a protectionist economic system; see Hough, *Russia and the West*, chap. 2; Ken Jowitt describes Stalinism as a "castle regime" in Jowitt, *New World Disorder*, 171.

7 See Matthews, *The Passport Society*.

8 Salitan explains the restrictiveness of Soviet emigration policy as the result of "an ideology that does not accept free emigration." See Salitan, "Domestic Pressures," 672.

9 Arendt, in 1951, wrote about the integral relationship of isolation to totalitarianism, in *Origins of Totalitarianism*, 172. For Brzezinski and Friedrich, in *Totalitarian Dictatorship and Autocracy*, closed borders were implicit in the totalitarian state's control of communications and its linkage of external and internal enemies. Andrew Janos saw closed borders as a way of preventing citizens in totalitarian regimes from becoming aware of the standard of living available in Western consumer society. Janos, *Politics and Paradigms*, 121–2.

10 Dowty, *Closed Borders*, 4.

11 Felshtinskii, *K istorii nashei zakrytosti*, 6.

12 William Zimmerman observes that despite the many similarities between Yugoslavia and the Soviet model, including a Communist Party monopoly on power and a considerable reliance on domestic repression, Yugoslav borders were opened in the 1950s, proving that variation was possible within the Communist model. Zimmerman, *Open Borders*, 6–9.

13 The conflict between the goal of a world socialist order and the development of the Soviet Union as a national state is explored by Elliot Goodman, who discusses the conflict between the Comintern and the Soviet state, and mentions the role of state borders in Soviet ideology. See *Soviet Design*, 31, 61.

14 V.I. Lenin, "The State and Revolution" (1918), in Tucker, ed., *Lenin Anthology*, 315–25.

15 Jean-Yves Calvez, "Doctrine de la Frontiére en URSS," in Duroselle, *Frontières européenes de l'URSS*, 6–7.

16 A philosophy most clearly articulated in *History of CPSU (Bolsheviks): Short Course*.

17 The idea that international uncertainty was an important influence on the nature of Soviet institutions is argued by Snyder, "International Leverage," 1–30.

18 This characterization is drawn from Lisa Anderson's discussion in "State in Middle East," 2. Anderson notes that many recognized states do not meet these criteria.

19 Examples include Rokkan and Unwin, eds., *Economy, Territory, Identity*; Clark and Dear, *State Apparatus*; and Shue, *Reach of the State*.

20 Michael Mann, "The Autonomous Power of the State: Its Origins, Mechanisms and Results," in Hall, ed., *States in History*, 109, 123.

21 David Easton's discussion of political science stresses that the role of the state has been overemphasized and we should look at politics from a broader perspective; he sees politics as being "the authoritative allocation of values." Yet when he refers to the obligation of all citizens to respect "policy and law," it seems clear that he is referring to the state. Easton, *Political System*, 134.

22 These three functions have been conceptualized by Stein Rokkan, who defines the dimensions as objects of economic exchange, people, and the communication of ideas. Rokkan, "Entries, Voices, Exits," 43. Samuel L. Finer defines border control as "the operational mechanism which gives effect to [system boundaries] by giving the system a *spatial dimension* and policing the territorial boundary so laid down." Finer, "State-Building, State Boundaries and Border Control," 85.

23 Kratochwil, "Of Systems, Boundaries and Territoriality," 27–52.

24 Hirschman, "Exit, Voice, and the State," 90–107.

25 Giddens, *Nation State and Violence*, 50–7.

26 Mitchell, "Limits of the State," 94–5.

27 Mann, *States, War and Capitalism*, 23–5.

28 See Callaghy, *State-Society Struggle*; Anderson, *State and Social Transformation*; Lustick, "Israeli State-Building," 151–71.

29 Gourevitch, "Second Image Reversed," 896–900.

30 Anderson, *Lineages of the Absolutist State*.

31 Levi, *Of Rule and Revenue*.

32 See Charles Tilly, "Reflections on the History of European State-Making," in Tilly, ed., *Formation of National States*.

33 Tilly, *Coercion, Capital and European States*, 29–31.

34 Seymour Martin Lipset and Stein Rokkan, "Cleavage Structures, Party Systems, and Voter Alignments," in Lipset and Rokkan, eds., *Party Systems and Voter Alignments*, 1–64.

35 See, for example, David H. Bayley, "The Police and Political Development in Europe," in Tilly, ed., *The Formation of National States*, 361–5, 378, and other essays in the Tilly volume.

36 Anderson, "State in the Middle East," 14–15.

37 A series of articles written by Stein Rokkan, Samuel Finer, and Albert O. Hirschman in the late 1970s, inspired by Hirschman's "exit-voice-loyalty" paradigm, explore the tendency of newly established states to try to close their borders. Again, they focus on the experiences of the states of early modern Europe. See Finer, "State-building, State Boundaries and Border Control," 79–82. Hirschman, "Exit, Voice and the State," 100–4. Rokkan, "Dimensions of State Formation and Nationbuilding: A Possible Paradigm for Research on Variations within Europe," in Tilly, ed., *Formation of National States*, 589–91. Michael Marrus also argues that in early modern Europe state-building was accompanied by restrictions on movement and emigration outside of the country. Marrus, *The Unwanted*, 6–7.

38 This would eventually lead to pressures from the population for a voice in political affairs, according to Hirschman; see "Exit, Voice and the State," 100, 104.

39 In discussing the case of society at the Franco-Spanish border, Peter

Sahlins argues that this could be a form of peasant resistance, in *Boundaries*, 129.

40 Rokkan, "Entries, Voices, Exits," 39–53.
41 Hirschman, "Exit, Voice and Loyalty: Further Reflections," 16–18.
42 Raimond Strassoldo, "Center-Periphery and System-Boundary: Culturological Perspectives," in Gottman, ed., *Center and Periphery*, 51.
43 Hirschman, "Exit, Voice and the State," 96–9.
44 Polanyi, *Great Transformation*, 23–4, 200. The 1920s and 1930s were a time when many countries adopted restrictive immigration and emigration policies; in addition, the reluctance of some countries to accept mass numbers of Jewish refugees during that period has been well documented. See, for example, Abella and Troper, *None Is Too Many*.
45 Gourevitch, *Politics in Hard Times*.
46 This point was noted by Day, *Leon Trotsky*, 56.
47 Marrus, *The Unwanted*; Dowty, *Closed Borders*.
48 Keohane and Nye, among others, have argued that increasing transborder contact is eroding and changing contemporary sovereignty; see *Power and Interdependence*.
49 Brown and Shue, eds., *Boundaries*; John F. Stack, Jr., "Ethnic Groups as Emerging Transnational Actors," in Stack, ed., *Ethnic Identities in a Transnational World*, 17–46.
50 Strassoldo, "Center-Periphery and System-Boundary," 47–9.
51 Weiner, "The Macedonian Syndrome," 681–2.
52 These are arguments suggested by Weiner, "The Macedonian Syndrome," 665–83, and developed in explicit detail by Sahlins, *Boundaries*, 7–8; see also Finer, "State-building, State Boundaries and Border Control," 83.
53 Sahlins, *Boundaries*, 8–9.
54 Kirchheimer, "Confining Conditions and Revolutionary Breakthroughs," 964–74.
55 By "Soviet-type" or "Leninist" regime I mean to describe the Soviet or East European variant of what scholars such as Juan J. Linz have described as the totalitarian regime, possessing its particular ideology, Communist leadership, and historical struggles. I do not mean to imply that this is a regime category in itself. See Linz's discussion, "Totalitarian and Authoritarian Regimes," in Greenstein and Polsby, eds., *Handbook of Political Science*, 3:175–371.
56 The idea that the Soviet system was the result of a regime developed in response to a revolutionary situation and an uncertain international environment, and that this system thus became an apparatus of entrenched institutions, is argued by Snyder, "International Leverage," 1–30.
57 Doyle, *Empires*, 46, 362–4.

58 Pipes, *Formation of the Soviet Union*, rev. ed.
59 Austin, "Soviet Karelian," 16–35.
60 See Park, *Bolshevism in Turkestan, 1917–1927*.
61 See Marie Bennigsen Broxup, "Introduction: Russia and the North Caucasus," and Fanny E.B. Bryan, "Internationalism, Nationalism and Islam before 1990," in Bennigsen Broxup et al., eds., *The North Caucasus Barrier*, 1–17 and 195–218 respectively; Gammer, *Muslim Resistance to the Tsar*.
62 This is discussed at length in Subtelny, *Ukraine*.
63 Skocpol argued that revolutions, notably the Russian case, are made possible by the breakdown of existing state authority; see *States and Social Revolutions*.
64 Proving the point that "Stalinism grew from preexisting conditions but created its own conditions"; Bialer, *Stalin's Successors*, 47.
65 William Zimmerman has suggested that closed borders followed certain policy choices. A "closed system," Zimmerman notes, seeks to minimize the role that international influences might play in its political system. Zimmerman discusses the opening of the "closed system" of borders in Yugoslavia after the break with Stalin in 1948, and how this opening fit Yugoslavia's economic and political decentralizing reforms and its policy of non-alignment. See Zimmerman, *Open Borders*, 7.
66 Hough, *Russia and the West*, chap. 2, and 80–4.
67 Bialer argues that Stalinism was a qualitatively different system from the early Bolshevik state; see *Stalin's Successors*, 10.
68 Bialer describes in depth these overlapping and arbitrary bureaucracies and the role of the secret police as a driving force; see *Stalin's Successors*, 13–16.
69 Katzenstein, *Small States in World Markets*, 192.
70 For example, Bendix, *Nation-Building and Citizenship*, 2nd ed., 21–4.
71 The other characteristics were "autonomy," "complexity," and "coherence." Huntington, *Political Order in Changing Societies*, 12.
72 March and Olsen, *Rediscovering Institutions*; Krasner, "Sovereignty: An Institutional Perspective," 66–94.
73 See Seymour Martin Lipset and Stein Rokkan, "Cleavage Structures, Party Systems, and Voter Alignments: An Introduction," in Lipset and Rokkan, eds., *Party Systems and Voter Alignments*, 3–64, and the essays in Charles Tilly, ed., *Formation of National States*.
74 Krasner, "Sovereignty: An Institutional Perspective," 80–6. As an example, Krasner points to the continued existence of state border controls in an era of increasing transnational interdependence. For institutions as creators of values, see March and Olsen, *Rediscovering Institutions*, 52; and also Meyer and Rowan, "Institutionalized Organizations," 340–63.
75 Ostrom, *Governing the Commons*, 51–2.

76 See Motyl's discussion of "totalitarian decay," in *Dilemmas of Independence*, 37–8; Roeder, *Red Sunset*; Odom, "Soviet Politics and After," 66–98.

CHAPTER THREE

1 Krasin, *Voprosy vneshnei torgovli*, 75.
2 Hingley, *Russian Secret Police*, 266; the Bolsheviks' awareness of cross-border communications and smuggling links is illustrated by Futrell, *Northern Underground*.
3 A.I. Chugunov and Iu.I. Korablev, intro. to P.I. Zyrianov, et al., eds., *Pogranichnye voiska SSSR*, 1:5.
4 "Ukazaniie komandovaniia vtorogo okruga pogranichnoi okhrany kommissaru 6 -ogo raiona pogranichnoi okhrany (Mogilevskaia Guberniia o raz'iasnenii naseleniiu znacheniia okhrany gosudarstvennoi granitsy" (Instruction … on Explaining the Significance of the Control of State Borders to the Population), July 1918, in Zyrianov, ed., *Pogranichnye voiska SSSR*, 1:396–7.
5 "Iz prikaza voennogo komissara vtorogo okruga pogranichnoi okhrany o sozdanii iacheek sochuvstvuiushchikh Kommunisticheskoi Partii" (From an Instruction … on the creation of cells of sympathizers of the Communist Party), 25 Jan. 1919, in Zyrianov, ed. *Pogranichnye voiska SSSR*, 1:441.
6 Chugunov, *Bor'ba na granitse*, 7–8.
7 Ivanov, *Chasovye Sovetskikh granits*, 18–19.
8 Gleason, *Federalism and Nationalism*, 42–3. See also Nation, *Black Earth, Red Star*; and Blank, *Sorceror's Apprentice*. In Blank's words, "All things being equal, the party would advance the cause of the largest possible state" (7).
9 Felshtinskii, *K istorii nashei zakrytosti*, 14.
10 Goliakov, *Sbornik dokumentov po istorii ugolovnogo zakonodatel'stva*, 23.
11 Skocpol, *States and Social Revolutions*, 95–9, 208–9.
12 For example, Rieber, "Landed Property," 29–38; Malle, *Economic Organization of War Communism*; Koenker, Rosenberg, and Suny, eds., *Party, State and Society*; Lih, *Bread and Authority in Russia*; Leggett, *Cheka: Lenin's Political Police*.
13 Memoirs of V.A. Dobrynin, *Oborona mugani: zapiski kavkazkogo pogranichnika* (Soiuz Georgievskikh Kavalerov, Paris 1925), 1 folder, Archives of the Hoover Institution on War, Revolution, and Peace (hereafter Hoover Institution Archives), Stanford University.
14 Thompson, *Russia, Bolshevism and the Versailles Peace*, 396.
15 Wandycz, *Soviet-Polish Relations*, 93.

16 Schulz, *Revolutions and Peace Treaties*, 160–2.

17 *Ibid.*, 205–6.

18 Western accounts of the activity of such political opposition on the Soviet border are sparse, and suffer from what Motyl has identified as the reluctance to take émigré and defeated political movements seriously; see *Sovietology, Rationality, Nationality*, chaps. 8 and 9. Soviet accounts tended to exaggerate the story and to be coloured by conspiracy theories that are poorly substantiated. See, for example, Pochs, *Sanitarnyi kordon.*

19 Schulz, *Revolutions and Peace Treaties*, 205–6.

20 On 22 April 1918 the Transcaucasus declared independence; on 26 May, Georgia, under a Menshevik-led government, declared its own sovereignty, followed by Armenia and Azerbaijan. Suny, *Making of the Georgian Nation*, 191–2. In Ukraine independence was declared by the *Rada* government on 22 January 1918, against the Bolshevik government's wishes to create a Soviet Ukrainian government by force; and its delegates attended the Brest-Litovsk peace conference with the recognition of the Germans, who gave their support to Hetman Skoropadsky in April. The allies, however, occupied Southern Ukraine and supported Petliura (to a limited extent) and Denikin. See Reshetar, *The Ukrainian Revolution*, 3–4; Pipes, *Formation of the Soviet Union.*

21 Mosely, "Aspects of Russian Expansion," 205–9.

22 There is a rich literature on the Civil War, for example, Bradley, *Civil War in Russia.*

23 Chugunov, *Bor'ba na granitse*, 39.

24 Lenin, "Pis'mo Petrogradskim rabochim o pomoshchi vostochnomu frontu" (Letter to the Petrograd Workers on Aid to the Eastern Front), 10 Apr. 1919, *KPSS o vooruzhennykh silakh*, 63.

25 Baron T. von Wrangel, "The Russian Problem and Its Solution," 23 Mar. 1919, George David Herron, Papers, Baron von Wrangel, document XIIA, Hoover Institution Archives, Stanford University.

26 At the very least, the White General Iudenich in the northwest did; I am unsure about other areas. In the northwest *oblast* there were customs authorities set up and resolutions passed prohibiting certain goods from crossing the border. *Prikaz*, 3 June 1919, Boris I. Nicolaevsky Collection, box 128, ser. 73, file 12, Hoover Institution Archives. In addition, they set up their own *pogranichniki* on the Estonian border but encountered serious supply problems; see Report, 9 Apr. 1919, Papers of Nikolai Nikolaevich Iudenich, box 11, opis 62, no. 6, Hoover Institution Archives.

27 Erickson, *Soviet High Command*, 289–91.

28 Ivanov, *Chasovye Sovetskikh granits*, 18. Of course, we have to ask why the Soviet leadership would aspire to the territory of the Russian empire,

a question difficult to answer. Bertram Wolfe wrote in 1950 that the state boundaries of the Soviet Union, as they evolved by the end of the Civil War, stemmed from military decisions made during the struggle to assert Bolshevik authority during that conflict; see "Influence of Early Military Decisions," 169–79.

29 Bradley, *Civil War in Russia 1917-1920*, 162.

30 See Motyl, *The Turn to the Right*, for the Ukrainian situation; Williams, *Culture in Exile*; Thompson, *Russia, Bolshevism and Versailles Peace*.

31 Telegram to the Ukrainian Division, to Moscow, People's Commissariat of Foreign Affairs, from General Consul Krzheminskiy, Kyïv, 4 Sept. 1918, USSR Central State Archives of the October Revolution, Moscow (hereafter TSGAOR), f. 130, op. 2, no. 520.

32 Alexander Park describes at length how communications between Turkestan and Russia were severed during the war and Civil War, and the importance of this in the growth and power of nationalist movements that rivalled the Bolsheviks' authority. See *Bolshevism in Turkestan 1917–1927*, 68.

33 Kulischer, *Europe on the Move*, 3.

34 For example, "Pis'mo voennogo rukovoditelia v Vyshii Voennyi Sovet ob uskorenii resheniia voprosa organizatsii pogranichnoi okhrany" (Letter of the Military Leader Bonch-Bruevich to the Higher Military Soviet on the Acceleration of Decision of Questions of Organization of Border Control), 8 May 1918, in Zyrianov, ed., *Pogranichnye voiska SSSR*, 1:71. This letter urged the staffing of border crossing-points because of the number of refugees. A decree called for border guards to halt the flow of refugees coming into the country and especially towards Moscow. "Postanovlenie STO o prekrashchenii besporiiadochnogo dvizheniia bezhentsev k Moskve i k zapadnoi granitse" (Resolution of the Council of Labour and Defence on the Prevention of the Disorderly Movement of Refugees to Moscow and the Western Border), 1 June 1921, in Zyrianov, ed., *Pogranichnye voiska SSSR*, 1:172–3. See also, for refugees trying to leave Ukraine, "Letter to Minister-President of the Ukrainian Soviet Republic T. Rakovskii from the Soviet of the Nikolaevskii Otdel," 19 Mar. 1919, Central State Archives of the October Revolution of the Ukrainian SSR (hereafter TSGAOR UKSSR), f. 2, op. 1, spr. 481, #8.

35 For example, "Letter from T. Rakovskii to the soviet of the Nikolaevskii Otdel," 19 Mar. 1919, TSGAOR UKSSR, f. 2, op. 1, spr. 481, #8. The letter discusses a telegram received forbidding the return of refugees to their home countries; he asks for permission to return them to Belorussia, the Baltic states, and Poland.

36 For example, see the Revvoensovet Decision, dated June 1919, TSGAOR, f. 130, op. 3, ed. khr. 202, p. 24.

37 In some cases appeals by the local authorities were successful in having

refugees returned to countries across the border, although, as this document verifying the return of thirty carloads of Poles demonstrates, not necessarily in providing the physical means to do this. Telegram from Ekaterinoslav *Guberniia* Committee on Prisoners of War and Refugees to the Main Commission on Prisoners of War and Refugees Evacuation Department, 2 May 1919, Kyïv, TSGAOR UkSSR, f. 2, op. 1, spr. 340, #4. The telegram was asking for trains and supplies.

38 Felshtinskii, *K istorii nashei zakrytosti*, 72–3.
39 Simpson, *Refugee Problem*, 63, 83–4.
40 Lorimer, *Population of the Soviet Union*, 39.
41 See Stephan, *Russian Fascists*, 31; Williams, *Culture in Exile*, 113; Fischer, ed., *Russian Emigré Politics*.
42 Motyl, *Sovietology, Rationality, Nationality*, chap. 8. See espec. 140.
43 Felshtinskii, *K istorii nashei zakrytosti*, 41.
44 Thompson, "Lenin's Analysis of Intervention," 151–60.
45 Ginsburgs, "Soviet Union and the Problem of Refugees," 329.
46 Felshtinsky, "Legal Foundations," 334–5.
47 Mukhachev, "Krakh burzhuaznogo restavratorstva," 94–5.
48 "Doklad" (Report) from the People's Commissar of Social Security Poznanskii to the Ukrainian Council of People's Commissars, ca 18 Apr. 1924, TSGAOR UkSSR, f. 2, op. 3, d. 1013.
49 Bukharin, "Programma Kommunistov (Bol'shevikov)," *Izbrannye proizvedeniia*, 65–68.
50 Telegram to Ukrainian Department of the People's Commissariat of Foreign Affairs, from General Consul Krzheminskiy, undated ca Aug. 1918, Kyïv, TSGAOR, f. 130, op. 2, ed. khr. 520.
51 Gladkov and Smirnov, *Menzhinskii*, 185.
52 Ivanov, *Chasovye Sovetskikh granits*, 24–6.
53 Iurovskii, *Denezhnaia politika Sovetskoi vlasti*, 38–41.
54 Ibid., 80–1, 107.
55 Ibid., 240.
56 Markov, *Ocherki po istorii tamozhennoi sluzhby*, 73–4.
57 "O razgranichenii prav tsentralnoi i mestnykh sovetskikh vlastei po sobiraniiu poshlin i o reguliravanii deiatel'nosti tamozhennykh uchrezhdenii" (On the Division of Powers of Central and Local Soviet Authorities in Collecting Duties and Regulating the Activity of Customs Institutions), 1 Sept. 1922, *Sobranie uzakonenii RSFSR*, 58 (1922):948–52.
58 "O natsionalizatsii vneshnei torgovli" (On the Nationalization of Foreign Trade), 22 Apr. 1918, *Resheniia partii i pravitel'stva po khoziaistvennym voprosam*, 1:50–2.
59 Khrabskov, *Tamozhniia i zakon*, 15–16.
60 Ibid., 17–18.
61 Ibid., 15–16.

62 "Iz ob'iasnitelnoi zapiski k proektu dekreta o polozhenii o tamozhennoi okhrane gosudarstvennoi granitsy" (Draft of a Decree of the RSFSR Council of People's Commissars on Customs Control of the State Border), Apr. 1919, in Zyrianov, ed., *Pogranichnye voiska SSSR*, 1:145.

63 This is certainly true of the Basmachi political resistance to Soviet rule in Turkestan, where their engagement in trade with Afghanistan and their political ties with the Bukharan emir were vital issues in their conflict with the Soviet Armed Forces over the policy of "sovietization"; the border guards sought to seal off the southern border. See Zyrianov, ed., *Pogranichnye voiska SSSR*, 1:582–701. For Krasin's point, see *Voprosy*, 44.

64 See Merle Fainsod, "Bureaucracy and Modernization: The Russian and Soviet Case," in LaPalombara, ed., *Bureaucracy and Political Development*, 233–67; Rigby, *Lenin's Government: Sovnarkom 1917–1922*, 14–16; Remington, *Building Socialism in Bolshevik Russia*; Service, *The Bolshevik Party in Revolution*.

65 Rigby, *Lenin's Government: Sovnarkom 1917–1922*, 16–17.

66 This was often described as a kind of "vicious circle" – in, for example, a document relating to the Central Asian border. See "Iz postanovleniia Tsentral'noi Komissii po bor'be s Basmachestvom pri Sredneaziatskom Biuro RKP(b) o rabote, prodelannoi v Zeravshanskoi Oblasti" (From a Decree of the Central Commission for the Struggle with Basmachism of the Central Asian Bureau of the Central Committee of the Communist Party on the Work being Carried out by the Zeravshanskoi Oblast), Dec. 1925, in Zyrianov, ed., *Pogranichnye voiska SSSR*, 1:664.

67 "Doklad upravliaiushchego Pos'etskoi tamozhennoi zastavoi vo Vladivostokskuiu tamozhniu i o kontrabande v pervom polugodii 1918 g." (Report of the Ruling Customs Organ of Vladivostok on Contraband in the First Half of 1918), 27 July 1918; "Iz prikaza glavnokomanduiushchego vsei Dal'nevostochnoi Respubliki o soznanii pogranichnykh raionov dlia bor'by s Belogvardeiskimi otriadami" (From an Instruction of the Main Command of the Armed Forces of the Far Eastern Republic on the Organization of Border Control), 17 Mar. 1921; both in Zyrianov, ed., *Pogranichnye voiska SSSR*, 1:778–9.

68 Intro. by Korablev and Chugunov to Zyrianov, ed. *Pogranichnye voiska SSSR*, 1:5.

69 Rigby, *Lenin's Government: Sovnarkom 1917–1922*, 14–16.

70 Ivanov, *Chasovye Sovetskikh granits*, 24–6.

71 Felshtinskii, *K istorii nashei zakrytosti*, 7.

72 File, "Passports and Visas," 1917–24, box 19; file, "Russia: *Narkomindel* regulations for obtaining entry visas, January 1918," box 30; both in Papers of the Russian Embassy in France, Basil Maklakoff, ambassador, Hoover Institution Archives. Meanwhile, the Whites in the Northern

Oblast sent the embassy notice that it had its own border rules, which cleaved to the 1916 regulations on entry and exit. They required a passport issued by the Russian (Rossiiskii) diplomatic representatives. See box 30, 14 Nov. 1919, letter from the Temporary Government of the Northern Oblast, Department of Foreign Affairs, to the Russian Embassy in Paris, and regulations, 9 Nov. 1919, in Papers of the Russian Embassy in France, Basil Maklakoff, ambassador, Hoover Institution Archives.

73 Leggett, *Cheka*, 90, 229–30.
74 Intro. by Korablev and Chugunov to Zyrianov, ed., *Pogranichnye voiska SSSR*, 1:8–9.
75 Telegram of V.I. Lenin to the Kursk Executive Political Committee, ca 14 June 1918, in Belov, et al., ed., *Iz istorii Vserossiiskoi Chrezvychainoi Komissii*, 140.
76 *Ezhenedel'nik Vecheka*, 1, 1918, 27.
77 "G," "O voprose zashchity granits" (On the Question of Defence of the Borders), *Ezhenedel'nik Vecheka* 4, 1918, 14.
78 Telegram from Krzheminskiy, General Consul in Kiev, to the Ukrainian Division of the People's Commissariat of Foreign Affairs, Moscow, 29 Aug. 1918, TSGAOR, f. 130, op. 2, ed. khr. 520, 2.
79 Chugunov, *Bor'ba na granitse*, 19, 24.
80 Intro. by Korablev and Chugunov to Zyrianov, ed. *Pogranichnye voiska SSSR*, 1:8–9.
81 "Polozhenie o chrezvychainykh kommissiiakh na mestakh" (Position on the Extraordinary Commissions in the Localities), adopted at the All-Russian Conference of Chekas, 11 June 1918, Boris I. Nicolaevsky Collection, box 143, ser. 89, no. 7, Hoover Institution Archives.
82 "Pis'mo Narodnogo Komissara Torgovli i Promyshlennosti v Revvoensovet Respubliki o sokhranenii samostoiatel'nosti chastei pogranichnoi okhrany i ikh vydelenii iz sostava Krasnoi Armii dlia pereformirovaniia po novym shtatam" (Letter ... on the Conservation of the Independence of Units of the Border Guard and Their Division from the Staff of the Red Army for Reformation to a New State), 28 Jan. 1919, in Zyrianov, ed., *Pogranichnye voiska SSSR*, 1:136–9.
83 "Pis'mo Glavnogo Upravleniia Pogranichnoi Okhrany v Narodnyi Komissariat Finansov ob uskorenii osvobozhdeniia voisk zavesy ot obiazannosti neseniia pogranichnoi okhrany i o formirovanii pogranichnoi okhrany" (Letter of the Main Administration of Border Control to the People's Commissariat of Finance on the Acceleration of the Liberation of the Troops at the Front from the Necessity of Carrying out Border Control Functions and on the Formation of Border Control), 30 July 1918, in Zyrianov, ed., *Pogranichnye voiska SSSR*, 1:93.
84 See von Hagen, *Soldiers in the Proletarian Dictatorship*, 50–51.

85 Intro. by Korablev and Chugunov to P. Zyrianov, ed., *Pogranichnye voiska SSSR*, 1:9–11.

86 "Pis'mo narodnogo komissara torgovli i promyshlennosti v Revvoensovet respubliki o sokhranenii samostoiatel'nosti chastei pogranichnoi okhrany i ikh vydelenii iz sostava krasnoi armii dlia pereformirovanii po novym shtatom" (Letter of the People's Commissar of Trade and Industry of *Revvoensovet* of the Republic on the Conservation of the Independence of Units of the Border Guard and Their Division from the Staff of the Red Army for Reformation to a New State), 28 Jan. 1919, in Zyrianov, ed., *Pogranichnye voiska SSSR*, 1:136–9. See also Chugunov, *Bor'ba na granitse*, 18–39.

87 "Iz prikaza Glavnogo Upravleniia Pogranichnoi Okhrany ob activizatsii nabora dobrovol'tsev v pogranichnoi okhrany i usilenie okhrany granitsy" (From an Instruction of the Main Administration of Border Control on the Activation of the Choice of Volunteers into Border Service and the Strengthening of Border Control), 28 July 1918, in Zyrianov, ed., *Pogranichnye voiska SSSR*, 1:92–3.

88 Leggett, *Cheka*, 90–3.

89 The People's Commissariat of Internal Affairs (NKVD), which was established at the republic level in Russia and in Soviet Ukraine shortly after the revolution; it remained at the republic level until its dissolution in 1929. It is thus to be distinguished from the USSR NKVD, which was formed in 1934 as a central government body and is most commonly identified as the political police responsible for the Stalinist purges of the late 1930s.

90 Felshtinskii, *K istorii nashei zakrytosti*, 14–15.

91 RSFSR, "Instruktsiia pogranichnym osobistam osobootdeleniia" (Instruction to Border Extraordinary Departments) no. 6, 23 Dec. 1921, Papers of Boris Aleksandrovich Bakhmeteff, box 62, no. 379, Bakhmeteff Archive, Rare Book and Manuscript Library, Columbia University.

92 "Pis'mo ..." (Letter from the Central Committee of the Jewish Social Democratic Workers' Party, to VTsIK, the Council of People's Commissars of the RSFSR, and the Council of People's Commissars of the Ukrainian SSR), Moscow, 20 Feb. 1921. TsGAOR, f. 1318, op. 1, no. 1261, 43–5, 56.

93 "Protokol zasedanii Komissii Organizovannoi SNK i VTsIK o Re-evaki Bezhentsev-Evreev na granitse" (Protocol of the Session of the Organizational Commission of the Council of People's Commissars and the Central Executive Committee on the Re-evacuation of Jewish Refugees on the Border), 11 Apr. 1921, TsGAOR, f. 1318, op. 1, ed. khr. 1261, 17–18.

94 "Pis'mo ..." (Letter from the Zavedotdel of the People's Commissariat of Nationalities to the People's Commissariat of Internal Affairs), undated, TsGAOR, f. 1318, op. 1, no. 1261, 191–2.

95 "Prikaz VChK okhrany Rymanskoi granitse" (Order of the VChK on Control of the Rumanian Border), ca early 1921, TSGAOR, f. 1318, op. 1, ed. khr. 1261, 77.

96 "Doklad ..." (Report from the Plenipotentiary of the Kyïv Obshch-estkom and the Commission for the Investigation of the Rumanian Border), 29 Mar. 1921, TSGAOR, f. 1318, op. 1, ed. khr. 147, 123.

97 Iz prikaza komandovaniia voiskami VChK respubliki s ob'iavleniem "Instruktsii Chastiam VChK Okhraniaiushchim Granitsy RSFSR" (Instruction to Units of the VChK Guard Controlling the Borders of the RSFSR), 15 Feb. 1921, in Zyrianov, ed. *Pogranichnye voiska SSSR*, 1:170–1.

98 Leggett, *Cheka*, 227–9.

99 See, for example, Telegram from Zavpolitdev Second Border Division, to the Roslavl Communist Party Committee, 5 Aug. 1920, Smolensk Archive of the RKP(b), roll 15, WKP 119, 11–12.

100 Translation from *Ekonomicheskaia zhizn'*, no. 154, 13 July 1922, in U.S. Department of State, *Records of the Department of State Relating to the Internal Affairs of Russia and the Soviet Union, 1910–1929*, roll 140, 861.70/15, 38.

101 For example, in 1921 there were reports that border regiments around Slutsk were evidencing anti-Bolshevik moods, and that they would side with the rebels if there were uprisings against Soviet rule. "Krasnaia armiia po dannym, poluchennym 15 Avgusta 1921 goda s Pol'sko-Sovet-skoi granitsy," Boris Aleksandrovich Bakhmeteff Papers, box 59, f. 2, #228, Bakhmeteff Archive, Rare Book and Manuscript Library, Columbia University.

102 Shapiro, ed., *Soviet Treaty Series*, 1: 83.

103 See ibid., 1:134–6, and Chugunov, *Bor'ba na granitse*, 8–14; DeQuirielle, *Le Gouvernement de Moscou*, 61–5.

104 Suny, *Making of the Georgian Nation*, 213.

105 Resolution of the Council of People's Commissars of Ukraine, 18 Oct. 1921, in *Sbirnik uzakonen' i rosporiadzhen'* 21 (1921): 709.

106 "Treaty Concerning the Establishment of the Union of Soviet Socialist Republics," in English translation in Shapiro, ed., *Soviet Treaty Series*, 1:199–201.

107 For example, there was the 20 March 1922 Georgia/Turkey protocol on border crossings, which allowed inhabitants of local areas to cross, at designated customs points, with twenty-one-day passes granted by district authorities (one year for those living within three kilometres), and also an agreement on the use of pastures. Special provisions were made for nomads. The five-year convention was quietly renewed by All-Union authorities in 1928. Shapiro, *Soviet Treaty Series*, 1:4–5.

108 De Quirielle, *Le Gouvernement de Moscou*, 69–72, 102.

109 *Mezhdunarodna politika* RSFSR *v 1922 g*, 34-42.
110 *Mezhdunarodna politika* RSFSR *v 1922 g*, 34-42.
111 X S'ezd RKP, *Stenograficheskii otchet* (Stenographic Record of the 10th Congress of the Russian Communist Party), (St Petersburg: Gosizdat 1921), 176–84.
112 The fact that the Cheka won control over the borders would give border control a highly politicized character. As George Leggett writes, the Cheka, developed as an extraordinary body, became institutionalized as an entity with many powers and relatively little accountability. *Cheka*, 357–60.

CHAPTER FOUR

1 Day, *Leon Trotsky*, 127.
2 Dyker, *Future of the Soviet*, 3.
3 Krasner, "State Power and the Structure," 317. Similarly, William Zimmerman, in discussing Marxist-Leninist states, defines as a "closed system" a polity that seeks to minimize the role played by international influences, including the market, in its political system; see *Open Borders*, 7.
4 Walt, *Origins of Alliances*, 46–8.
5 See Hirschman, *National Power*; Tilly, *Coercion, Capital and European States*, 54.
6 Hirschman, "Exit, Voice, and the State," 96–9.
7 Hough, *Russia and the West*, 52–4.
8 *Spravochnik partiinogo rabotnika* 2 (1922): 178, cited in Waxmonsky, *Police and Politics in Soviet Society*, 287.
9 See Malle, *Economics of War Communism*. Nikolai I. Bukharin wrote with concern about the need for the Bolsheviks to struggle with scarcity and the black-market abuses that accompanied it in "Programma Kommunistov (Bol'shevikov)," written 1918, *Izbrannye proizvedeniia*, 65–71.
10 See Davies, *Industrialization of Soviet Russia*, 3.
11 *Customs Organization and Administration*, 3.
12 In 1926 passport fees were raised; passports could only be obtained in provincial capitals; and foreign steamships were taxed for each person leaving the country. Report, "Difficulties Affecting Emigration from Russia of Immigrants to the United States," by Harry H. Hall, vice-consul, Riga, 6 May 1926, U.S. Department of State, *Records of the Department of State Relating to the Internal Affairs of Russia and the Soviet Union 1910–1929.* #861.56/71.
13 N.I. Bukharin, "Mirovoe khoziaistvo i imperializm" (The World Economy and Imperialism), in *Problemy teorii i praktiki sotsializma*, 27.
14 *Sistematicheskoe sobranie deistvuiushchikh zakonov* SSSR, 1:277.

15 Decree of the Soviet of People's Commissars Establishing a Permanent Commission at the Soviet of Labour and Defence for Regulation of Agricultural and Industrial Immigration. (translated from *Izvestiia*, 2 Dec. 1922), trans. in U.S. Department of State, *Records*, roll 128, 861.55/14.

16 Commission on Immigration of the Council of Labour and Defense (STO), "Prohibition of Entering the USSR without Permission," from *Pravda*, 12 June 1924, trans. in U.S. Department of State, *Records*, roll 128, #861.55/15.

17 Confidential Report, "German Immigration into Russia," 1 Feb. 1924, U.S. Department of State, *Records*, roll 128, #861.5562.

18 Resolution of the Council of People's Commissars, no. 119, *Sobranie zakonov i rasporiiazhenii* 16 (25 Mar. 1925): 197–9.

19 Certificates of permission were required for professional articles, articles of art, books, bicycles, sewing machines, eyeglasses, stamp collections, and inventions. "Permit to Export from Russia Personal Luggage of Passengers," from regulations of the Council of People's Commissars, 1 Sept. 1922, in Harry H. Hall, American Consul General in Riga, report, "Difficulties Affecting Emigration from Russia of Immigrants to the United States," U.S. Department of State, *Records*, roll 128, 861.56/71.

20 Hough, *Russia and the West*, 46.

21 Krasin, *Voprosy vneshnei torgovli*, 75.

22 For this paragraph generally, see Hough, whose brief discussion of the issue first drew my attention to this debate; *Russia and the West*, chap. 2.

23 Bukharin, "Programma Kommunistov (Bol'shevikov)," *Izbrannye proizvedeniia*, 79.

24 Leon Trotsky, letter to V.I. Lenin, 12 Dec. 1922, T-764, Papers of Leon Trotsky, Houghton Library, Harvard University.

25 V.I. Lenin, "O monopolii vneshnei torgovli" (On the Monopoly on Foreign Trade), in *Pol'noe sobranie sochinenii* 45:333–7.

26 Letter from Lenin to Trotsky, 15 Dec. 1922, T-769, Trotsky Papers, Houghton Library, Harvard University.

27 Day, *Leon Trotsky*, 74–6, 127.

28 Khrabskov, *Tamozhniia i zakon*, 15–16.

29 Resolution of the October 1925 plenum of the RKP(b), "O vneshnei torgovli" (On Foreign Trade), in *KPSS v rezoliutsiiakh i resheniiakh s'ezdov, konferentsii i plenumov TsK*, 3:407–13.

30 Krasin, "Gosudarstvennyi khoziaistvennyi plan," 27.

31 Krasin, *Planovoe khoziaistvo i monopoliia*, 34.

32 Vinokur et al., *Praktika tamozhennogo dela*, 1.

33 According to Vinokur, the border zone was 50 kilometres in the European parts of the country and those bordering Turkey and Persia, but 100 kilometres in the Asian part of the country; see *Praktika tamozhennogo dela*, 191–6.

34 Ibid., 201–2.
35 Tamozhennyi kodeks (Customs Code), *Sobranie zakonov i raspori-iazhenii sssr*, 1, 1929.
36 Sahlins, *Boundaries*, 129.
37 David Phillipson estimates that one-half the population was involved in smuggling directly or indirectly; see *Smuggling*, 13–19. See also Nicholls, *Honest Thieves*, 193.
38 Vinokur, ed., *Praktika tamozhennogo dela*, 3–4.
39 Ball, *Russia's Last Capitalists*, 122–4.
40 E. Iaroslavskii, "Izuchaite bogatsva Rossii," *Pravda*, 30 Nov. 1922, 1.
41 The quotation is translated from the original Russian source, *Na strazhe* (Pskov), 1 Oct. 1923, 1.
42 Draft: "O v'ezde za granitsu grazhdan rsfsr i inostrantsev dlia prove-deniia v zhizn' v administrativnom poriadke," 13 May 1922. This is from the former Central Party Archive of the Institute of Theory and History of Socialism of the Central Committee of the Communist Party of the Soviet Union, renamed, as of December 1991, Rossiiskii Tsentr Khraneniia i Izucheniia Dokumentov Noveishei Istorii (the Russian Cen-tre for the Preservation and Study of Documents of Contemporary His-tory of the Russian Federation Committee on Archival Affairs), Moscow, (hereafter, rtskhidni/Former Central Party Archive for purposes of clari-ty and brevity), f. 19 (rsfsr Council of People's Commissars), op. 1, d. 485, point 5, 88.
43 *Sbirnik uzakonenii ta raspirizhenii*, no. 4, 24 Feb. 1923, 94–5.
44 From the rsfsr People's Commissariat of Foreign Trade to the Council of Labour and Defence, Moscow, 25 Jan. 1922, tsgaor, f. 130 (rsfsr Council of People's Commissars), op. 6, ed. khr. 642, 5.
45 Koldaev, *Istoriia i sovremennye sposoby*, 10–11.
46 Vinokur, *Praktika tamozhennogo dela*, 209.
47 Ibid., 217.
48 Figures for 1922 claimed that 8,251 instances of smuggling in foreign goods, with a value of 522,001 rubles were apprehended, as opposed to 1,321 cases of smuggling in Russian goods for a value of 199,913 rubles, were apprehended. Most of the smuggling took place on the western border, though it seems to have been widespread on every bor-der. See *Torgovo-promyshlennaia gazeta*, no. 126 (373), 9 June 1923.
49 Iurovskii, *Denezhnaia politika Sovetskoi vlasti*, 80–1, 107.
50 Ibid., 214.
51 "Soobshchenie s Pol'sko-Sovetskoi granitsy" (Report from the Polish-Soviet Border), May 1922, box 60, Reports on Conditions in Russia, no. 453, 2–4, Bakhmeteff Papers, Rare Book and Manuscript Library, Columbia University.

52 *Torgovo-promyshlennaia gazeta*, no. 91 (632), 20 Apr. 1924, 5.
53 For example, as evidenced by the pages of the monarchist paper *Na granitse* (begun 1936), at Pogranichnaia on the Manchurian border near Harbin.
54 M. Makotinskii, "Bor'ba s kontrabandoi i nadzor prokuratory" (The Struggle with Contraband and the Role of Procuracy Control), *Vestnik Sovetskoi iustitsii* (Kharkov) 8, no. 42 (1925): 329–31. I am grateful to Peter Solomon for this reference.
55 The quotation is translated from the original Russian source, S. Ippa, "Kontrabanda i dela tamozhennye" (Contraband and Customs Matters), *Rabochii sud* 39–40 (1925): 1483.
56 Lev Kamenev, speech, 30 Jan. 1924, S'ezd Sovetov sssr, 2nd session, *Stenograficheskii otchet 1924*, 86–7.
57 "Comrade" Mendeshev, in ibid., 101–3.
58 S. Ippa, "Kontrabanda i dela tamozhennye," 1481–8.
59 sssr, S'ezd Sovetov, *Stenograficheskii otchet* 4 (Apr. 1927): 142–3.
60 Iukovskii, *Denezhnaia politika Sovetskoi vlasti*, 241.
61 See, for example, "Iz svodki glavnogo upravleniia pogranichnoi okhrany i voisk ogpu o bor'be s kontrabandoi 1929-30 g.g." (From a Survey of the Main Administration of Border Protection and ogpu Troops on the Struggle with Contraband 1929–1930), in Zyrianov, ed. *Pogranichnye voiska sssr*, 2:707–8.
62 "Iz protokola soveshchaniia pri upravlenii upolnomochennogo po vnesh-nei torgovle pri snk uzssr o bor'be s kontrabandoi" (From a Protocol of a Meeting of the Plenipotentiary Administration on Foreign Trade of the Council of People's Commissars of the Uzbek ssr on the Struggle with Contraband) 22 Nov. 1926, in Zyrianov, ed., *Pogranichnye voiska sssr*, 1:712.
63 Josef C. Brada, Vladimir Popov, Marie Lavigne, Alexander Belov, Scott Pardee, Alexander Parkansky, and Francis Scotland, "A Phased Plan for Making the Ruble Convertible: A Multilateral Proposal," in Brada and Claudon, eds., *Reforming the Ruble*, 93–4.
64 Arnold, *Banks, Credit and Money*, 262–3.
65 Ibid. See also Bettelheim, *Class Struggles in the ussr 1923-1930*, 60.
66 "ussr Summary of Currency Regulations," Moscow, State Bank of the ussr, Mar. 1930, in Great Britain, Foreign Office, *Russia: Correspondence, 1930–1940*, no. 10, #33346, 13 May 1931.
67 Frunze, *Krasnaia armiia*, 11.
68 See Dyker, *Soviet Economy*, 1–23.
69 Krasin, "Gosudarstvennyi khoziaistvennyi plan i monopoliia," 24–5.
70 A. Rozengolts, "Stalinskaia konstitutsiia i monopoliia vneshnei torgov-li," *Vneshniaia torgovliia*, 1 (1937): 4.

71 Alan A. Brown, "Towards a Theory of Centrally Planned Foreign Trade," in Brown and Neuberger, eds., *International Trade and Central Planning*, 59–62.
72 Richard Day has written of Trotsky's positions favouring greater economic contact with the outside world; see *Leon Trotsky*.
73 Letter from Leon Trotsky to V.I. Lenin, 17 Oct. 1919, T-36, Papers of Leon Trotsky, Houghton Library, Harvard University.
74 Leon Trotsky, "Teoriia sotsializma v otdel'noi strane," manuscript, 1926, T-3007, Trotsky Papers, Houghton Library, Harvard University.
75 Leon Trotsky, "SSSR v voine," manuscript, 1939, T-4633, Trotsky Papers, Houghton Library, Harvard University.
76 Leon Trotsky, "Natsionalizm i khoziaistvo," manuscript, 4 Jan. 1934, T-3636, Trotsky Papers, Houghton Library, Harvard University.

CHAPTER FIVE

1 See Shue, *The Reach of the State*, 31–71.
2 See, for example, Shils, "Center and Periphery," in *The Constitution of Society*, 93–109; Vivienne Shue, *The Reach of the State*; Rokkan and Urwin, *Economy, Territory, Identity*.
3 Giddens, *Nation-State and Violence*, 50–7.
4 Alvin W. Gouldner categorizes Soviet politics in terms of centre-periphery relations, characterizing the "internal colonialism" of a dominant centre that imposes its value-system on a recalcitrant periphery as part of a state-building process; see "Stalinism," 5–48. Another approach is Gerald Easter, "Personal Networks, Institutional Constraints, and State Formation."
5 Sahlins, *Boundaries*, 8.
6 See Daniel C. Matuszewski, "Empire, Nationalities, Borders: Soviet Assets and Liabilities," in Wimbush, ed., *Soviet Nationalities in Strategic Perspective*, 75–100.
7 Chugunov, *Bor'ba na granitse*, 9.
8 Shils, "Center and Periphery," in Shils, *Constitution of Society*, 102.
9 Rokkan and Urwin, *Economy, Territory, Identity*.
10 Letter from Deputy Chairman of VSNKh of the Ukrainian SSR P. Zhigalko ca autumn 1923, TSGAOR UkSSR, f.2, op. 2, spr. 653, #44. (The title given of the document in question is incomplete as it is partially illegible in the original.)
11 However, these areas became more developed after the Second World War, once this proximate threat was removed. See I.S. Koropeckyj, "Growth and Productivity," in Koropeckyj and Schroeder, *Economics of Soviet Regions*, 105–6.
12 This was the argument of a delegate from Belorussia to the Fourth Con-

gress of Soviets, who claimed that border areas should not be kept undeveloped for strategic reasons because industry would strengthen the socialist base that would help, not weaken, the country in the event of a war with imperialism. SSSR, S'ezd Sovetov, *Stenograficheskii otchet* 4 (Apr. 1927): 291–2. In Ukraine in particular there were strong feelings that the republic was being deliberately kept backward while areas in the interior of Russia were being developed, and this, it has been argued, contributed to the development of anti-Soviet nationalism in Ukraine during the Second World War. See "The Nature and Extent of Disaffection and Anti-Soviet Activity in the Ukraine," 16 Jan. 1947, U.S. Department of State, *Intelligence and Research Reports*, OSS, part VI, reel 7, 7. This report cites an editorial of 28 Aug. 1946 in *Pravda* that claimed the Western industries evacuated during the war would not be restored.

13 V.I. Lenin, "Instructions of the Council of Labour and Defence to Local Soviet Bodies – Draft," 21 May 1921, in *V.I. Lenin on the Soviet State Apparatus*, 299–300. The notes claim that the draft was endorsed by the Presidium of the All-Russia Central Executive Committee on 30 June 1921.

14 Prikaz no. 50, "Po Osobpogranpunktu no. 2, Osobotdeleniia no. 7 Kievskogo Voennogo Okruga," 13 June 1921. Papers of Boris Aleksandrovich Bakhmeteff, box 59, file 2, #235, Bakhmeteff Archive, Rare Book and Manuscript Library, Columbia University.

15 Transl. from Fomin, *Zapiski starogo chekista*, 164.

16 Ibid., 168.

17 For example, "Prikaz komandovaniia voisk VchK respubliki o podgotovke k pomoshchi sel'skomu naseleniiu v uborke urozhaiu i privedenii voisk v boevuiu gotovnost' dlia bor'by s vozmoznymi vystupleniami kontrrevoliutsionnykh elementov, sviazennykh s neurozhaem" (Order of the Command of the VChK troops on Preparation To Assist the Rural Population in Bringing in the Harvest and Putting Guards on Military Readiness for the Struggle with Possible Manifestations of Counterrevolutionary Elements Linked with a Bad Harvest), 15 July 1921, in Zyrianov, ed., *Pogranichnye voiska SSSR*, 1:176–9; "Iz ukazanii Glavnogo Upravleniia pogranichnoi okhrany i voisk OGPU ob osnovnykh zadachakh raboty pogranokhrany na period s 1 noiabria 1928 g. po 1 maia 1929 g."(From Instruction of the GUPO and OGPU Troops of the Basic Tasks for Border Protection in the Period from 1 November 1928 to 1 May 1929), in Zyrianov, ed., *Pogranichnye voiska SSSR* 1:258–62. Discussions in the border-troop press of these roles include *Na Krasnom Rubezhe* (Shepetevo), 20 Dec. 1928; *Klinok Pogranichnika* (Mogilev), no. 6, 19 Dec. 1923. The military's role as an agent of Soviet socialization of the peasantry has been written about extensively by von Hagen, *Soldiers in the Proletarian Dictatorship*.

18 Resolution "O poriadke pokrytiia raskhodov po raskvartirovaniu chastei uchrezhdenii i zavedenii voisk GPU" (On the Procedure for Covering Expenses for the Quartering of Units of Institutions of GPU Troops), *Vestnik TSIK, Sovnarkoma i Soveta Truda i Oborony SSSR* 4 (1923): 65.

19 Lt-General G. Zaboletnyi, "Polveka na strazhe Sovetskikh granits," *Kommunist vooruzhennykh sil* 9 (May 1968): 37.

20 *Na strazhe* (Pskov), 3 June 1924.

21 "Iz ukazanii OGPU komandovaniiu pogranichnoi okhrany Karel'skoi ASSR o povyshanii bditel'nosti i boegotovnosti v sviazi s aktivizatsiei zarubezhnoi kontrrevoliutsii" (From an Instruction of the OGPU Border Control Command of the Karelian ASSR on Increasing Vigilance and Military Preparedness in Connection with the Activation of Foreign Counterrevolution) 14 Jan. 1925, in Zyrianov, ed., *Pogranichnye voiska SSSR*, 1:360.

22 Resolution, Secretariat of the VTSIK, 18 August 1926, Central State Archive of the October Revolution of the USSR, hereafter TSGAOR, f. 1235, op. 49, ed. khr. 12, 9. However, at least in the Ukraine, the Central Commission on National Minorities seems to have been told it would not have a role or representation in border policy, at least in the creation of the Committee on Border Zones composed of representatives of various government departments, despite that commission's entreaty so to participate. See Note to the Central Commission of National Minorities pri vutsVK from the Council of People's Commissars of the UKSSR (in Ukrainian) 21 December 1926, TSGAOR UKSSR, f. 2, op. 5, d. 1334, 1.

23 *Na strazhe* (Pskov), 1 Oct. 1923, 1. In 1921 there were reports that inexperienced people, unaccustomed to guarding newly liberated border posts, were allowing citizens to congregate on the border and talk freely with Polish soldiers. Polish soldiers also allegedly felt free to cross the border to engage in "boozing and carousing" (*popoika i kutezh*), sometimes with Soviet border guards (*pogranichniki*) participating in the revelry. Moreover, Poles and Soviets would take turns guarding the border to let each other sleep(!). This behaviour was criticized as "inappropriate" and "criminal" conduct, and post leaders were asked to stop this fraternizing immediately because it would "open up the border and give the Poles a great deal of information." The same order reprimands one particular border post for drunkenness, which seems to have been a chronic problem of Soviet border troops. Prikaz 31, "Po Osob-pogranpunktu no. 2 Osobotdeleniia no. 7, Kievskogo Voennogo Okruga," 19 May 1921, Bakhmeteff Papers, box 59, file 2, Bakhmeteff Archive, Rare Book and Manuscript Library, Columbia University.

24 See, for example, telegram, 12 Aug. 1919, American Historical Association, Committee for the Study of War Documents, Communist Party of the Soviet Union, Smolensk Oblast Committee, Records 1917–1941, roll

15, WKP 199, p 89. The telegram discusses a highway worker who fled to Poland with money and was now lurking in the border area causing trouble.

25 See, for example, Smolensk Archives, roll 15, WKP 119 (1920), 11–12, on the lack of supplies and newspapers for border troops; and on the lack of participation by border guards in the 1923 party census "O ne proshedshikh partperipis' chlenakh partii rabotaiushchikh v pogranich-nykh chastiiakh GPU" (On the Lack of Participation in the Party Re-Registration of Members of Border Units of the GPU), *Spravochnik partiinogo rabotnika*, 4 (1924): 150.

26 See American Historical Association, Committee for the Study of War Documents, Communist Party of the Soviet Union, Smolensk Oblast Committee, Records 1917–1941, roll 15, WKP 119 (1920), 175, and newspaper sources.

27 A 27 July 1923 decree of the Central Executive Committee and the Council of People's Commissars required local budgets to provide for the billeting of troops, their sanitation, electricity, etc. I am unsure but believe that this also applied to border troops. United States, Department of State, Records of the Department of State Relating to the Internal Affairs of Russia and the Soviet Union, 1910–1929, roll 90, 861.22/50.

28 *Na krasnom rubezhe* (Shepetevo), 31 May 1926, 1.

29 "Predlozheniia. Prilozhenie k protokolu Biuro TsK n. 84," 21 Aug. 1925, Russian Centre for the Conservation and Study of Documents of Recent History (hereafter RTskhIDNI), formerly the Central Party Archive, Moscow, fond 17, op. 68, d. 635, 149.

30 "Dokladnaia zapiska o sostoianii partiinoi organizatsii i partapparatov pogranichnykh oblastei" (Report on the Composition of Party Organizations and the Party Apparatus in Border Oblasts), 7 Sept. 1925, RTskhIDNI, f. 17, op. 68, d. 635, 121.

31 At least, as this document shows, the Red Army's control over border-guard party organizations was in 1924 transferred to local party organizations to ensure greater communication and contact between the border-control authorities and local party and soviet organs. "Odesskomu, Podol'skomu i Volynskomu gubkomam i kontrol'nym kommissiam KP(b)U," 2 Aug. 1925, RTskhIDNI, f. 17, op. 68, d. 28, 2.

32 "Osnovnye vyvody po sostoianie pogranichnoi polosy [UkSSR, BSSR, i severnaia-zapadnaia oblast]" (Basic Conclusions on Conditions in the Border Strip of the Ukrainian SSR, Belorussian SSR, and North-West Oblast), [1925], RTskhIDNI, f. 17, op. 68, d. 635, 161–5.

33 While simultaneously trying to step up vigilance in border areas, according to Chugunov, who also noted this twofold policy drive. *Bor'ba na granitse*, 14.

34 Particularly in the Soviet Far East, according to remarks to this effect at a 1925 session of the Amur *guberniia* branch of the Communist Party in the Far Eastern Oblast. RTSkhIDNI, f. 17, op. 16, d. 199, 48–9.

35 For Ukraine, "Postanovlenie Buro TsK KP(b)U po dokladu kommissii po obsledovaniiu pogranichnykh okrugov" (Resolution of the Bureau of the Central Committee of the Communist Party of Ukraine on the Report of the Commission for the Investigation of Border Okrugs), 28 Aug. 1925, f. 17, op. 68, d. 635, 155. On the greater participation of central party authorities and nationality policymakers, "Proekt postanovleniia orgburo ob ozdorovlenii i ukreplenii partorganizatsii v pogranichnoi polosy" (Draft Resolutions on the Improvement and Intensification of the Party Organization in the Border Zone), 1925, f. 17, op. 68, d. 635, 126. For Central Asia, f. 17, op. 16, d. 1178, 9. All references RTSkhIDNI.

36 The rest of the catch would go in fixed amounts to Narkomfin, the customs authorities, and the OGPU. *Sobranie zakonov i rasporiiazhenii SSSR* 11 (1924): 160–1.

37 "Mnenie" to GPU UkSSR po proektu postanovleniia VUkTsIK, "O slozhenii i sokrashchenii nedoimok i shtrafov za kontrabandu," 9 Feb. 1925, TSGAOR UkSSR, f. 2, op. 5, spr. 1091, no. 10.

38 Provision of 19 Dec. 1928, Tamozhennyi Kodeks, *Sobranie zakonov i rasporiiazhenii SSSR*, 1 (1929).

39 An example of this two-tier approach: "Predlozheniia. prilozhenie k protokolu Biuro TsK, No. 84." This document, cited above, emphasizes that the approach to the peasants regarding the border regime must be "softened," while the GPU should struggle against "professional contraband, banditry, and espionage." 21 Aug. 1925, RTSkhIDNI, f. 17, op. 68, d. 635, 149.

40 Chugunov argues that the Ukrainian Council of People's Commissars had considerable authority over resolving questions of the western border in the 1920s. See *Bor'ba na granitse*, 70.

41 The link between these two threats is a common concern in archival documents on the Ukrainian border situation. See, for example, "Zasedanii komissii po obsledovanii sostoianiia granits, sovmesto s biurogubkom, sekretaryami raikomov, fraktsiei gubispolkomov, Prezident VTSSPS i predsedatelyam Krasnoi armii i GPU" (Session of the Commission for the Investigation of the Composition of Borders ...), 5 June 1923, Party Archive of the Institute of History of the Party of the Central Committee of the Ukrainian Communist Party, Kiev, Ukraine, f. 1 (Central Committee of the Ukrainian Communist Party), op. 20, d. 1758, 3–12.

42 According to this document, border guards in the Ukraine were 44.14 per cent Russian, 44.71 per cent Ukrainian. See "Tezisi k sodokladu po natsional'nomu voprosu" (Theses towards the Joint Report on the

National Question), 1923. Party Archive of the Institute of History of the Party of the Central Committee of the Ukrainian Communist Party, Kiev, Ukraine, f. 1, op. 20, d. 1660, 17–19.

43 Circular to all Party Organizations of Border Okrugs, 16 Jan. [1928?], Party Archive of the Institute of History of the Party of the Central Committee of the Ukrainian Communist Party, Kiev, Ukraine, f. 1, op. 20, d. 2810, 1928, 131.

44 See for example, on Jews; "Memorandum Vseukrainskomu Tsentral'nomu TSK Sovetov rabochikh i krestianskikh deputatov po voprosu i polozhenii evreiskikh mass na Ukraine v sviazi s massovoi emigratsiei" (Memorandum ... on the Position of the Jewish Masses in Ukraine in Connection with Mass Emigration), 1921, Party Archive of the Institute of History of the Party of the Central Committee of the Ukrainian Communist Party, Kiev, Ukraine, f. 1, op. 20, d. 799, 1–8. On Germans: "Ob emigratsii nemtsev iz SSSR" (On the Emigration of Germans from the USSR), 4 Sept. 1929, RTSKhIDNI, f. 17, op. 74, d. 37, 106.

45 "Protokol zasedaniia sredne-Aziatskogo buro TsK RKP" (Protocol of the Session of the Central Asian Bureau of the Central Committee of the Russian Communist Party), 24 Aug. 1924, RTSKhIDNI, f. 17, op. 16, d. 1174, 121.

46 "Politicheskoe sostoianie," report of the Russian Communist Party Central Asian Party Bureau, [ca end of 1925], RTSKhIDNI, f. 17, op. 16, d. 1178, 9–12.

47 "O rabote PPO GPU," report of T. Belskogo, in "Materialy, doklady i postanovleniia plenuma Sredne-Aziatskogo biuro TSK RKP(b)," no. 7, 2–4, July 1925, RTSKhIDNI, f. 17, op. 16, d. 1173, 98–103. Belskii argues that attempts to nativize the Central Asian GPU were futile, as they attracted only a few "thugs."

48 Title illegible due to damaged microfilm, [RKP Central Asian Bureau Report, 1925], RTSKhIDNI, f. 17, op. 16, d. 1178, 9–10.

49 "Postanovlenie biuro TSK KP(b)U po dokladu komissii po obsledovaniiu pogranichnykh politicheskikh okrugov" (Resolution of the Bureau of the Central Committee of the Communist Party of Ukraine on the Report of the Commission on the Investigation of Border Political Okrugs), 28 Aug. 1925, RTSKhIDNI, f. 17, op. 68, d. 635, 155.

50 The quotation provided is translated from the original Russian source: "Osnovye vyvody po sostoianiiu pogranichnoi polosy UKSSR, BSSR, i severo-zapadnoi oblasti" (Basic Conclusions on the Composition of the Border Zone of the Ukrainian SSR, the Belorussian Republic, and the Northwest Oblast), ca 1925, RTSKhIDNI, f. 17, op. 68, d. 635, 161–5.

51 Ibid.

52 For example, in 1926 the Central Committee of the RKP(b) requested a summary of conditions in border territories of all republics except the

RSFSR from the USSR Central Executive Committee: 1 Feb. 1926, RTskhIDNI, f. 17, op. 68, d. 635, 203.

53 Speech by Kaganovich, 4 Dec. 1927, XV S'ezd VKP(b), *Stenograficheskii otchet* (Moscow: Gosizdat 1928), 132.

54 Circular letter from General Secretary Kaganovich, "Vsem partorgani-zatsiiam pogranichnykh okrugov" (To All Party Organizations of the Border Okrugs), 16 Jan. 1928, Party Archive of the Institute of History of the Party of the Central Committee of the Ukrainian Communist Party, Kiev, Ukraine, f. 1, op. 20, d. 2810, 1.

55 "Dokladnaia zapiska," 9 June 1928, to Lazar Kaganovich from GPU Chairman V. Balitskii, Party Archive of the Institute of History of the Party of the Central Committee of the Ukrainian Communist Party, Kiev, Ukraine, f. 1, op. 20, d. 2810, 65–6.

56 "Circular #6654 from Pskov Provincial branch of OGPU to Commanders of the 9th, 10th, and 11th frontier detachments of the OGPU," 1 (in English trans.), Records, roll 89, 861.20260 P/7, 22 Aug.1927, and similar documents in same enclosure, U.S. Department of State. These documents refer to the Latvian border.

57 Secretariat of the Central Committee, "Ob emigratsii nemtsev iz SSSR," 4 Sept. 1929, RTskhIDNI, f. 17, op. 74, d. 37, 106.

58 "Na oznakomlenie," 17 May 1932, RTskhIDNI, f. 17, op. 120, d. 82, 135.

59 "Polozhenie ob okhrane gosudarstvennykh granits Soiuza SSR" (Regulation on the Protection of the State Border of the USSR), *Sobranie zakonov i rasporiiazhenii*, no. 62 (15 June 1927): 1218–25.

60 Felshtinskii, *Iz istorii nashei zakrytosti*, 153.

61 A 1930 report to Kuibyshev from the OGPU on *kolkhoz* construction in the western border area said as much: 17 Dec. 1930, RTskhIDNI, f. 79 (Papers of V.V. Kuibyshev), op. 1, d. 652.

62 Z. Ostrovskii, "Polozhenie natsional'nykh men'shinstv v zapadnoi oblasti" (The Position of National Minorities in the Western Oblast), *Sovetskoe stroitel'stvo* 2, no. 43 (Feb. 1930): 114, 123–4.

63 Instruction to All Party-Soviet Workers and All Organs of the OGPU, Court and Procuracy from Molotov (as representative of SNK) and Stalin, 8 May 1933, Smolensk Archive of the RKP(b), roll 22, WKP 178, 134–5.

64 "Fugitives from the USSR," Sergei Melgunov Papers, box 15, 1930, Archives of the Hoover Institution on War, Revolution, and Peace; see also box 16, 1932. Great Britain, Foreign Office, Russia–Correspondence 1930–1940, roll 7, 1932, 371/16336, various reports.

65 S.I. Ilianov, "Korennoe preobrazovanie sel'skogo khoziaistva v Kirgizii" (The Fundamental Transformation of Agriculture in Kirgizia), in Danilov, ed., *Ocherki istorii kollektivizatsii*, 408.

66 "Nekotorye vazhneishie itogi i zadachi politicheskoi i partiinoi raboty
   P.O. i VOGPU Ukrainy" (Several Important Results and Tasks of the
   Political and Party Work of the Border and OGPU Troops of Ukraine), 24
   June 1930, Party Archive of the Institute of History of the Party of the
   Central Committee of the Ukrainian Communist Party, Kiev, Ukraine, f.
   1, op. 20, d. 3202, 15–19.
67 Pashkov, *Stranitsy geroicheskoi letopisy*, 28–30.
68 *Prikordonna pravda* (Slavutsk), 25 June 1931; a report of local border
   troops boasted that 97.8 per cent of those coming from villages were
   collectivized peasants.
69 *Chervonyi kordon* (Mogilev), 27 July 1929, 2.
70 As they did in the rayon of Sebezh, at the northwestern border:
   Pogranichnaia pravda (Sebezh), 20 Aug. 1931, 4.
71 Resolution, "O vypolnenii postanovleniia SNK SSSR ot 11/XII/31 g. ob
   ukreplenii pogranotriadov," 29 May 1932, RTskhIDNI, f. 17, op. 120, d.
   82, 126–9.
72 XVII S'ezd VKP(b), *Stenograficheskii otchet* (Moscow: Partizdat 1934), 27
   Jan., 71–3.
73 Ibid., 213.
74 File 1, "NKVD SSSR (po materialam byvshikh sotrudnikov NKVD SSSR
   1939–1941 g.g.)," Nicolaevsky Archive, box 294, series 227, 274–84.
   Hoover Institution Archives.
75 Ibid.
76 Erickson, *The Soviet High Command*, 406–7.
77 I. I. Petrov, "Zabota partii ob ukreplenii pogranichnykh voisk
   (1939–1941 g.g.)" (The Concern of the Party on the Intensification of
   Border Troops), *Voprosy istorii KPSS*, no. 5 (1968): 94–9.
78 Central Executive Committee and Council of People's Commissars of the
   USSR, "O nakazanii za vyezd za granitsu ili v'ezd v Soiuz SSSR bez
   ustanovlennogo pasporta ili razresheniia" (On the Punishment for Exit
   or Entry across the Border of the USSR without the Necessary Passport
   or Permission), in I.T. Goliakov, *Sbornik dokumentov po istorii
   ugolovnogo zakonodatel'stva*, 393.
79 V.P. Artemiev and B.S. Burlutsky, "Personnel, Conditions of Service and
   Training in the Border Troops," in Wolin and Slusser, eds, *The Soviet
   Secret Police*, 280.

CHAPTER SIX

1 It also was, in the paternalistic view of Soviet social organizations, a
   means of protecting an ignorant populace from the lures of capitalist
   entrapment, the enticements to emigrate into exploitation and misery.

See, for example, "Otchet o deiatel'nosti Postoiannoi Komissii po tru-
dovoi sel'skokhoziaistvennoi i promyshlennoi immigratsii i emigratsii,"
25 Oct. 1925, RTSKhIDNI, f. 17, op. 68, d. 368, 38.

2. Trotsky, *The Revolution Betrayed.*

3 Fainsod, *Smolensk under Soviet Rule.*

4 Bialer, *Stalin's Successors,* 12–16.

5 Gary Richard Waxmonsky argues this point in the case of the secret
police in the 1920s; the scope of the early NKVD in local politics was an
important contributing factor in the development of the all-powerful
secret police in the 1920s. See *Police and Politics in Soviet Society
1921–1929.*

6 See March and Olsen, *Rediscovering Institutions,* 64–5; David Stark and
Victor Nee, "Toward an Institutional Analysis of State Socialism," in
Stark and Nee, with Mark Selden, eds., *Remaking the Economic Institu-
tions,* 17–31; Ickes, "Obstacles to Economic Reform," 53–64.

7 This may be partly a function of the available source material; at the
time of research it was still a subject treated as secret, and party and
state leaders' insights may be closeted away in closed archives still
unavailable as of early 1992. It is none the less striking how silent leaders appear to have been on the subject in their published works, in those
archival materials that are available, and in state archives, where border
control shows every sign of having been the preserve of faceless bureaucrats, policemen, and border guards.

8 See, for example, Fomin, *Zapiski starogo chekista.*

9 Krasin, *Voprosy vneshnei torgovli,* 75.

10 One of these rare comments is a note from (name illegible) in the Russian Communist Party Central Committee Secretariat to the Commissariat of Nationalities in 1921, directing that the Commissariat (Narkomnats) produce an anti-emigration pamphlet for nationalities that were
inclined to try to leave the country, a request clearly directed at Jews. See
"Note from RKP(b) Secretary to Narkomnats," [ca 1921], TSGAOR, f.
1318, op. 1, ed. khr. 1261, 202.

11 To Pskov NKVD Administrative Department (Adminotdel) from Central
Administrative Upravlenie Deputy Zaitsev, [ca 1926], TSGAOR, f. 393,
op. 64, no. 185, 89.

12 According to a *polozhenie* of 24 Oct. 1923, TSGAOR, f. 3316, op. 1, 42.

13 "Polozhenie o Narodnom Komissariate po Inostrannym Delam SSSR,"
Vestnik TSIK, Sovnarkom, i Soveta Truda i Oborony 10 (1923): 178.

14 This is revealed by the formation of the Council of Labour and Defence
Permanent Commission on Immigration and Emigration in 1925, with
representatives from the Commissariats of Communications, Agriculture,
Foreign Affairs, Labour, and the TSIK, Vesenhkha, and the OGPU. The
commission was to work out policy on immigration, and regulate emi-

gration to and from the USSR. The *postanovlenie* establishing the commission was established 17 Feb. 1925. TSGAOR, f. 5446 (Council of People's Commissars), op. 1, no. 9b, 350–3.

15 Evidently, at the least the Commissariats of Foreign Affairs, Internal Affairs, Labour, and the OGPU had this veto power, according to a protocol of the commission, 17 Dec. 1926. TSGAOR, f. 5515 (People's Commissariat of Labour), op. 24, ed. khr. 82.

16 This was also observed by Felshtinskii, *K istorii nashei zakrytosti*, 38.

17 One example is provided by the General Inspector for the Observation of the Activity of Shipping Societies in a report discussing whether to let a group of people emigrate to Brazil. Brazil, he argued, was being subsidized by those who wanted cheap, exploitable labour. The immigrants' labour was hard; the climate was bad for Europeans; disease was rife, and the low pay barred return to the USSR. The Council of Labour and Defence commission resolved subsequently that the USSR should stop allowing such emigration except where applicants had close relatives who had sent them an invitation (*priglashenie*). See Resolution of the Permanent Commission on Immigration and Emigration, "Ob emigratsii v Shtat Sao-Paolo, Brazil," (1926), TSGAOR, f. 393, op. 64, ed. khr. 198, 27.

18 Here referring to the loss of Mennonites, a large number of whom wanted to leave for Canada. See Protocol of the commission, 6 Oct. 1926, TSGAOR, f. 5515, op. 24, d. 82, 52; also, Resolution of the Council on Labour and Defence Permanent Commission, on emigration to Brazil, 1926, f. 393 (Russian NKVD), op. 64, 198, 36.

19 Felshtinskii, *K istorii nashei zakrytosti*, 39–40.

20 Remarks by F. Dzerzhinskii, 4 Apr. 1924, RTSKhIDNI, f. 76, op. 2, d. 172.

21 Felshtinskii, *K istorii nashei zakrytosti*, 38.

22 Letter to E.D. Stasovaia from F. Dzerzhinskii, 4 Apr. 1924, RTSKhIDNI, f. 76, op. 2, 18.

23 RSFSR NKVD, various correspondence, 1927, TSGAOR, f. 393, op. 71, 128, 1927.

24 "Utverzhdenii pravil ob usloviiakh truda rabotnikov uchrezhdenii SSSR za granitsu," *Izvestiia Narkomtruda*, no. 45 (10 Nov. 1927): 674–9.

25 "Pravila ob usloviiakh truda rabotnikov uchrezhdeniia SSSR za granitsei," *Izvestiia Narkomtruda* 22 (20 Aug. 1930): 482.

26 Postanovlenie of the People's Commissariat of Labour, 28 Dec. 1931, TSGAOR, f. 5515, op. 16, no. 16, 59–63.

27 For those who lacked funds, had good reasons for leaving, and whose departure did not, in the estimation of the authorities, hurt the state. TSGAOR, Resolution of the Central Executive Committee and Council of People's Commissars, 6 Apr. 1926, f. 393, op. 64, no. 198, 9.

28 See TSGAOR, f. 393, op. 71, devoted to this issue.

29 "Instruktsiia o poriadke vyezda iz Predelov SSSR voenno-sluzhashchikh i voenno-ob'iazannykh," 2 Feb. 1925. TSGAOR, f. 393, op. 64, ed. khr. 191, 425.

30 Postanovlenie of NKVD of the Ukrainian SSR, "Instruktsiia o vydache obhchegrazhdanskikh zagranichnykh pasportov dlia grazhdan Soiuza SSR i viz dlia inostrantsev" (Instruction on the Issue of Foreign Passports for Citizens of the USSR and Visas for Foreigners), 20 Nov. 1926, TSGAOR, f. 393, op. 71, ed. khr. 155, 14.

31 "Instruktsiia o poriadke vydachi grazhdanam SSSR obshchegrazhdan- skikh zagranichnykh pasportov i viz dlia inostrantsev" [ca 1927], TSGAOR, f. 393, op. 87, ed. khr. 6, 89.

32 Spravka from Moscow Guberniia Finansovyi Otdel [ca 1927], TSGAOR, f. 393, op. 71, ed. khr. 160, 17.

33 Communication from RSFSR NKVD Administrative Otdel to NKVD Central Administrative Upravlenie, [c.1927]. TSGAOR, f. 393, op. 71, ed. khr. 157, 303.

34 Letter to the Permanent Commission of the STO on Agricultural and Industrial Immigration and Emigration, from NKVD Tsentral'noe Admin- istrativnoe Upravlenie, 26 Oct. 1926, TSGAOR, f. 393, op. 64, ed. khr. 198, 27.

35 "O poriadke vydachi vidov na zhitel'stvo, prebyvaniia, inostrantsev na territorii RSFSR, v'ezda i vyezda inostrantsev i grazhdan SSSR," 15 June 1927, TSGAOR, f. 393, op. 64, ed. khr. 199, 112–17.

36 V. Vasiliev, "Likvidatsiia Narodnykh Komissariatov Vnutrennikh Del" (Liquidation of the People's Commissariats of Internal Affairs), *Sovet- skoe stroitel'stvo* (organ of the USSR Central Executive Committee) 1, no. 54 (Jan. 1931): 28–9.

37 See NKVD correspondence, 24 May 1926, TSGAOR, f. 393, op. 64, ed. khr. 185, 165, on adoption of Soviet citizenship.

38 Draft, "O vyezd za granitsu grazhdan RSFSR i inostrantsev dlia prove- deniia v zhizn' v administrativnom poriadke," (On Exit Abroad of RSFSR Citizens and Foreigners in Accordance with the Administrative Proce- dure), 13 May 1922, RTSKhIDNI, f. 19 (RSFSR Council of People's Com- missars), op. 1, d. 485, point 5, 88.

39 See, for example, a communication from the NKVD TSAU to the Penzen Guberniia NKVD Adminotdel, 1 Oct. 1925, TSGAOR, f. 393, op. 57, no. 182, 11.

40 Secret communication from [illegible] to the head of the NKVD TSAU, 22 Apr. 1925, TSGAOR, f. 393, op. 57, ed. khr. 180.

41 "Sluzhebnaia zapiska," from F. Dzerzhinskii to Comrade Gurevich, 25 July 1926, RTSKhIDNI, f. 76, op. 2, d. 172, 4.

42 Correspondence, 1927, RTSKhIDNI, f. 17, op. 74, d. 64, 8–10.

43 Evidence of Stalin's intervention in one case is a letter from Stalin to

Comrade Kozlov, 17 Feb. 1925, RTSKHIDNI, f. 558 (Papers of Joseph Stalin), op. 1, d. 2684; Dzerzhinskii's complaint of "red tape" surrounding the application process is rather cheeky considering his contribution to it: f. 76, op. 2, d. 172, 30 Aug. 1924, 2.

44 11 July 1925, RTSKHIDNI, f. 17, op. 68, d. 630, 10. As early as 1919 the Commissariat of Foreign Affairs was told to give foreign passports to those working for Soviet institutions only if they had been given the stamp of good conduct and political loyalty to Soviet rule: "Postanovlenie SNK o poriadke vydache zagranichnykh pasportov" (Resolution of the Council of People's Commissars on the Procedure for Issuing Foreign Passports), 3 June 1919, RTSKHIDNI, f. 19, op. 1, d. 292, punkt 22, 89.

45 I.e., calling the OGPU on the carpet in the event that someone went abroad and defected or deviated from the prescribed plan of activities. See, for example, a letter to Kaganovich from a OGPU chairman absolving himself of responsibility in just such a case: 31 July 1930, RTSKHIDNI, f. 17, op. 74, d. 64, 7.

46 11 July 1925, RTSKHIDNI, f. 17, op. 68, d. 630, 10.

47 The concern with counter-revolutionary literature became more obvious in 1928; see 31 Aug. 1928, "Iz telegrammy nachal'nika Glavnogo upravleniia pogranichnoi okhrany i voisk OGPU o pereprave kontrrevolutsionnykh proklamatsii cherez granitsu na territoiriu SSSR" (From a Telegram of the Boss of the GUPO and OGPU Troops on Counterrevolutionary Proclamations coming into USSR Territory), in Zyrianov, ed., Pogranichnye voiska SSSR, 1:540–2.

48 Elistratov, Administrativnoe pravo, 210.

49 Respectively, articles 148, 123–5, 25, and 24. Trainin, Ugolovnoe pravo RSFSR. There were more serious penalties for helping others to cross the border illegally or for crossing the border for purposes of espionage. Kareva, Ugolovnoe zakonodatel'stvo SSSR i Soiuznykh Respublik, 18, Articles 26 and 25 respectively.

50 Felshtinskii considers that year to have been an important benchmark of the solidification of Soviet policy. See K istorii nashei zakrytosti.

51 It defined as its duties the following tasks: guaranteeing the inviolability of borders and struggling against their violation, including political control (the prevention of the infiltration of counter-revolutionaries, subversive literature, and illicit weaponry) and interception of contraband; maintaining "revolutionary order" in the 22-kilometre border zone; defence of the population of border areas against armed attacks; and ensuring that Soviet territorial waters were not violated.

52 V.P. Artemiev, "Protection of the Frontiers of the USSR" in Wolin and Slusser, eds., The Soviet Secret Police, 241–73. See also Reitz, "The Soviet Security Troops," 280–91.

53 Here I am influenced by the ideas of Michel Foucault, particularly in

Discipline and Punish, although he does not specifically talk about border control by the state.

54 *Na krasnom rubezhe* (Shepetevo), exact date unknown, 1928.

55 Ibid., 2 (35), 28 Apr. 1928.

56 For example, L. Zakovskii, "O nekotorykh metodakh i priemakh inostrannykh rasvedyvatel'nykh organov i ikh Trotskistsko-Bukharinskoi agentury," *Pogranichnaia pravda* (Opochka), 22 July 1937.

57 V. Vitalin, "Oborona Sovetskoi rodiny," *Sovetskoe stroitel'stvo* 1, no. 126 (Apr. 1937): 42.

58 "Iz istorii boevoi deiatel'nost' Dzhebrail'skogo pogranichnogo otriada" (From the History of the Military Activity of the Dzhebrail Border Detachment), 3 Dec. 1927, in Zyrianov, ed., *Pogranichnye voiska SSSR*, 1:564–5.

59 The invoking of the names of these two leaders, who were portrayed as among the ranks of imperialist spies trying to penetrate Soviet borders and undermine the socialist system, was used in, for example, N. Satarov and S. Dmitriev, "Monopoliia vneshnei torgovli i bor'ba s kontrabandoi," *Vneshniaia torgovlia*, nos. 4–5 (1938): 88.

60 "Vsem mestnym partorganizatsiiam ot TSK VKP(b)," 18 January, 1928. RTSKhIDNI, f. 17, op. 120, d. 18, 2–4.

61 This can be noticed, for example, in NKVD Belorussia, Trial Reports, 1935, RTSKhIDNI, f. 17, op. 120, d. 181. This *opis*, in the Central Committee's innocuously titled "Otdel delami," consisted of reports by the NKVD to the party.

62 See, for example, this accusation that many Polish "political immigrants" into the Soviet Union were actually working for Polish intelligence: "Dokladnaia zapiska o predvoritel'nykh itogakh operativnoi raboty v sviazi s proverkoi partiinykh dokumentov," 23 Nov. 1935, RTSKhIDNI, f. 17, op. 120 (Central Committee Otdel Delami), d. 181, 74.

63 Letter to Ezhov, 5 Nov. 1935, RTSKhIDNI, f. 17, op. 120, d. 181, 164–5.

64 "Predvaritel'nye itogi proverki partiinykh dokumentov v partorganizatsiiakh chastei pogranichnoi i vnutrennoi okhrany NKVD SSSR," [1935], RTSKhIDNI, f. 17, op. 120, d. 181, 287–300.

65 From Iagoda, NKVD, to Ezhov, 2 Mar. 1936, RTSKhIDNI, f. 17, op. 120, d. 270.

66 A typical example: B. Nikiforov, "Sovetskoe ugolovnoe zakonodatel'stvo o narusheniiakh gosudarstvennoi granitsy," *Pogranichnik* 11 (June 1947): 51–2.

67 Felshtinskii, *K istorii nashei zakrytosti*, 153–8.

68 Report by Stalin at the Plenum of the Central Committee of the Russian Communist Party (bol'shevik), 3 Mar. 1937, "O nedostatkakh partiinoi raboty i merakh likvidatsii trotskistkikh i inykh dvurushnikov" (On the Shortcomings of Party Work and Measures for the Liquidation of Trot-

skyites and Other Double-dealers), *Vneshniaia torgovliia*, no. 3 (1937): 2–4.

69 *Pogranichnaia pravda* (Opochka), 8 Oct. 1937. In Kalinin Oblast, a resolution of the All-Union Council of People's Commissars called for the significant improvement of *kolkhozy* in the border zone, adding tractor facilities, local transport, housing, and other developments: *Pogranichnaia pravda* (Opochka), 10 Oct. 1937.

70 Vladimir Paperny, "Moscow in the 1930s and the Emergence of a New City," in Gunther, ed., *Culture of the Stalin Period*, 235–6.

71 Clark, *Soviet Novel: History as Ritual*, 114.

72 Again, while Foucault does not specifically discuss border control, see the discussion of surveillance in *Discipline and Punish*.

73 British Foreign Office, Correspondence, report by Leslie Potts, 26 May 1935, reel 3, 1935, 371/19454. The events were linked by Potts to Sergei Kirov's assassination.

74 British Foreign Office, Correspondence, letter from Chilston, British Embassy in Moscow, 7 Aug. 1936, roll 6, 1936, 371.20353, no. 4117.

75 Postanovlenie Tsentralnogo Ispolnitelnogo Komiteta i Soveta Narodnykh Komissarov no. 45, "O v'ezde i prozhivanii v pogranichykh polosakh" (On Entry into and Residence in Border Zones), *Sobranie zakonov i rasporiiazhenii*, no. 377, 685–6.

76 Introduction by S. Presman to first issue of *Pogranichnik: Journal of the Political Administration of Border Troops of the* USSR NKVD (Moscow), 1 (Sept. 1939): 1–2.

77 "Pogranichniki na strazhe 1-6 zavoevanii oktiabria," *Pogranichnik* 3 (Oct. 1939): 5.

78 I. Maevskii and P. Orlov, "Sovetskaia Pribaltika," *Pogranichnik* 15 (Aug. 1940): 38–46.

79 Chugunov, *Granitsa nakanune voiny 1939–1941*, 72–3.

80 Gross, *Revolution from Abroad*, 152, 188–197.

81 "Pervye shagi NKVD v zapadnoi Belorussii," Radio Liberty Informational Department, Nicolaevsky Archive, box 296, ser. 227, doc. 19, undated, Hoover Institution Archives.

82. "NKVD SSSR (Po materialam byvshikh sotrudnikov NKVD SSSR 1939–1941 g.g.)," Nicolaevsky Archive, box 294, ser. 227, file 1, 274–84.

CHAPTER SEVEN

1 The reader will note that the sources for this chapter rely heavily on the Soviet press, articles in journals such as *Pogranichnik*, and published laws. Available sources on this period continue to be sparse in comparison with both the earlier period already discussed and the *perestroika* period.

2 This is an application to border control of the argument made by S.

Frederick Starr about the effect of new communications technologies on the USSR; his argument has proved a very influential theme for this chapter. See "New Communications Technologies and Civil Society," in Graham, ed., *Science and Soviet Social Order*, 19–50. The importance of international technological progress in producing a crisis of the Soviet system in the 1980s is explored by Seweryn Bialer in *The Soviet Paradox*, 78–9.

3 P. Alampiev, "Granitsy nashei velikoi sotsialisticheskoi rodiny" (The Borders of Our Great Socialist Motherland), *Pogranichnik* 3 (1951): 31.

4 See Zyrianov, ed., *Pogranichnye voiska SSSR*, 4.

5 The Vlasov movement was an anti-Soviet resistance army led by the former Soviet general. The OUN was a Ukrainian nationalist organization favouring armed opposition to Soviet rule. See, for example, Dallin and Mavrogordata, "The Soviet Reaction to Vlasov," 307–22.

6 For example, A. Egorov, "Granitsy SSSR okhraniaet ves' Sovetskii narod" (The Borders of the USSR Protect the Entire Soviet People), *Pogranichnik* 3 (1951): 61.

7 The Harvard Interview Project, performed in 1950–51, drew on the experiences of these refugees, many of whom claimed that they took advantage of the chaotic war situation in order to escape the hated Soviet regime. Some were military deserters. The project's results are deposited in the Hoover Institution Archives.

8 Ginsburgs, "Soviet Union and Problem of Refugees," 325.

9 Vyshinskii, "Text of Speech, November 6, 1946," 4.

10 For instance, in the 1920s and 1930s agreements were signed with Greece for the repatriation of Armenians to that country, and with various Slavic countries in the aftermath of the Second World War. Other measures allowed for the return to the Soviet Union of prisoners of war and former Russian citizens who wished to return. See Ginsburgs, "Soviet Union and Problem of Refugees," 348–52.

11 Although in the case of Poland they were more relaxed as of the late 1970s. Relatively little has been written on East European border control and emigration. For an example of the resemblance to Soviet legislation, see Solyom-Fekete, "Travel Abroad and Emigration." In 1985 the USSR signed agreements with Hungary, Poland, and Czechoslovakia to simplify border crossings for local residents. See Dinis, *Mezhdunarodno-pravovaia osnova prigranichnykh otnoshenii*, 141.

12 For example, F. Pomitiaev, "O znachenii okhrany gosudarstvennykh granits" (On the Significance of the Protection of State Borders), *Pogranichnik* 9 (1947): 14.

13 The Soviet literature dwells on this theme, without seeing the paradox of continuing border controls on its Soviet border, rather emphasizing that the Soviet bloc presented a united front to the capitalist world by estab-

lishing similar border regimes in all the East European countries. The regimes of Eastern Europe are beyond the scope of this study, but it seems fair to conjecture that, like the Soviet Union, their border controls served internal more than external political objectives. See Alampiev, "Granitsy," 31.

14 Dinis, *Mezhdunarodno-pravovaia osnova prigranichnykh otnoshenii*, 15–16.

15 A theoretical discussion of the nature of state borders under socialism is *Soldatenko, Sotsial'no-politicheskaia priroda gosudarstvennykh granits.* See also Ivanov, *Chasovye Sovetskikh granits*, 209.

16 I am grateful to Thane Gustafson for bringing this point to my attention.

17 Pravda, 4 Sept. 1956, 1; see also Knight, KGB.

18 "Polozhenie ob okhrane gosudarstvennoi granitse SSSR," *Vedomosti Verkhovnogo Soveta SSSR*, 30 Aug. 1960, no. 34 (1018): 747–56.

19 Rubinstein, "Lumumba University," 64–9.

20 Probably the first to notice and write about this trend was the scholar Frederick C. Barghoorn, who none the less met with KGB-sponsored misfortune when he attempted to visit the country. See "Cultural Relations," 323–44.

21 Bialer, *Stalin's Successors*, 142.

22 Salitan, *Politics and Nationality*, 35.

23 Stavis and Wishnevsky, "Impact of *Glasnost'*," 3–4; Alova, "Pered Podemom Zanavesa," 7, 28–9.

24 O'Keefe, "Soviet Legal Restrictions," 323, 327.

25 The Ministry of Internal Affairs, MVD, was, along with the KGB, one of the two bodies created to succeed the NKVD after Stalin's death. The MVD contains the militia and organs of social control, including passport matters, residence permits, and other social-control functions.

26 "Polozhenie o v'ezde v Soiuz Sovetskikh Sotsialisticheskikh Respublik i o vyezde iz Soiuza Sovetskikh Sotsialisticheskikh Respublik" (Resolution on Entry into and Exit from the USSR), Resolution of the Council of Ministers, no. 801, 22 Sept. 1970. *Sobranie Postanovlenii Pravitel'stva SSSR* 18 (1970): 362–6.

27 Ibid., 164.

28 Those eligible for diplomatic passports included leading members of the central and regional Communist Party, parliamentary deputies, government ministers, and high-ranking military officers, as well as diplomats. Foreign correspondents for the most prestigious state media outlets and civil servants travelling abroad on government business were eligible for what were known as "official passports." See ibid., 165.

29 See Barghoorn, *Detente*; Zaslavsky and Brym, *Soviet-Jewish Emigration*; and the writings of Peter Reddaway.

30 Article 13, no. 2, of United Nations, *Universal Declaration on Human Rights* (Washington, DC, 1948), 3; Korey, *The Soviet Cage*, 188–90.

31 Carle, *Consensus Formation*, 57.

32 Molineu, "Negotiating the Helsinki Agreement," 6–39.

33 Notably the Moscow Helsinki Monitoring Group, which provided an umbrella and perhaps the most important voice for Soviet dissident groups. See Moscow OGS, "General Observations about Documents 11–14 on Flagrant Violation of a Citizen's Right To Leave the Country in Which he Lives," *Arkhiva samizdata*, AS2832, 2 Dec. 1976.

34 O. Berdnik, et al., members of the Ukrainian Helsinki Monitoring Group, "Memorandum no. 18 to Belgrade Conference of 35 States on the Discrimination against Ukrainians with Respect to the Right To Emigrate," Dec. 1977, AS3330, *Arkhiva samizdata*, no. 33 (8 Sept. 1978); The Right to Emigrate Committee, "The Right to Emigrate," *Chronicle of Current Events* 36 (Oct.-Dec. 1979): 27–31.

35 Mickiewicz, *Split Signals*, 21.

36 Motyl, *Will the Non-Russians Rebel?* 146–7.

37 Motyl, *Sovietology, Rationality, Nationality*, 132–5.

38 A new customs code was introduced in 1964 that basically routinized the Soviet customs system and reinforced the state monopoly on foreign trade. The code made clear that *valiuta*, precious metals and other articles valuable to the state, were not to leave the country without permission. Still, the code probably aimed to provide a blueprint for the Soviet Union's new push for involvement in foreign trade in the 1960s. See *Tamozhennyi kodeks Soiuza SSSR*. Later customs measures added in 1971 (amendments to the code) and 1976 (*ukaz*) aimed to cut down on the problem of hard-currency smuggling and the black market in *valiuta*. See *Vedomosti Verkhovnogo Soveta SSSR*, no. 13 (1585), 30 July 1971, and no. 21 (2147), 30 Nov. 1976. In 1986 amendments to the code added further bureaucratization to customs responsibilities and gave customs officials greater powers to search for and charge customs violations: *Vedomosti*, no. 21 (2147), 17 May 1982.

39 Kolosova, *Otvetsvennost' za kontrabandu*, 47–9.

40 Ibid., 3.

41 V. M. Koldaev, *Istoriia i sovremennye sposoby*, 78.

42 Koldaev, *Istoriia i sovremennye sposoby bor'by*, 80–3.

43 Thane Gustafson, "The Crisis of the Soviet System of Power and Mikhail Gorbachev's Political Strategy," in Bialer and Mandelbaum, eds., *Gorbachev's Russia*, 196–7.

44 As tends to happen when such methods are used by Communist regimes in the long term, according to Andrew C. Janos. Janos argues that Communist regimes use such methods of isolation as an instrument of rule, to shield their citizens from the "international demonstration effect" of

observing the superior material position of the Western countries. See *Politics and Paradigms*, 122.

45 In his discussion of the causes of the First World War, Jack Snyder persuasively argues that institutional and individual biases (dogmatically held beliefs, bureaucratic politics, and feelings of threat) can undermine "rational" calculations of policy and lead to undesirable or unintended consequences for the state. His work also hints at how political leaders may delegate important policy matters to "professionals", thereby losing the big picture of how the policy in question fits into the state's general interest. See *Ideology of the Offensive*, 15–40.

46 Johnson, ed. *Change in Communist Systems.*

47 Bialer, *Soviet Paradox*, 144–5; Gustafson, "The Crisis of the Soviet System"; Goldman, *Gorbachev's Challenge.*

48 V. Rubanov, "Ot kul'ta sekretnosti," 24–36.

49 Krasner, "Global Communications," 336–66.

50 V.V. Fedorchuk, Doklad "O proekte zakona o gosudarstvennoi granitse SSSR" (On the Draft Law on the State Border of the USSR) *Pogranichnik* 1, (Jan. 1983): 6.

51 Earlier published measures had been the statute of 1927 and the *ukaz* of 1960, which had the status of decrees or regulations.

52. "Zakon SSSR o gosudarstvennoi granitse SSSR" (USSR Law on the State Border), *Pogranichnik* 1, (Jan. 1983): 12 [USSR Supreme Soviet, 24 Nov. 1982].

53 In January of that year, a decree was passed that stiffened penalties for persons guilty of "anti-Soviet agitation and propaganda" where the persons involved had received money or resources from foreign sources. In May a Supreme Soviet Presidium decree provided for administrative penalties for both Soviet citizens and foreigners who participated in the violation of the regulations whereby foreigners could travel, reside, and hold visas in the USSR. While these regulations attracted wide concern both in the West and inside the country, Julia Wishnevsky cautions that their significance should not be overestimated; see Wishnevsky, "The Decree on Administrative Liability."

54 Stavis and Wishnevsky, "The Impact of *Glasnost* on Soviet Emigration Policy," 3–6.

55 Sobraniie Postanovlenii Pravitel'stva SSSR: Otdel Pervyi no. 31, 563–66, trans. in Foreign Broadcast Information Service, *Daily Report on the Soviet Union*, 20 Nov. 1986, R43–45.

56 This latter part is presumably aimed at people who had applied to emigrate to Israel but had "dropped out" to go to the United States, a phenomenon that became common in the late 1970s and that Soviet authorities seemed to take as a sign of bad faith. On the "drop-out" controversy, see Salitan, *Politics and Nationality*, 45–55. See 1986 amendments in

Sobranie postanovlenii pravitel'stva sssr: otdel pervyi, 31, 563–6 trans. in Foreign Broadcast Information Service, *Daily Report on the Soviet Union,* 20 Nov. 1986, R43–45.
57 Text of 1986 amendments in ibid.
58 Ibid.
59 Ibid.
60 Medvedev, *Andropov,* 120.
61 Philip Taubman, "New Emigration Law Takes Effect," *New York Times,* 25 Mar. 1987, 1.

CHAPTER EIGHT

1 A very preliminary exploration of some of the ideas developed at length in this chapter appears in my paper "The Iron Curtain and Gorbachev: Recent Changes in the Soviet System of Border Control," *Soviet Observer* 1, no. 1 (Apr. 1990): 4–6.
2 See Gorbachev, *Perestroika.*
3 Ivanov, "From Self-Imposed Isolation," 70–2.
4 Shiriaev, "Sotsialisticheskii transnatsionalism i mirovoi rynok," 114–15.
5 P. Smirnov, "Tamozhennaia politika," 46.
6 Gorbachev's speech to the United Nations, 7 Dec. 1988, in Black, ed., *ussr Documents Annual 1988,* 409, 415.
7 Gorbachev, *Perestroika,* 131–2.
8 For example, Abel Aganbegyan, "Economic Reforms," and Ivan D. Ivanov, "Perestroika and Foreign Economic Relations," in *Perestroika 1989.*
9 The first comment was made by L. Anisimov, consultant to the Ministry of Foreign Affairs, in an interview in *Argumenty i fakty,* no. 40 (1989): 2; the second, A. Lukianov and A. Liuty, "Za rubezh po lichnomy delu – budin otdelov viz i registratsii" (Abroad for Personal Business – the Routine of ovir), *Pravda,* 25 March 1989, 6.
10 For example, A. Lukianov and A. Liuty, ibid.; interview by Alla Alova with Professor V.A. Kartashkin, Doctor of Juridical Sciences, member of the Commission for Humanitarian Co-operation and Human Rights, "Pered pod'emom zanavesa," 7, 28–9. A similar argument was made in an interview with Kartashkin by Vladimir Kuznetsov, Literaturnaia gazeta, 7 December 1988, 14, trans. in Foreign Broadcast Information Service, *Daily Report on the Soviet Union,* 21 December 1988, 91–2.
11 "V Tsentral'nom Komitete kpss," *Pravda,* 3 Mar. 1988, 2.
12 E. Nastin, "Po priglasheniiu za granitsu" (Abroad by Invitation), *Izvestiia,* 17 Mar. 1988, 6.
13 F. Ivanov, "Customs – A Concept of Trust," *Izvestiia,* 1 August 1989, 8, trans. in *Current Digest of the Soviet Press* 40, no. 34 (1989); 35.

14 Interview with Lt-Gen. Ilia Iakovlevich Kalinichenko, chief of staff of the
   USSR KGB Border Guard Troops; Doctor of Military Sciences Maj-Gen.
   Georgii Petrovich Sechkin, chief of the Red Banner Border Guards High-
   er Command Courses Military Science Dep.; and Border Guards Maj.
   Sergei Vasilevich Demchenko, by correspondents Col. R. Makushkin and
   Lt-Col. S. Kalinaev, *Krasnaia zvezda*, 28 May 1988, 6.
15 Interview with Chebrikov by A. Karpychev and A. Cherniak, *Pravda*, 2
   Sept. 1988, 3. In some respects this had already occurred in some areas:
   in 1987 people living in Moldavia were permitted to travel across the
   border to Romania for one week without a visa. A. Plutnik, "Visa v
   Moldaviu," *Izvestiia*, 7 Sept. 1987, 2.
16 Interview with Chairman of the KGB Vladimir Aleksandrovich Kriuch-
   kov, *Pogranichnik* 6 (1990): 9–10.
17. "Tamozhennyi kodeks SSSR," *Izvestiia*, 18 Apr. 1991, 3.
18 Including the Ministry of Internal Affairs, the Ministry of Foreign
   Affairs, the Ministry of Justice, the KGB, the Ministry of Finance, Procuracy, the Party Central Committee, experts from the Institute of State
   and Law, scientific institutes, and "social organizations," according to
   the remarks of A.G. Kovalev, first deputy of the Ministry of Foreign
   Affairs, who introduced the draft. Verkhovnyi Sovet SSSR, *Stenograficheskii otchet*, 2nd session, no. 27 (13 Nov. 1989): 37.
19 V. Prokopenko, "Granitsa bez zamka" (The Border Unlocked) *Komsomol'skaia pravda*, 17 Nov. 1989, 4.
20 Fiodor Burlatskii, "Kommunizm ili sotsial'naya demokratiia?" (Communism or Social Democracy), *Literaturnaia gazeta*, no. 9 (1991): 4.
21 Examples cited in interview with Ministry of Foreign Affairs representative B.N. Chaplin, in S. Mushkaterov, "Zakon o vyezde i v'ezde v SSSR:
   kak k nemu gotoviats'ia v nashei strane i za rubezhom" (The Law on
   Exit and Entry: How To Prepare for It in Our Country and Abroad),
   Izvestiia, 8 Feb. 1991, 6.
22 Despite the fact that he was on the commission that considered ministries' submissions of their estimated costs associated with the law,
   Burlatskii openly challenged these costs, claiming the ministries were taking advantage of the opportunity to advance their own agendas. Verkhovnyi Sovet SSSR, *Stenograficheskii otchet*, no. 52 (7 May 1991): 19.
23 "Soviets Stalling Bill To Permit Free Emigration," *New York Times*, 14
   May 1991, 1, 9.
24 Interview with V.A. Volokh, Administration of Migration and Resettlement, Ministry of Labour, "Ulitsa s dvustoronnim dvizheniem" (A Two-
   Way Street), *Literaturnaia gazeta*, no. 13 (3 April 1991): 6.
25 See remarks by F.M. Burlatskii, Verkhovnyi Sovet SSSR, *Stenograficheskii
   otchet* no. 52 (7 May 1991): 15–19; I.D. Laptev, 54 (12 May 1991):
   5–6.

26 See remarks by F. M. Burlatskii, Verkhovnyi Sovet sssr, *Stenograficheskii otchet* no. 52 (7 May 1991): 15–19; I.D. Laptev, 54 (12 May 1991): 5–6; and A.E. Sebentsov, chairman of the Supreme Soviet Committee on Legislation and Law, ibid., 7–8.

27 With reference to the argument that free emigration would enable the ussr to overcome the limits of the Jackson-Vanik amendment on u.s.-Soviet trade, one deputy argued in the Supreme Soviet that it was more important to address the needs of Soviet society than those of the American legislature. Verkhovnyi Sovet sssr, *Stenograficheskii otchet*, 5th session, no. 54 (12 May 1991): 16.

28 A typical comment by a deputy who worked in a machine factory in Southern Russia: "I am not against anybody going abroad. As a worker I see it this way: I will not be among the first to leave. My turn will not come for a long time yet. I have nothing to go for." Verkhovnyi Sovet sssr, *Stenograficheskii otchet*, 5th session, no. 52 (7 May 1991): 15.

29 Verkhovnyi Sovet sssr, *Stenograficheskii otchet*, 5th session, no. 59 (20 May 1991): 5.

30 See ibid., no. 55 (13 May 1991): 31.

31 The final law declared listed the reasons: if the applicant knowingly had access to state secrets or had other contractual obligations to the state; if s/he had criminal charges against him/her or was facing criminal or civil proceedings; if s/he was serving a penal sentence; if s/he had given false information; if s/he was due for military service; or if s/he was considered dangerous.

32 Contrast the final law in *Izvestiia*, 6 June 1991, 4, with the 1989 draft, text translated in Sidney Heitman, "Soviet Draft Law," 41–5.

33 Interview with Ivan Laptev by Liudmilla Telens, "Can We Afford Freedom?" *Moscow News*, 21, 26 May–2 June 1991, 8.

34 "Zakon sssr O poriadke vyezda iz sssr i v'ezda v sssr grazhdan sssr," (Law of the ussr on the Procedure for Exit from and Entry into the ussr for Citizens of the ussr), *Izvestiia*, 6 June 1991, 4.

35 Gleason, *Federalism and Nationalism*, 2.

36 Radio Free Europe/Radio Liberty *Daily Report* no. 233, 8 Dec. 1989, reported by Riina Kionka.

37 The border violations were condemned by a ussr Supreme Soviet Resolution, 10 Jan. 1990, *Pravda*, 11 Jan. 1990, 1.

38 For example, in September 1990 an armed terrorist seeking to cross the Soviet border into Poland from Latvia threatened to blow up the border post unless it was opened to crossings. See Foreign Broadcast Information Service, *Daily Report on the Soviet Union*, 11 Sept. 1990, 62. In November 1991 a customs agent was killed in Moldova in a clash with separatists.

39 Remarks by Central Asian Border District General Markevitsky,

Moscow Radio to Great Britain and Ireland, 18 Feb. 1990, in FBIS, *Daily Report on the Soviet Union*, 2 Mar., 101; also Moscow Television Service, 27 Feb., in FBIS, *Daily Report on the Soviet Union*, 2 Mar. 1990, 101.

40 Interview by Col. R. Makushin of Col. Gen. I. Kalinichenko, *Krasnaia zvezda*, 27 May 1990, 2, trans. in FBIS, *Daily Report on the Soviet Union*, FBIS-SOV-90-120, 21 June 1990, 68.

41 For text of the draft Union treaty, see FBIS, *Daily Report on the Soviet Union*, 26 Nov. 1990, 39–42.

42 "On Additional Measures to Guarantee the Rights of Soviet Citizens and the Protection of Sovereignty on the Territory of the Lithuanian SSR": see Moscow, TASS International Service, 21 Mar. 1990, in FBIS, *Daily Report on the Soviet Union*, 22 Mar. 1990, 87–8; and V. Iurteev, "Obstanovka na granitse," in *Pravitel'stvennyi vestnik* 14 (Apr. 1990): 1, 9.

43 Remarks by Baltic Frontier District Lt-Gen. Valentin Gaponenko, Moscow, TASS International Service, 1300 GMT, 23 Mar. 1990, in FBIS, *Daily Report on the Soviet Union*, 23 Mar. 1990, 64.

44 See FBIS, *Daily Report on the Soviet Union*, 21 Aug. 1990, 66.

45 See ibid., 30 July 1990, 72.

46 Francis X. Clines, "A Theme Song for the Baltics: March of the Customs Posts," in *New York Times*, 19 Nov. 1990, A9.

47 *New York Times*, 28 May 1991, A3.

48 See article by Vasilii Fedorov, *Kommersant*, no. 13 (25 Mar.–1 Apr. 1991): 4.

49 The customs law is published in *Izvestiia*, 18 Apr. 1991, 3–6.

50 Although a lone delegate warned that the law would be unpalatable to the republics, and succeeded in pressuring for more republics' participation in the new central customs body. Verkhovnyi Sovet SSSR, *Stenograficheskii otchet*, 4th session, no. 52, (27 Nov. 1990): 29–51; and 5th session, no. 26 (26 Mar. 1991): 17–24.

51 Georgia passed a swift resolution on the development of its own customs service: *Vedomosti Verkhovnogo Soveta Respubliki Gruzii*, no. 4 (604) (Apr. 1991): 119. Ukraine passed its law affirming its own sovereignty over customs, 25 June 1991, *Vedomosti Verkhovnogo Soveta Ukrainy*, no. 44 (1991): 1247–50. Lithuania had passed its first customs law on 9 October 1990 and added various supplementary measures: *Vedomosti Verkhovnogo Soveta i Pravitel'stva Litovskoi Respubliki*, no. 30 (1990): 994–7. Estonia passed a similar law almost concurrently: *Vedomosti Estonskoi Respubliki*, no. 15 (1990): 359–63.

52 Estonia's law on immigration, passed in early 1990, was quite drastic: *Vedomosti Estonskoi Respubliki*, no. 2 (1990): 39–47. Lithuania passed repeated measures asserting control over passports and visas starting in 1990.

CHAPTER NINE

1 See Terry, "Thinking about Post-Communist Transitions," 333–7.
2 Przeworski, *Democracy and the Market*, 189.
3 See, for example, Mikhail Tsypkin, "The Politics of Russian Security Policy," in Parrott, ed., *State Building and Military Power*, 11; Lepingwell, "The Russian Military," 70–92; Olcott, "Sovereignty and the Near Abroad," 353–68. Both Olcott and Tsypkin consider the definition of Russia's security interests to be contentious and subject to debate by various constituencies.
4 Snyder, "Nationalism and the Crisis," 5–26; Rubin, "The Fragmentation of Tajikistan," 71–91.
5 This conflict is noted in Palei and Petr, "Integration vs. Independence," 1–12.
6 Bahry, "Union Republics and Contradictions," 236–7.
7 See Shevardnadze, "No One Can Isolate Us," 119.
8 Tatyana Korotkova, "Federal Customs Service Dissolved," *Commersant*, 6 Jan. 1992, 14.
9 "Agreement on the Creation of a Commonwealth of Independent States," text of agreement in RFE/RL *Research Report*, 10 Jan. 1992, 4–5.
10 Ibid., 4.
11 CIS, "Agreement on the Principles of Customs Policy," Foreign Broadcast Information Service, Daily Report on Central Eurasia, FBIS-SOV-92-051, 16 Mar. 1992, 38–41.
12 After this point I pay less attention to the republics of the Caucasus and Tajikistan, partly out of a problem in finding sources, partly because I assume that states in a situation tantamount to civil war are not in a position to develop a coherent customs policy or to patrol their borders in a meaningful way.
13 Nikolai Lashkevich, "Gosudarstvennye granitsy vnutri sodruzhestva bystro teriaiut svoiu prozrachnost'" (State Boundaries within the Commonwealth Are Quickly Losing Their Transparency), *Izvestiia*, 6 June 1992, 1.
14 Mariia Kuz'menkova, "Ne vynesla tamozhniia 'prozrachnoi' granitsy" (Customs controls Have Not Removed from the "Transparent" Border), *Rossiiskaia gazeta*, 2 Sept. 1992, 1.
15 *Izvestiia*, 30 Sept. 1992, 1.
16 Nikolai Gritchin, "Stavropol' zakryvaet granitsu s trudnym sosedom" (Stavropol' Closes its Border with a Difficult Neighbour), *Izvestiia*, 17 Sept. 1992, 2.
17 A 14 Dec. 1992 decree provided for customs duties for certain goods exported to CIS from Russia: FBIS-USR-93-003, 8 Jan. 1993, 10.
18 For perceptive, early analyses of the faults of the CIS, see Maksimova,

"Ot imperskogo soiuza," 5. Ann Sheehy, "Unloved, Ill-fed Infant Faces an Uncertain Future," *RFE/RFL Research Report* 1, 8 (21 Feb. 1992): 1–3.

19 Shaposhnikov, *Vybor: Zapiski glavnokomandiushchego*, 104–7.

20 Teresa Rakowska-Harmstone, "Russia's Monroe Doctrine: Peacekeeping, Peacemaking or Imperial Outreach?" in Molot and von Riekhoff, eds., *A Part of the Peace*, 231–65.

21 Pavel K. Baev, "Old and New Border Problems in Russia's Security Policy," in Forsberg, ed., *Contested Territory*, 93.

22 Raymond L. Garthoff, "Russian Military Doctrine and Deployments," in Parrott, ed., *State Building and Military Power*, 49–50.

23 Dunlop, "Will a Large-Scale Migration," 605–11.

24 Oleg Vladykin, Iurii Pirogov, "Pomeniaet li granitsa shirotu?" (Does the Border Change Its Breadth?), *Krasnaia zvezda*, 28 Nov. 1992, 5.

25 I. Andreev, "Russia Closes Its Borders," *Izvestiia*, 7 Nov. 1992, 2, trans. in FBIS-USR-92-149, 20 Nov. 1992, 1–2.

26 FBIS, Daily Report on Central Eurasia, SOV-92-240-S, 14 Dec. 1992, 29–30.

27 See Anna Kreikemeyer, "Renaissance of Hegemony and Spheres of Influence – The Evolution of the Yeltsin Doctrine," in Ehrhart, Kreikemeyer, and Zagorski, eds., *Crisis Management*, 99–102.

28 For example, the point that unilateral Ukrainian moves to monitor its boundary influenced the establishment of Russian border controls on the Ukrainian border was made, by Maj.-Gen. Anatolii Parakhin, first deputy commander of Russian Border Troops, in an interview by Sergei Nagaev, *Rossiiskaia gazeta*, 4 May 1993, 2, trans. in FBIS-SOV-93-085, 5 May 1993, 41.

29 Tuomas Forsberg, "The Collapse of the Soviet Union and Historical Border Questions," in Forsberg, *Contested Territory*, 4–5.

30 Ursel Schlichting, "Conflicts in the Former Soviet Union: Chances and Limits of their Settlement," in Ehrhart, Kreikemeyer, and Zagorski, eds., *Crisis Management*, 19–21.

31 "Foreign Ministry Official on Border Control in Chechnia," Interfax, FBIS-SOV-93-239, 15 Dec. 1993, 69.

32 "Checkpoints set up on Border with Chechnia," ITAR-TASS, in FBIS-SOV-94-157, 15 Aug. 1994, 26.

33 Hanson, "Local Power," 48–9.

34 An early exception to the Western consensus favouring integration can be found in Palei and Petr, "Integration vs. Independence," 1–12.

35 Constantine Michalopoulos and David Tarr, "Energizing Trade of the States of the Former USSR," *Finance and Development* (IMF/World Bank), Mar. 1993, 24; Constantine Micholopoulos, "Trade Issues in the New Independent States," World Bank, *Studies of Economies in Transition* 7 (1993): 11.

36 Havrylyshyn and Williamson, *From Soviet disUnion*, 17–23.
37 Grant H. Spender with Paul S. Ross, "Common Issues and Interrepublic Relations in the Former USSR," *Economic Review*, Washington, D.C.: International Monetary Fund, Apr. 1992, 7–8.
38 Drebentsov, "Rebuilding the Interrepublic Ties," 4.
39 Constantine Michalopoulos and David Tarr, "Trade and Payments Arrangements for States of the former USSR," World Bank, *Studies of Economies in Transition* 2 (1993): 20.
40 See Bomsdorf, et al., "Confronting Insecurity," 35.
41 Erik Whitlock, "Obstacles to CIS Economic Integration," *RFE/RL Research Report* 27 (2 July 1993): 35.
42 Granville, "Price and Currency Reform."
43 Havrylyshyn and Williamson, *From Soviet disUnion*, 27; also Noren and Watson, "Interrepublican Economic Relations," 89–129.
44 Beverly Crawford, "Post-Communist Political Economy: A Framework for Analysis of Reform," in Crawford, ed., *Markets, States and Democracy*, 19–21.
45 Ibid., 17–18.
46 Constantine Micholopoulos, "Trade Issues in the New Independent States," World Bank, *Studies of Economies in Transition* 7 (1993): 5–6.
47 Constantine Michalopoulos and David Tarr, "Trade and Payments Arrangements for States of the former USSR," World Bank, *Studies of Economies in Transition* 2 (1993): 20.
48 Anatolii Kruglov, chairman of the Russian Federation State Customs Committee, interview in *Ekonomika i zhizn*, Jan. 1993, trans. in Foreign Broadcast Information Service, Central Eurasia, FBIS-USR-93-045, 10 Apr. 1993, 89.
49 "On Strengthening Currency and Export Controls and Developing the Currency Market," FBIS-USR-9333-045, 10 Apr. 1993, 97–100.
50 Vadim Ogurtsov, "Granitsa na zamke. Iz zhesti" (The Border is Closed with a Tin Lock), interview with head of the North Caucasus customs administration Aleksandr Epifanov, *Rossiiskaia gazeta*, 26 Feb. 1993, 2.
51 Hanna Tuhai, "Prokhidnyy dvir dlia kontrabandistiv i ... komariv" (A Door Forbidden to Smugglers and ... Mosquitoes), *Pravda Ukraïny*, 25 May 1993, 2.
52 N. Palkina, "Tamozhnia: v Rossii poiavilsia novyi vid prestupnosti – kommercheskaia kontrabanda" (Customs: A New Type of Crime Has Appeared in Russia: Commercial Smuggling), *Ekonomika i zhizn'*, no. 17 (May 1993): 16.
53 As Timothy Mitchell writes, border controls are a symbol and a manifestation of modern coercive organization that help to "manufacture" a sense of the nation-state, exaggerating its power and mystery: "Limits of the State," 94.

54 Haus, *Globalizing the* GATT, 17–22.

55 Ibid., 102.

56 The link between the new tariff and Yeltsin's intentions regarding the GATT was made in Vladimir Lisakov, "Customs Rules Have Been Changed," *Izvestiia*, 2 July 1993, trans. in FBIS-USR-93-089, 106.

57 Sabelnikov, "Russia on the Way," 345–7.

58 Vadim Bardin and Alexander Volynets, "Foreign Trade Still a Swamp of Subsidy and Privilege," *Commersant*, 14 Apr. 1993, 21.

59 Nadezhda Garifullina, "Chernye dyry biudzheta" (Black Holes of the Budget), *Sovietskaia Rossiia*, 20 July 1993, 2. At the same time, conservatives do not always seem to favour Russia's establishment of customs boundaries with the successor states. See Aleksandr Shinkin, "Granitsa na zamok. i Rossiian – tozhe" (The border Is Under Lock and Key. And So Is the Russian Citizen), *Pravda*, 29 Apr. 1993, 2.

60 See, for example, the debate over "shock therapy": Brada, "The Transformation from Communism," 87–110, and Murrell, "What Is Shock Therapy?" 111–40.

61 Text of law, "O tamozhennom tarife" (On the Customs Tariff), *Ekonomika i zhizn'*, no. 23 (June 1993): 18–20.

62 V. Oreshkin, "Gosudarstvennoe regulirovanie vneshneekonomicheskoi deiatel'nosti v Rossii" (State regulation of foreign economic activity in Russia), *Ekonomika i zhizn'*, no. 29 (July 1993): 23.

63 Valery Oreshkin, "Customs regulation changes again," *Moscow News*, no. 29 (16 July 1993): 8.

64 For details on Russia's application, see "Russia Applies for GATT Membership," GATT *Focus* 100 (July 1993): 2.

65 Text of law, in FBIS-USR-93-080, 28 June 1993, 67.

66 Resolution, 24 May 1993, "O neotlozhnykh merakh po usileniiu tamozhennogo kontrolia na gosudarstvennoi granitse Rossiiskoi Federatsii" (On Necessary Measures To Strengthen Customs Control on the State Border of the Russian Federation), *Ekonomika i zhizn'*, no. 22 (June 1993): 17.

67 "Tamozhennyi Kodeks Rossiiskoi Federatsii," *Vedomosti s'ezda narodnykh deputativ* RF *i verkhovnogo soveta* RF, no. 31 (5 Aug. 1993): 3–166. This has been translated in a special issue of FBIS-USR-93-109, 19 Aug. 1993.

68 From interview with V.F. Kruglikov, first deputy chairman of Russia's State Customs Committee, published in *Ekonomika i zhizn'*, no. 24 (June 1993): 16, trans. in FBIS-USR-93-092, 21 July 1993, 67.

69 N. Palkina, interview with M.V. Vanin, head of the administration for the struggle with contraband and violations of customs rules, GTK., "Tamozhennyi kodeks: teper', kontrabandist, derzhis'!" (Customs code: From Now On, Watch Yourself, Smuggler!) *Ekonomika i zhizn'*, no. 33 (Aug. 1993): 16.

70 David A. Dyker, "Recentralization or Liberalization in Foreign Trade?" *RFE/RL Research Report*, 23 July 1993, 6–9.

71 Havrylyshyn and Williamson, *From Soviet disUnion*, 18.

72 Sergei Stepashin, "On the Agenda of the Sixth Session: The Law and the Border," *Rossiiskaia gazeta*, 4 Jan. 1993, 2, trans. in FBIS-SOV-93-003, 6 January 1993, 29–30.

73 Anatolii Stasovskii, "A Border without a Law Is No Border; A State without a Border Is No State," *Krasnaia zvezda*, 3 Apr. 1993, 1, trans. in FBIS-SOV-93-065, 42–43.

74 Zakon Rossiiskoi Federatsii, "O gosudarstvennoi granitse Rossiiskoi Federatsii," *Vedomosti S'ezda Narodnykh Deputatov Rossiiskoi Federatsii i Verkhovnogo Soveta Rossiiskoi Federatsii*, no. 17 (29 Apr. 1993): 987–1014.

75 For Kazakhstan, Marat Salimov, "Kazakhstan has Established Its Customs Tariffs: Importers Have a Liberal Treatment in Kazakhstan," in *Kommersant Daily*, 3 Dec. 1992, 3, trans. in FBIS-USR-93-007, 16 Jan. 1993, 44; Ukaz, "O tamozhennoi tarife respubliki Kazakhstan na eksportiruemye tovary" (On the Customs Tariff of the Republic of Kazakhstan for Export Goods), *Kazakhstanskaia pravda*, 16 Mar. 1993, 1.

76 *Pravda vostoka*, 5 Jan. 1993, 2; 10 Nov. 1992, 2.

77 FBIS-USR-92-161, 16 Dec. 1992.

78 For example, Porter and Saivetz, "Once and Future Empire," 75–90.

79 Erik Whitlock, "Obstacles to CIS Economic Integration," *RFE/RL Research Report* 27 (2 July 1993): 34.

80 Leonid Krasnov, "Ekonomicheskii soiuz stran SNG vozmozhen. No tol'ko na ravnopravnoi dlia vsekh osnove" (Economic Union of the CIS Countries is Possible. But Only on an Equal Basis for All), *Rossiiskaia gazeta*, 7 Sept. 1993, 7.

81 Havrylyshyn and Williamson, *From Soviet disUnion*, 16.

82 "Russia, Tajikistan, Others Sign Border Control Accord," FBIS-SOV-94-137, 18 July 1994, 59.

83 Tatiana Shakleina, "Russian Policy toward Military Conflicts in the Former Soviet Union," in Parrott, ed., *State Building and Military Power*, 95.

84 Anatolii Rozanov, "Belarusian Perspectives on National Security and Belarusian Military Policy," in Parrott, ed., *State Building and Military Power*, 204.

85 See Elaine M. Holoboff, "National Security in the Baltic States: Rolling Back in the Bridgehead," in Parrott, ed., *State Building and Military Power*, 118; Olcott, "Sovereignty and the Near Abroad," 353; "Council Discusses Army Measures, Border Control," Vilnius Radio, trans. in FBIS-SOV-92-122, 24 June 1992, 85; "Official Says Russian Army Adding to Border Control Problems," ETA (Tallinn), in FBIS-SOV-93-081, 29 Apr. 1993, 55.

86 Dzintra Bungs, "Seeking Solutions to Baltic-Russian Border Issues," RFE/RL *Research Report* 3, no. 13 (1 Apr. 1994): 25–32.
87 "Guards Close Border with Abkhazia," ITAR-TASS, in FBIS-SOV-92-164, 24 Aug. 1992, 9.
88 See Charles Tilly, "Reflections on the History of European State-Making," in Tilly, ed., *The Formation of National States in Western Europe,* 3–83; Binder, et al., *Crises and Sequences.*

CONCLUSION

1 An early diagnosis, written before the collapse of the Soviet Union, was "Z," "To the Stalin Mausoleum," 295–343. Another example is Odom, "Soviet Politics and After," 66–98.
2 Dallin, "Causes of the Collapse," 279–302.
3 Huntington, *Political Order in Changing Societies,* 8, 17; Colton, *Dilemma of Reform,* rev. ed., 8–60; Chalmers Johnson, "Comparing Communist Nations," in Johnson, ed., *Change in Communist Systems,* 12.
4 Bendix, *Nation Building and Citizenship,* 2nd ed.
5 Motyl, *Sovietology, Rationality, Nationality,* chap. 12; Gail W. Lapidus, "From Democratization to Disintegration: The Impact of Perestroika on the National Question," in Lapidus and Zaslavsky with Goldman, eds., *From Union to Commonwealth,* 45–70.
6 Motyl, *Dilemmas of Independence,* 39.
7 di Palma, "Legitimation from Top to Civil Society," 49–80.
8 See Holloway, "State, Society and Military," 5–24; Meyer, "How the Threat," 5–38.
9 Jack Snyder stresses the causal role of entrenched strategic ideas among imperial elites as leading to the problem of "overextension": *Myths of Empire,* 1–6. The role of domestic political coalitions and interests in contributing to the rise or decline of states in the international environment is stressed in Peter J. Katzenstein, introduction to Katzenstein, ed., *Between Power and Plenty,* 3–22. Edward N. Luttwak focuses on the high costs that the Soviet territorial commitment was incurring in *The Grand Strategy of Soviet Union,* 111–12. Luttwak has earlier written about the burdens involved in the upkeep of the Roman Empire in *Grand Strategy of Roman Empire.*
10 See Katzenstein, ed., *Between Power and Plenty*; Snyder, *Myths of Empire*; Gilpin, *War and Change*; Strachey, *The End of Empire*; Mann, ed., *Rise and Fall of the Nation State*; Kennedy, *Rise and Fall of the Great Powers*; Luttwak, *Grand Strategy of Roman Empire*; Doyle, *Empires.*
11 Motyl, *Dilemmas of Independence,* 37–41.
12 Philip G. Roeder makes this argument, suggesting that the Soviet sys-

tem's "authoritarian constitution" allowed it to effect revolutionary changes in its first decades in power but eventually contributed to its fall because the leadership was unable to respond to new demands from society or to scale down its own power. See *Red Sunset*, 4–7. Roeder, it should be pointed out, is concerned with the Soviet elite as a hierarchical organization rather than with the territorial or national dimensions of Soviet power.

13 Max Weber, "Politics as a Vocation," in Gerth and Mills, eds., *Max Weber*, 78.

14 Snyder, "Nationalism and the Crisis," 5–26.

15 See Hirschman's discussion of exit and voice in "Exit, Voice and the State," cited in chap. 2.

16 Brzezinski, "The Premature Partnership," 67–82.

17. Thank you, Mum (my mother, Joan Chandler), for letting me yet again spread out my computer on your kitchen table, and for the conversation that we had as I wrote these final words; thanks for never tiring of talk about borders.

Bibliography

ARCHIVES AND DOCUMENT
COLLECTIONS

American Historical Association, Committee for the Study of War Documents. Communist Party of the Soviet Union, Smolensk Oblast Records 1917–41. Microfilm. United States National Archives, 1957.

Bakhmeteff, Boris. Papers. Rare Book and Manuscript Library, Columbia University.

Central State Archive of the National Economy of the USSR, Moscow (TSGANKh USSR):
– Fond 3527, Narkom Pocht i Sviazei (People's Commissariat of Post and Communications).

Central State Archive of the October Revolution of the Ukrainian SSR, Kiev, Ukraine (TSGAOR UkSSR):
– Fond 1, All-Ukrainian Central Executive Committee of Workers', Peasants', and Red Army Deputies, Kiev/Kharkiv. 1917–20.
– Fond 2, Council of People's Commissars of the Ukrainian SSR. 1917–30.
– Fond 5, Commissariat of Internal Affairs (NKVD) Ukrainian SSR.

Central State Archive of the October Revolution of the USSR, Moscow, Russian Federation (TSGAOR USSR):
– Fond 130, Council of People's Commissars (SNK), RSFSR.
– Fond 393, NKVD (People's Commissariat of Internal Affairs), RSFSR.
– Fond 1235, Central Executive Committee (TSIK), RSFSR.
– Fond 1318, People's Commissariat of Nationalities (Narkomnats), USSR.
– Fond 3316, Central Executive Committee (TSIK), USSR.

– Fond 5283, All-Soviet Society for Cultural Relations (Vsesoyuznoe Obshchestvo Kul'turnykh Sviazei).
– Fond 5446, Council of People's Commissars, USSR.
– Fond 5515, People's Commissariat of Labour, USSR.
– Fond 5674, Council of Labor and Defence (STO), USSR.
Great Britain, Foreign Office. *Russia – Correspondence*, 1930–40. Microfilm.
Hoover Institution Archive on War, Revolution and Peace, Stanford, Calif.:
– American Relief Administration, Russian Unit, William N. Haskell, director. Files 1922.
– Dal'nevostochnaia Respublika. Miscellaneous records 1919–21.
– Dobrynin, V.A. Papers.
– Harvard University Russian Research Center, Refugee Interview Project. Transcripts 1950–51.
– Heroys, Alexandre. Papers.
– Herron, George David. Papers.
– Iudenich, Nikolai Nikolaevich. Papers.
– Krupenskii, Aleksandr Nicolaevich. Papers 1918–35.
– Laserson, Maurice. Papers 1920–49.
– Lonzinov, V. Memorandum ca 1930. 1 folder.
– Maklakoff, Basil A. Papers.
– Mel'gunov, Sergei Petrovich. Papers 1918–33.
– Nikolaevsky, Boris I. Papers.
– Russia. Posol'stvo. France.
– Russia. Posol'stvo. United States.
The Party Archive of the Institute of History of the Party of the Central Committee of the Ukrainian Communist Party, Kiev, Ukraine:
– Fond 1, Central Committee of the Ukrainian Communist Party.
The Russian Centre for the Preservation and Study of Documents of Contemporary History of the Russian Federation Committee on Archival Affairs (RTSIKHDNI), Moscow, Russian Federation (until December 1991, Central Party Archive of the Institute of Theory and History of Socialism of the Central Committee of the Communist Party of the Soviet Union):
– Fond 17 (includes documents of the Central Committee of the Communist Party).
– Fond 19, Protocols of the Council of People's Commissars 1917–22.
– Fond 76, Personal Papers of Feliks E. Dzerzhinskii.
– Fond 79, Personal Papers of V. V. Kuibyshev.
– Fond 588, Personal Papers of Joseph Stalin.
Trotsky, Leon. Papers. Houghton Library, Harvard University, Cambridge, Mass.
United States, Department of State. Records of the Department of State Relating to the Internal Affairs of Russia and the Soviet Union, 1910–29. Microfilm.

ENGLISH-LANGUAGE SOURCES

Abella, Irving, and Harold Troper. *None Is Too Many: Canada and the Jews of Europe, 1933–1948.* Toronto: Lester and Orpen Dennys 1982

Anderson, Lisa. *The State and Social Transformation in Tunisia and Libya.* Princeton, NJ: Princeton University Press 1986.

– "Lawless Government and Illegal Opposition: Reflections on the Middle East." *Journal of International Affairs* 40, no. 2 (Winter/Spring 1987): 219–32.

– "The State in the Middle East and North Africa." *Comparative Politics* 20, no. 1 (Oct. 1987): 1–18.

Anderson, Perry. *Lineages of the Absolutist State.* London: New Left Books 1974.

Arendt, Hannah. *The Origins of Totalitarianism.* 4th ed. New York: Harcourt, Brace, and World 1968.

Armstrong, John A. "Federalism in the USSR: Ethnic and Territorial Aspects." *Publius* (Fall 1977): 89–105.

Arnold, Arthur Z. *Banks, Credit and Money in the Soviet Union.* New York: Columbia University Press 1937.

Artemyev, Vyacheslav P. "Manning the Iron Curtain." *Bulletin of the Institute for the Study of the USSR* (July 1962): 14–21.

Austin, Paul M. "Soviet Karelian: The Language That Failed." *Slavic Review* 51, no. 1 (Spring 1992): 16–35.

Bahry, Donna. "The Union Republics and Contradictions in Gorbachev's Economic Reform." *Soviet Economy* 7, no. 3 (1991): 215–55.

Bailey, Geoffrey. *The Conspirators.* New York: Harper and Row 1960.

Ball, Alan H. *Russia's Last Capitalists: The Nepmen, 1921–1929.* Berkeley: University of California Press 1987.

Barghoorn, Frederick C. "Cultural Relations and Soviet Foreign Policy." *World Politics* 8, no. 3 (Apr. 1956): 323–44.

– *Detente and the Democratic Movement in the USSR.* New York: Free Press 1976.

Barth, Fredrik, ed. *Ethnic Groups and Boundaries: The Social Organization of Culture Difference.* Boston: Little, Brown, and Company 1969.

Baykov, Alexander. *The Development of the Soviet Economic System.* Cambridge: Cambridge University Press 1980.

Bayley, David H. *Patterns of Policing: A Comparative International Analysis.* New Brunswick, NJ: Rutgers University Press 1985.

Bendix, Reinhard. *Nation Building and Citizenship.* 2nd ed. Berkeley: University of California Press 1977.

Bennigsen Broxup, Marie, et al., eds. *The North Caucasus Barrier: The Russian Advance towards the Muslim World.* London: Hurst and Company 1992.

Bettelheim, Charles. *Class Struggles in the USSR 1923–1930*. Sussex: Harvester Press 1978.

Bialer, Seweryn. *Stalin's Successors: Leadership, Stability and Change in the Soviet Union*. Cambridge: Cambridge University Press 1980.

– *The Soviet Paradox: External Expansion, Internal Decline*. New York: Vintage 1987.

– and Michael Mandelbaum, eds. *Gorbachev's Russia and American Foreign Policy*. Boulder: Westview 1988.

– ed. *Inside Gorbachev's Russia: Politics, Society and Nationality in the USSR*. Boulder, Colo.: Westview Press 1989.

Binder, Leonard, James S. Coleman, Joseph LaPalombara, Lucian W. Pye, Sidney Verba, and Myron Weiner. *Crises and Sequences in Political Development*. Princeton, NJ: Princeton University Press 1971.

Black, Cyril Edwin, ed. *The Transformation of Russian Society: Aspects of Social Change since 1861*. Cambridge: Harvard University Press 1969.

Black, J.L., ed. *USSR Documents Annual*. Gulf Breeze, Fla.: Academic International Press, 1989

– *Into the Dustbin of History: The USSR from Coup to Commonwealth August–December 1991*. Gulf Breeze, Fla.: Academic International Press 1993.

Blank, Stephen. *The Sorceror's Apprentice: Stalin as Commissar of Nationalities, 1917–1924*. Westport, Conn.: Greenwood Press 1994.

Boguslavskii, M.M. "The Legal Status of Free Economic Zones in the USSR." *Soviet Law and Government* 29, no. 4 (1991): 78–91.

Bomsdorf, Fal, et al. *Confronting Insecurity in Eastern Europe: Challenges for the European Community*. London: Royal Institute of International Affairs, Dec. 1992.

Borkenau, Franz. "State and Revolution in the Paris Commune, the Russian Revolution and the Spanish Civil War." *Sociological Review* 29, no. 41 (1937): 41–75.

Brada, Josef C. "The Transformation from Communism to Capitalism: How Far? How Fast?" *Post-Soviet Affairs* 9, no. 2 (Apr.–June 1993): 87–110.

Brada, Joseph C., and Michael P. Claudon, eds. *Reforming the Ruble: Monetary Aspects of Perestroika*. New York: New York University Press 1990.

Bradley, J.F.N. (John Francis Nejez). *Civil War in Russia 1917–1920*. London: B.T. Batsford 1975.

Bremmer, Ian, and Ray Taras, eds. *Nations and Politics in the Soviet Successor States*. New York: Cambridge University Press 1993.

Brown, Alan A., and Egon Neuberger, eds. *International Trade and Central Planning*. Berkeley: University of California Press 1968.

Brown, Peter G., and Henry Shue. *Boundaries: National Autonomy and its Limits*. Totowa, NJ: Rowman and Littlefield 1981.

Broxup, Marie Bennigsen, et al., eds. *The North Caucasus Barrier: The Russ-

ian Advance towards the Muslim World. London: Hurst and Company 1992.

Brzezinski, Zbigniew. "The Premature Partnership." *Foreign Affairs* 73, no. 2 (Mar./Apr. 1994): 67–82.

– and Carl J. Friedrich. *Totalitarian Dictatorship and Autocracy.* New York: Praeger 1956. 2nd. ed., Cambridge: Harvard University Press 1965.

Callaghy, Thomas. *The State-Society Struggle: Zaire in Comparative Perspective.* New York: Columbia University Press 1984.

Calvez, Jean-Yves. *Droit international et souveraineté en URSS.* Cahiers de la Fondation Nationale des Sciences Politiques no. 48, Paris: Librairie Armand Colin 1953.

Carle, François. *Consensus Formation at the Conference on Security and Cooperation in Europe.* MA, Carleton 1976.

Carnoy, Martin. *The State and Political Theory.* Princeton: Princeton University Press 1984.

Clark, Gordon L., and Michael Dear. *State Apparatus: Structures and Language of Legitimacy.* Boston: Allen & Unwin 1984.

Clark, Katerina. *The Soviet Novel: History as Ritual.* Chicago: University of Chicago Press 1981.

Cohen, Stephen F. *Rethinking the Soviet Experience: Politics and History since 1918.* New York: Oxford University Press 1985.

Colton, Timothy J. *The Dilemma of Reform in the Soviet Union.* Rev. ed. New York: Council on Foreign Relations 1986.

Connor, Walter D. *Socialism's Dilemmas: State and Society in the Soviet Bloc.* New York: Columbia University Press 1988.

Conquest, Robert. *The Harvest of Sorrow: Soviet Collectivization and the Terror-Famine.* New York: Oxford University Press 1986.

Crawford, Beverly, ed. *Markets, States and Democracy: Political Economy of Post-Communist Transformation.* Boulder, Colo.: Westview 1995.

Dallin, Alexander. "Causes of the Collapse of the USSR." *Post-Soviet Affairs* 8, no. 4 (Oct.–Dec. 1992): 279–302.

Dallin, Alexander, and Ralph S. Mavrogordata. "The Soviet Reaction to Vlasov." *World Politics* 8, no. 3 (Apr. 1956): 307–22.

Davies, R.W. (Robert William). *The Industrialization of Soviet Russia: The Soviet Economy in Turmoil, 1929–1930.* Cambridge: Cambridge University Press 1980.

Day, Richard B. *Leon Trotsky and the Politics of Economic Isolation.* Cambridge: Cambridge University Press 1973.

De Quirielle, Louis. *Le Gouvernement de Moscou et les Republiques Sovietiques.* Paris: Librairie de Recueil Sirey 1932.

Degras, Jane, ed. *Soviet Documents on Foreign Policy.* Vol. 2, 1925–1932. London: Oxford University Press 1952.

Deutscher, Isaac. *Stalin: A Political Biography.* New York: Penguin 1949.

di Palma, Guiseppe. "Legitimation from the Top to Civil Society: Politico-Cultural Change in East Europe." *World Politics* 44, no. 1 (Oct. 1991): 49–80.

Dima, Nicholas. *Bessarabia and Bukovina: The Soviet Rumanian Territorial Dispute*. Boulder, Colo.: East European Monographs 1982.

Dowty, Alan. *Closed Borders: The Contemporary Assault on Freedom of Movement*. New Haven: Yale University Press 1987.

Doyle, Michael. *Empires*. Ithaca: Cornell University Press 1986.

Drebentsov, Vladimir. "Rebuilding the Interrepublic Ties That Once Bound." *Geonomics*, 5, no. 2 (1993): 3–5.

Dunlop, John B. "Will a Large-Scale Migration of Russians to the Russian Republic Take Place over the Next Decade?" *International Migration Review* 27, no. 3 (103) (Fall 1993): 605–11.

Duroselle, Jean-Baptiste, ed. *Les Frontières Européennes de l'URSS, 1917–1941*. Cahiers de la Fondation Nationale des Sciences Politiques no. 85. Paris: Librairie Armand Colin 1957.

Dyker, David A. *The Soviet Economy*. London: Crosby Lockwood Staples 1976.

– *The Future of the Soviet Economic Planning System*. London: Croom Helm 1985.

Easter, Gerald. "Personal Networks, Institutional Constraints, and State Formation: The Dynamics of Center-Periphery Relations in Postrevolutionary Soviet Russia, 1921–1939." PhD, Columbia 1991.

Easton, David. *The Political System: An Inquiry into the State of Political Science*. New York: Knopf 1968.

Ehrhart, Hans-Georg, Anna Kreikemeyer, and Andrei V. Zagorski, eds. *Crisis Management in the CIS: Whither Russia?* Baden-Baden: Nomosverlagsgesellschaft 1995.

Elazar, Daniel J. "International and Comparative Federalism." *PS: Political Science and Politics* 26, no. 2 (June 1993): 190–5.

Ernst and Whinney. *The Cost of Non-Europe*. Vol. 4, *Border-Related Controls and Administrative Formalities*. Luxembourg: Commission of the European Communities 1988.

Erickson, John. *The Soviet High Command: a Military-Political History 1918–1941*. London: Macmillan 1962.

Evans, Peter, Dietrich Rueschemeyer, and Theda Skocpol, eds. *Bringing the State Back In*. New York: Cambridge University Press 1985.

Fainsod, Merle. *Smolensk under Soviet Rule*. Cambridge: Harvard University Press 1958.

Feierbend, I. K. "Expansionist and Isolationist Totalitarian Regimes." *Journal of Politics* 24, 4 (1962): 733–42.

Felshtinskii, Yuri."The Legal Foundations of the Immigration and Emigration Policy of the USSR 1917–1928." *Soviet Studies* 34, no. 3 (July 1982): 327–48.

Finer, Samuel E. "State-Building, State Boundaries and Border Control: An

Essay on Certain Aspects of the First Phase of State-Building in Western Europe Considered in the Light of the Rokkan-Hirschman Model." *Social Science Information* 13, no. 4/5 (Aug./Oct. 1974): 79–126.

Fischer, George, ed. *Russian Emigre Politics*. New York: East European Fund 1951.

Fitzpatrick, Sheila. *Education and Social Mobility in the Soviet Union, 1922–1934*. New York: Cambridge University Press 1979.

Fleron, Frederic J., and Erik P. Hoffman, eds. *Post-Communist Studies and Political Science: Methodology and Empirical Theory in Sovietology*. Boulder, Colo.: Westview 1993.

Forsberg, Tuomas, ed. *Contested Territory: Border Disputes at the Edge of the Former Soviet Empire*. Aldershot: Edward Elgar 1995.

Forster, Thomas M. *The East German Army: A Pattern of a Communist Military Establishment*. London: George Allen & Unwin 1967.

Foucault, Michel. *Discipline and Punish: The Birth of the Prison*. New York: Vintage 1979.

– *Power/Knowlege: Selected Interviews and other Writings, 1972-1977*. Ed. Colin Gordon. New York: Pantheon 1980.

Futrell, Michael. *Northern Underground: Episodes of Russian Revolutionary Transport and Communications through Scandinavia and Finland*. London: Faber 1963.

Gammer, Moshe. *Muslim Resistance to the Tsar: Shamil and the Conquest of Chechnia and Daghestan*. London: Frank Cass 1994.

Geertz, Clifford. *The Interpretation of Cultures*. New York: Basic Books 1973.

Gerson, Lennard D. *The Secret Police in Lenin's Russia*. Philadelphia: Temple University Press 1976.

Gerth, H.H., and C. Wright Mills, eds. *Max Weber: Essays in Historical Sociology*. New York: Oxford University Press 1946.

Giddens, Anthony. *The Nation-State and Violence*. Berkeley: University of California Press 1987.

Gilpin, Robert. *War and Change in World Politics*. New York: Cambridge University Press 1991.

Ginsburgs, George. "The Soviet Union and the Problem of Refugees and Displaced Persons 1917-1956." *American Journal of International Law* 51 (1957): 325–61.

Gleason, Gregory. *Federalism and Nationalism: the Struggle for Republican Rights in the USSR*, Boulder, Colo.: Westview 1990.

– "De-Colonization in the Former Soviet Borderlands: Politics in Search of Principles." *PS: Political Science and Politics*, 26, no. 3 (Sept. 1993): 522–5.

Godrechot, Jacques. *The Counter-Revolution: Doctrine and Action 1789–1804*. London: Routledge and Kegan Paul 1961.

Goldman, Marshall I. *Gorbachev's Challenge: Economic Reform in the Age of High Technology*. New York: Norton 1987.

Goodman, Elliot. *The Soviet Design for a World State*. New York: Columbia University Press 1957.

Gorbachev, Mikhail Sergeevich. *Perestroika: New Thinking for Our Country and the World*. New York: Harper and Row 1987.

Gottman, Jean, ed. *Centre and Periphery: Spatial Variation in Politics*. Beverly Hills: Sage 1980.

Gouldner, Alvin W. "Stalinism: a Study of Internal Colonialism." *Telos*, no. 34 (Winter 1977–78): 5–48.

Gourevitch, Peter. "The Second Image Reversed: The International Sources of Domestic Politics." *International Organization* 32, no. 4 (Aug. 1978): 881–911.

– *Politics in Hard Times: Comparative Responses to International Economic Crises*. Ithaca: Cornell University Press 1986.

Graham, Loren R., ed. *Science and the Soviet Social Order*. Cambridge: Harvard University Press 1990.

Granville, Brigitte. *Price and Currency Reform in Russia and the CIS, Post-Soviet Business Forum*. London: Royal Institute of International Affairs, May 1992.

Green, Timothy. *The Smugglers*. New York: Walker and Company 1969.

Greenstein, Fred I., and Nelson W. Polsby. *Handbook of Political Science* 3. Reading, Mass.: Addison-Wesley 1975.

Greer, Donald. *The Incidence of the Emigration during the French Revolution*. Cambridge: Harvard University Press 1951.

Gregor, A. James. *Italian Fascism and Developmental Dictatorship*. Princeton: Princeton University Press 1979.

Gross, Jan T. *Revolution from Abroad: the Soviet Conquest of Poland's Western Ukraine and Western Belorussia*. Princeton, NJ: Princeton University Press 1988.

Gunther, Hans, ed. *The Culture of the Stalin Period*. London: Macmillan 1990.

Gurr, Ted Robert. "War, Revolution and the Growth of the Coercive State." *Comparative Political Studies* 21, no. 1 (Apr. 1988): 45–65.

Hagopian, Mark N. *The Phenomenon of Revolution*. New York: Harper and Row 1974.

Hall, John A., ed. *States in History*. Oxford: Basil Blackwell 1986.

Hamilton, Malcom B. "The Elements of the Concept of Ideology." *Political Studies* 34, no. 1 (Mar. 1987): 18–38.

Hamilton, William B., ed. *The Transfer of Institutions*. Durham, NC: Duke University Press 1964.

Hanson, Philip. "Local Power and Market Reform in Russia." *Communist Economies and Economic Transformation* 5, no. 1 (1993): 45–60.

Harding, Neil, ed. *The State in Socialist Society*. London: Macmillan 1984.

d'Hartoy, Maurice. *Histoire du passeport français depuis l'antiquité de nos jours*. Paris: Librairie Ancienne Honoré Campion, ca 1938.

Haus, Leah A. *Globalizing the* GATT: *the Soviet Union's Successor States, Eastern Europe, and the International Trade System.* Washington, DC: Brookings Institution 1992.

Havrylyshyn, Oleh, and John Williamson. *From Soviet DisUnion to Eastern Economic Community?* Washington, DC: Institute for International Economics 1991.

Heitman, Sidney. "A Soviet Draft Law on Emigration." *Soviet Jewish Affairs* 19, no. 3 (1989): 33–46.

Hingley, Ronald. *The Russian Secret Police.* New York: Simon and Schuster 1970.

Hirschman, Albert O. *National Power and the Structure of Foreign Trade.* Berkeley: University of California Press 1945.

– "Exit, Voice and Loyalty: Further Reflections and a Survey of Recent Contributions." *Social Science Information* 13, no. 1 (Feb. 1974): 7–26.

– "Exit, Voice and the State." *World Politics* 31, no. 1 (Oct. 1978): 90–107.

History of the CPSU *(Bolsheviks): Short Course.* Edited by a Commission of the Central Committee of the CPSU. New York: International Publishers 1939.

Hoffman, Erik P., and Robbin F. Laird, eds. *The Soviet Polity in the Modern Era.* New York: Aldine Publishing Company 1984.

Holloway, David. "State, Society and the Military under Gorbachev." *International Security* 14, no. 3 (Winter 1989–90): 5–24.

Hollifield, James F. "Immigration and the French State: Problems of Policy Implementation." *Comparative Political Studies* 23, no. 1 (Apr. 1990): 56–79.

Holzman, Franklyn D. *International Trade under Communism: Politics and Economics.* New York: Basic Books 1976.

Horowitz, Dan. *The Israeli Army.* New York: Harper and Row 1975.

Hough, Jerry F. *How the Soviet Union is Governed.* Cambridge: Harvard University Press 1979.

– *Russia and the West: Gorbachev and the Politics of Reform.* 2nd ed. New York: Touchstone 1990.

House, J.W. "Frontier Studies: An Applied Approach." In A.D. Burnett and P.J. Taylor, eds., *Political Studies from Spatial Perspectives.* Chichester: John Wiley & Sons 1981. 291–312

Hunter, Holland. *Soviet Transportation Policy.* Cambridge: Harvard University Press 1957.

Huntington, Samuel P. *Political Order in Changing Societies.* New Haven: Yale University Press 1968.

Ickes, Barry W. "Obstacles to Economic Reform of Socialism: An Institutional-Choice Approach." *Annals of the* AAPSS 507 (Jan. 1990): 53–64.

Innis, Harold. *Empire and Communications.* Rev. Mary Q. Innis. Toronto: University of Toronto Press 1972.

Iurovskii, L.N. *Currency Problems and Policy of the Soviet Union*. London: Leonard Parsons Limited 1925.

Ivanov, Ivan. "From Self-Imposed Isolation to an Open Economy." *International Affairs* (Moscow) (Apr. 1989): 70–72.

Jackson, Robert H., and Carl G. Rosberg. "Why Africa's Weak States Persist: The Empirical and the Juridical in Statehood." *World Politics* 35, no. 1 (Oct. 1982): 1–25.

Janos, Andrew C. *Politics and Paradigms: Changing Theories of Change in Social Science*. Stanford: Stanford University Press 1988.

Johnson, Chalmers, ed. *Changes in Communist Systems*. Stanford: Stanford University Press 1970.

Jones, William Milton. *Maintaining Public Order in the Soviet Union: The Militia and MVD in the Post-Khrushchev Era*. PhD, Duke 1976.

Jowitt, Ken. *New World Disorder: The Leninist Extinction*. Berkeley: University of California Press 1992.

Katzenstein, Peter J., ed. *Between Power and Plenty: Foreign Economic Policies of Advanced Industrial States*. Madison: University of Wisconsin Press 1978.

– *Small States in World Markets: Industrial Policy in Europe*. Ithaca: Cornell University Press 1985.

Kennedy, Paul. *The Rise and Fall of the Great Powers: Economic Change and Military Conflict from 1500–2000*. London: Fontana Press 1988.

Keohane, Robert O., and Joseph Nye. *Power and Interdependence*. Toronto: Little, Brown 1978.

Kirchheimer, Otto. "Confining Conditions and Revolutionary Breakthroughs." *American Political Science Review* 59, no. 4 (Dec. 1965): 964–74.

Knight, Amy. *The KGB: Police and Politics in the Soviet Union*. Boston: Unwin Hyman 1988.

Koenker, Diane P., William G. Rosenberg, and Ronald Grigor Suny, eds. *Party, State and Society in the Russian Civil War: Explorations in Social History*. Bloomington: Indiana University Press 1989.

Korey, William. *The Soviet Cage*. New York: Viking 1973.

Koropeckyj, I.S., and Gertrude E. Schroeder, ed. *Economics of Soviet Regions*. New York: Praeger 1981.

Krasner, Stephen D. "State Power and the Structure of International Trade." *World Politics*, 28, no. 3 (Apr. 1976): 317–47.

– "Approaches to the State." *Comparative Politics* 16, no. 2 (1984): 223–46.

– "Sovereignty: An Institutional Perspective." *Comparative Political Studies* 21, no. 1 (Apr. 1988): 66–94.

– "Global Communications and National Power: Battle of Sexes versus Prisoner's Dilemma, or, Life on the Pareto Frontier." *World Politics* 43, no. 3 (Apr. 1991): 336–66.

Kratochwil, Friedrich. "Of Systems, Boundaries, and Territoriality: an Inquiry into the Formation of the World System." *World Politics* 39, no. 1 (Oct. 1986): 27–52.

Kulischer, Eugene M. *Europe on the Move: War and Population Changes, 1917–1947.* New York: Columbia University Press 1948.

Kruszewski, Z. Anthony. *The Oder-Neisse Boundary and Poland's Modernization: The Socioeconomic and Political Impact.* New York: Praeger 1972.

La Palombara, Joseph G., ed. *Bureaucracy and Political Development.* Princeton University Press 1963.

Lapidus, Gail, and Victor Zaslavsky, with Philip Goldman, eds. *From Union to Commonwealth: Nationalism and Separatism in the Soviet Republics.* New York: Cambridge Soviet Paperbacks 1992.

Leggett, George. *The Cheka.* Oxford: Clarendon Press 1981.

Lepingwell, John W.R. "The Russian Military and Security Policy in the Near Abroad." *Survival* 36, no. 3 (Autumn 1994): 70–92.

Levi, Margaret. *Of Rule and Revenue.* Berkeley: University of California Press 1988.

Lewin, Moshe. *The Making of the Soviet System: Essays in the Social History of Interwar Russia.* New York: Pantheon 1985.

– *The Gorbachev Phenomenon: A Historical Interpretation.* Expanded ed. Berkeley: University of Califronia Press 1991.

Lih, Lars Thomas. *Bread and Authority in Russia, 1914–1921.* Berkeley: University of California Press 1990.

Lipset, Seymour Martin, and Stein Rokkan, eds. *Party Systems and Voter Alignments.* New York: Free Press 1967.

Lorimer, Frank. *Population of the Soviet Union: History and Prospects.* Geneva: League of Nations Economic, Financial and Transit Department 1946.

Lustick, Ian. *Arabs in the Jewish State: Israel's Control of a National Minority.* Austin: University of Texas Press 1980.

– "Israeli Statebuilding in the West Bank and Gaza Strip: Theory and Practice." *International Organization* 41, no. 1 (Winter 1987): 151–71.

Luttwak, Edward N. *The Grand Strategy of the Roman Empire: From the First Century AD to the Third.* Baltimore: Johns Hopkins University Press 1976.

– *The Grand Strategy of the Soviet Union.* London: Weidenfeld 1983.

McCagg, William O., Jr. and Brian D. Silver, eds. *Soviet Asian Ethnic Frontiers.* New York: Pergamon 1979.

Malle, Silvana. *The Economic Organization of War Communism.* Cambridge: Cambridge University Press 1985.

Mann, Michael. *States, War and Capitalism: Studies in Political Sociology.* London: Basil Blackwell 1988.

– *The Rise and Fall of the Nation State.* Oxford: Basil Blackwell 1990.

– "Nation-States in Europe and Other Continents: Developing, Diversifying, Not Dying." *Daedalus* 122, no. 3 (Summer 1993): 115–40.

Mannheim, Karl. *Ideology and Utopia.* New ed. London: Routledge 1991.

March, James G., and Johan P. Olsen. *Rediscovering Institutions: the Organizational Basis of Politics.* New York: Free Press 1989.

Marrus, Michael R. *The Unwanted: European Refugees in the Twentieth Century.* New York: Oxford 1985.

Martinez, Oscar J. *Across Boundaries: Transborder Interaction in Comparative Perspective.* El Paso: Texas Western Press 1986.

Matthews, Mervyn. *The Passport Society: Controlling Movement in Russia and the USSR.* Boulder: Westview 1993.

Medvedev, Zhores A. *Andropov.* London: Basil Blackwell 1983.

Meyer, Alfred G. *Leninism.* New York: Praeger 1957.

– "The Functions of Ideology in the Soviet Political System." *Soviet Studies,* 17, no. 3 (Jan. 1966): 273–285.

Meyer, John W., and Brian Rowan. "Institutionalized Organizations: Formal Structure as Myth and Ceremony." *American Journal of Sociology* 83, no. 2 (1977): 340–63.

Meyer, Stephen M. "How the Threat (and the Coup) Collapsed: The Politicization of the Soviet Military." *International Security* 16, no. 3 (Winter 1991–92): 5–38.

Michalopoulos, Constantine, and David Tarr. "Energizing Trade of the States of the Former USSR." *Finance and Development,* Mar. 1993.

– *Trade and Payments Arrangements for States of the Former USSR.* World Bank, Studies of Economies in Transition no. 2, 1993.

– *Trade Issues in the New Independent States.* World Bank: Studies of Economies in Transition no. 7, 1993.

Mickiewicz, Ellen. *Split Signals: Television and Politics in the Soviet Union.* New York: Oxford University Press 1988.

Midlarsky, Manus I. "Boundary Permeability as a Condition of Political Violence." *Jerusalem Journal of International Relations* 1, no. 2 (Winter 1975): 53–70.

Mitchell, Timothy. "The Limits of the State: Beyond Statist Approaches and Their Critics." *American Political Science Review* 85, no. 1 (Mar. 1991): 77–96.

Molineu, Harold. "Negotiating the Helsinki Agreement." *World Affairs* 141, no. 1 (Summer 1978): 36–50.

Molot, Maureen Appel, and Harald von Riekhoff, eds. *A Part of the Peace: Canada among Nations 1994.* Ottawa: Carleton University Press 1994.

Morrison, John A. "The Evolution of the Territorial-Administrative System of the USSR." *American Quarterly on the Soviet Union* 1, no. 3 (1938): 25–46.

Mosely, Philip E. "Aspects of Russian Expansion." *American Slavic and East European Review* 7, no. 3 (1948): 197–213.

Motyl, Alexander J. *The Turn to the Right: The Ideological Origins of Ukrainian Nationalism, 1919–1929.* Boulder, Colo.: East European Monographs 1980.

- *Will the Non-Russians Rebel? State, Ethnicity and Stability in the* USSR. Ithaca: Cornell University Press 1987.
- *Sovietology, Rationality, Nationality: Coming to Grips with Nationalism in the* USSR. New York: Columbia University Press 1990.
- "The Modernity of Nationalism: Nations, States and Nation-States in the Contemporary World." *Journal of International Affairs* 45, no. 2 (Winter 1992): 307–22.
- *Dilemmas of Independence: Ukraine after Totalitarianism.* New York: Council on Foreign Relations Press 1993.

Murrell, Peter. "What Is Shock Therapy? What Did It Do in Poland and Russia?" *Post-Soviet Affairs* 9, no. 2 (Apr.-June 1993): 111–40.

Nation, R. Craig. *Black Earth, Red Star: A History of Soviet Security Policy 1917–1991.* Ithaca, NY: Cornell University Press 1992.

Nicholls, F.F. *Honest Thieves: The Violent Heyday of English Smuggling.* London: Heinemann 1973.

Nimigeanu, Dumitru. *Hell Moved Its Border.* Trans. Margaret Aull. London: Blandford Press 1960.

Nordlinger, Eric. *On the Autonomy of the Democratic State.* Cambridge: Harvard University Press 1981.

Noren, James H., and Robin Watson. "Interrepublican Economic Relations after the Disintegration of the USSR." *Soviet Economy* 8, no. 2 (Apr.-June 1992): 89–129.

Odom, William E. "Soviet Politics and After: Old and New Concepts." *World Politics* 45, no. 1 (Oct. 1992): 66–98.

O'Keefe, Gerald F. "Soviet Legal Restrictions on Emigration." *Soviet Union/Union Sovietique* 14, no. 3 (1987): 301–41.

Olcott, Martha B. "The *Basmachi* or Freemen's Revolt in Turkmenistan 1918–1924." *Soviet Studies* 33, no. 3 (July 1981): 352–69.
- "Sovereignty and the Near Abroad." *Orbis* 39, no. 3 (Summer 1995): 353–68.

Olson, Mancur. "Dictatorship, Democracy, and Development." *American Political Science Review* 87, no. 3 (Sept. 1993): 567–76.

Ostrom, Elinor. *Governing the Commons: the Evolution of Institutions for Collective Action.* Cambridge: Cambridge University Press 1990.

Palei, L.V., and Jerry L. Petr. "Integration vs. Independence for the Successor States in the USSR: When Might Economics' Right Answers Be Wrong?" *Comparative Economic Studies* 34, no. 1 (Spring 1992): 1–12.

Park, Alexander G. *Bolshevism in Turkestan 1917–1927.* New York: Columbia University Press 1957.

Parrott, Bruce. *Politics and Technology in the Soviet Union.* Cambridge, Mass.: MIT Press 1983.

Parrott, Bruce, ed. *State Building and Military Power in Russia and the New States of Eurasia.* Armonk, NY: M.E. Sharpe 1995.

Perestroika 1989. New York: Scribner 1988.

Phillipson, David. *Smuggling: A History 1700–1900*. Newton Abbott: David and Charles 1973.

Pinder, John. *European Community: The Building of a Nation*. Oxford: Oxford University Press 1991.

Pipes, Richard. *The Formation of the Soviet Union: Communism and Nationalism 1917–1923*. Cambridge, Mass.: Harvard University Press 1954. Rev. ed. Cambridge, Mass.: Harvard University Press 1964.

Plender, Richard. *International Migration Law*. 2nd ed. Dordrecht, Netherlands: Martinus Nijhoff 1988.

Poggi, Gianfranco. *The Development of the Modern State: a Sociological Introduction*. Stanford, Calif.: Stanford University Press 1978.

Polanyi, Karl. *The Great Transformation*. Boston: Beacon Press 1944.

Porter, Bruce D. and Carol R. Saivetz. "The Once and Future Empire: Russia and the Near Abroad." *Washington Quarterly* 17, no. 3 (1994): 74–90.

Przeworski, Adam. *Democracy and the Market: Political and Economic Reforms in Eastern Europe and Latin America*. New York: Cambridge University Press 1991.

Quester, George H. "Transboundary Television." *Problems of Communism* 33, no. 5 (Sept.-Oct. 1984): 76–87.

Rakowska-Harmstone, Teresa. *Russia and Nationalism in Central Asia: The Case of Tadzhikistan*. Baltimore: Johns Hopkins University Press 1970.

– "The Dialectics of Nationalism in the USSR." *Problems of Communism* 23, no. 3 (May–June 1974): 1–22.

Reddaway, Peter. "Soviet Policies on Dissent and Emigration: The Radical Change of Course since 1979." Washington: Kennan Institute for Advanced Russian Studies occasional paper no. 192, 1984.

Reitz, James T. "The Soviet Security Troops – The Kremlin's Other Armies," in David R. Jones, ed., *Soviet Armed Forces Review Annual* 6 (1982): 279–327.

Remington, Thomas F. *Building Socialism in Bolshevik Russia: Ideology and Industrial Organization, 1917–1921*. Pittsburgh: University of Pittsburgh Press 1984.

Reshetar, John S. *The Ukrainian Revolution: A Study in Nationalism*. New York: Arno Press 1972.

Rieber, Alfred J. "Landed Property, State Authority and Civil War." *Slavic Review* 47, no. 1 (Spring 1988): 29–38.

Rigby, T. H. (Thomas Henry). *Lenin's Government: Sovnarkom 1917–1922*. Cambridge: University Press 1979.

Roberts, Barbara. *Whence they Came: Deportation from Canada 1900–1935*. Ottawa: University of Ottawa Press 1988.

Robinson, Neil. "What Was Soviet Ideology? A Comment on Joseph Schull and an Alternative." *Political Studies* 43, no. 2 (June 1995): 325–32.

Roeder, Philip G. *Red Sunset: The Failure of Soviet Politics.* Princeton, NJ: Princeton University Press 1993.

Rokkan, Stein. "Entries, Voices, Exits: Towards a Possible Generalization of the Hirschman Model." *Social Science Information* 13, no. 1 (Aug./Oct., 1974): 39–53.

– and Derek W. Unwin, eds. *Economy, Territory, Identity: Politics of West European Peripheries.* London: Sage 1983.

Rubin, Barnett R. "The Fragmentation of Tajikistan." *Survival* 35, no. 4 (Winter 1993-94): 71–91.

Rubinstein, Alvin Z. "Lumumba University: An Assessment." *Problems of Communism* 20, no. 5 (Nov.-Dec. 1971): 64–9.

Sabelnikov, Leonid. "Russia on the Way to the World Trade Organization." *International Affairs* (London) 72, no. 2 (1996): 345–55.

Sahlins, Peter. *Boundaries: The Making of France and Spain in the Pyrenees.* Berkeley: University of California Pres, 1989.

Salas, Luis. *Social Control and Deviance in Cuba.* New York: Praeger 1979.

Salitan, Laurie P. "Domestic Pressures and the Politics of Exit: Trends in Soviet Emigration Policy." *Political Science Quarterly* 104, no. 4 (Winter 1989–90): 671–87.

– *Politics and Nationality in Contemporary Soviet-Jewish Emigration, 1968-89.* London: Macmillan 1992.

Schapiro, Leonard Bertram. *The Communist Party of the Soviet Union.* 2nd edition. New York: Vintage Books 1971.

Schull, Joseph. "What Is Ideology? Theoretical Problems and Lessons from Soviet-Type Societies." *Political Studies* 40, no. 4 (Dec. 1992): 728–41.

Schulz, Gerhard. *Revolutions and Peace Treaties, 1917–1920.* Trans. Marian Jackson. London: Methuen 1967.

Scott, James C. *Weapons of the Weak.* New Haven: Yale University Press 1985.

Service, Robert. *The Bolshevik Party in Revolution: A Study in Organizational Change 1917–23.* London: MacMillan 1979.

Shain, Yossi. "The Shifting Character of Loyalty: The Dilemma of Exiles in Times of War." *Comparative Politics* 22, no. 3 (Apr. 1990): 322–39.

Shapiro, Leonard. *Soviet Treaty Series.* Vol. 1, *1917–1928.* Washington: Georgetown University Press 1950.

Sharpe, L.J. "Fragmentation and Territoriality in the European State System." *International Political Science Review* 10, no. 3 (1989): 223–38.

Shevardnadze, Eduard. "No One Can Isolate us, Save Ourselves: Self-Isolation is the Ultimate Danger." *Slavic Review* 51, no. 1 (Spring 1992): 117–21.

Shotwell, James T., and Max M. Laserson. *Poland and Russia, 1919–1945.* New York: Carnegie Endowment for International Peace and King's Crown Press 1945.

Shils, Edward Albert. *The Constitution of Society.* Chicago: University of Chicago Press 1982.

Shue, Vivienne. *The Reach of the State: Sketches of the Chinese Body Politic.* Stanford: Stanford University Press 1988.

Siegelbaum, Lewis H. *Soviet State and Society between Revolutions 1918–1929.* New York: Cambridge University Press 1992.

Sills, David L., ed. *Encyclopedia of the Social Sciences.* New York: MacMillan 1968.

Simpson, Sir John Hope. *The Refugee Problem: Report of a Survey.* London: Oxford University Press 1939.

Singh, Jyoti Shankar, ed. *World Population Policies.* New York: Praeger 1979.

Skilling, H. Gordon, and Franklyn Griffiths, eds. *Interest Groups in Soviet Politics.* Princeton: Princeton University Press 1970.

Skocpol, Theda. *States and Social Revolutions: A Comparative Analysis of France, Russia, and China.* Cambridge: Cambridge University Press 1979.

Slezkine, Yurii. "The USSR as Communal Apartment, or How a Socialist State Promoted Ethnic Particularism." *Slavic Review* 53, no. 2 (Summer 1994): 414–52.

Snyder, Jack. *The Ideology of the Offensive: Military Decisionmaking and the Disasters of 1914.* Ithaca: Cornell University Press 1984.

– "International Leverage on Soviet Domestic Change." *World Politics* 42, no. 1 (Oct. 1989): 1–30.

– *Myths of Empire: Domestic Politics and International Ambition.* Ithaca: Cornell University Press 1991.

– "Nationalism and the Crisis of the Post-Soviet State." *Survival* 35, no. 1 (Spring 1993): 5–26.

Soemardjian, S. "Bureaucratic Organization in a Time of Revolution." *Administrative Science Quarterly* 2 (Sept. 1957): 182–199.

Solyom-Fekete, William. *Travel Abroad and Emigration under New Rules Adopted by the Government of Hungary.* Washington, DC: Library of Congress Law Library 1979.

Spender, Grant A., with Paul S. Ross. "Common Issues and Interrepublic Relations in the Former USSR." *Economic Review.* Washington, DC: International Monetary Fund, Apr. 1992.

Stack, John F. *Ethnic Identies in a Transnational World.* Westport, Conn.: Greenwood Press 1981.

Stark, David, and Victor Nee, with Mark Selden, eds. *Remaking the Economic Institutions of Socialism: China and Eastern Europe.* Stanford: Stanford University Press 1989.

Starr, Harvey, and Benjamin A. Most. "The Substance and Study of Borders in International Relations Research." *International Studies Quarterly* 20, no.4 (Dec. 1976): 581–617.

Stavis, John, and Julia Wishnevsky. "The Impact of *Glasnost* on Soviet Emigration Policy." *Radio Liberty Report on the USSR,* 6 Oct. 1989, 3–6.

Stepan, Alfred. *The State and Society: Peru in Comparative Perspective.* Princeton: Princeton University Press 1981.

Stephan, John J. *The Russian Fascists: Tragedy and Force in Exile, 1925–1945.* New York: Harper and Row 1978

Strachey, John. *The End of Empire.* New York: Praeger 1960.

Subtelny, Orest. *Ukraine: A History.* 2nd ed. Toronto: University of Toronto Press 1994.

Suny, Ronald Grigor. *The Making of the Georgian Nation.* Bloomington: Indiana University Press 1988.

Terry, Sarah Meiklejohn. "Thinking about Post-Communist Transitions: How Different Are They?" *Slavic Review* 42, no. 2 (Summer 1993): 333–7.

Thomas, George M., John W. Meyer, Francisco O. Ramirez, and John Boli, eds. *Institutional Structure.* Newbury Park, Calif.: Sage 1987.

Thompson, John M. "Lenin's Analysis of Intervention." *American Slavonic and East European Review* 17, no. 2 (1955): 151–60.

– *Russia, Bolshevism and the Versailles Peace.* Princeton, NJ: Princeton University Press 1966.

Tillett, Lowell. "The National Minorities Factor in the Sino-Soviet Dispute." *Orbis* 21, no. 2 (Summer 1977): 241–60.

Tilly, Charles. *The Vendée.* Cambridge: Harvard University Press 1964.

– ed. *The Formation of National States in Western Europe.* Princeton: Princeton University Press 1975.

– *From Mobilization to Revolution.* New York: Random House 1978.

– *Coercion, Capital and European States, AD 990–1990.* Oxford: Basil Blackwell 1990.

Tlemcani, Rachid. *State and Revolution in Algeria.* Boulder, Colo.: Westview Press 1986.

Trotsky, Leon. *The Revolution Betrayed: What is the Soviet Union and Where Is it Going?* Trans. Max Eastman. New York: Pathfinder Press 1972.

Tucker, Robert C., ed. *The Lenin Anthology.* New York: Norton 1975.

United Nations. *Universal Declaration on Human Rights.* Washington, DC: 1948

– Department of Economic and Social Affairs. *Customs Organization and Administration in Developing Countries: Major Considerations.* New York, 1977

– *Population Policy Compendium.* 1979–85.

United States Library of Congress. Legislative Reference Service. *Passports and the Right To Travel: A Study of Administrative Control of the Citizen.* Washington, DC: U.S. Government Printing Office 1966.

von Hagen, Mark. *Soldiers in the Proletarian Dictatorship: The Red Army and the Soviet Socialist State, 1917–1930.* Ithaca: Cornell University Press 1990.

Vyshinskii, A.Y. "Text of Speech Delivered in Committee III of the General Assembly of the United Nations, November 6, 1946." Washington, DC: USSR Embassy 1946.

Walker, R.B.J., and Saul H. Mendlovitz, eds. *Contending Sovereignties:*

Redefining Political Community. Boulder, Colo.: Lynne Rienner Publishers 1990.

Walker, Rachel. "Thinking about Ideology and Method: A Comment on Schull." *Political Studies* 43, no. 2 (June 1995): 333–42.

Walt, Stephen M. *The Origins of Alliances.* Paper ed. Ithaca: Cornell University Press 1990.

Wandycz, Piotr S. *Soviet-Polish Relations, 1917–1921.* Cambridge, Mass.: Harvard University Press 1969.

Waxmonsky, Gary Richard. "Police and Politics in Soviet Society 1921–1929." PhD, Princeton 1982.

Weiner, Myron."The Macedonian Syndrome: An Historical Model of International Relations and Political Development." *World Politics* 23, no. 4 (July 1971): 665–83.

Weiner, Myron, and Samuel P. Huntington, eds. *Understanding Political Development.* Boston: Little Brown 1987.

Whelan, Frederick. "Citizenship and the Right To Leave." *American Political Science Review* 75, no. 3 (1981): 636–53.

Williams, Howard. *Concepts of Ideology.* New York: St. Martin's Press 1988.

Williams, Robert C. *Culture in Exile: Russian Emigrés in Germany, 1881–1914.* Ithaca: Cornell University Press 1972.

Wimbush, S. Enders, ed. *Soviet Nationalities in Strategic Perspective.* London: Croom Helm 1985.

Wishnevsky, Julia. "The Decree on Administrative Liability for Violation of the Rules on Contacts with Foreigners." *Radio Liberty Research* RL 287/84, 25 July 1984, 1–4.

Wittmer, Jurg. "Les Frontières nationales à l'heure de l'intégration européene (Le Cas de la frontière Suisse." In Louis-Edouard Roulet, ed. *Frontiéres et contacts de civilisation.* Colloque Universitaire Franco-Suisse, Neuchatel: Etudes et Documents d'Histoire 1979. 215–23.

Wolfe, Bertram D. "The Influence of Early Military Decisions upon the National Structure of the Soviet Union." *American Slavonic and East European Review* 9, no. 3 (1950): 169–79.

Wolin, Simon, and Robert M. Slusser, eds. *The Soviet Secret Police.* New York: Praeger 1957.

Workum, Fifeld, et al. *Freedom to Travel: Report of the Special Committee to Study Passport Procedures of the Association of the Bar of the City of New York.* New York: Dodd, Mead & Company 1958.

Yaney, George. "War and the Evolution of the Russian State." *South Atlantic Quarterly* 66, no. 3 (Summer 1967): 292–300.

"Z." "To the Stalin Mausoleum." *Daedalus* 119, no. 1 (Winter 1990): 295–343.

Zaslavsky, Victor, and Robert J. Brym. *Soviet-Jewish Emigration and Soviet Nationality Policy.* London: MacMillan 1983.

Zhukov, S.I. "The Geography of the USSR's Foreign Trade with Bordering Socialist Countries." *Soviet Geography* 31, no. 1 (Jan. 1990): 46–53.

Zimmerman, William. *Open Borders, Nonalignment and the Political Evolution of Yugoslavia.* Princeton, NJ: Princeton University Press 1987.

Zolberg, Aristide R. "The Formation of New States as a Refugee-Generating Process." *Annals of the American Academy of Political and Social Sciences* 467 (May 1983): 24–38.

– "International Migrations in Political Perspective." In Mary M. Kritz, Charles B. Keely, and Silvano M. Tomasi, eds., *Global Trends in Migration: Theory and Research in International Population Movements.* New York: Centre for Migration Studies 1983.

RUSSIAN- AND UKRAINIAN-LANGUAGE SOURCES

Alova, Alla. "Pered pod'emom zanavesa" (Before the Rising Curtain). *Ogonëk*, no. 5 (Jan. 1989): 28–31.

Aripov, R. and N. Mil'shtein. *Iz istorii organov gosbezopasnosti Uzbekistana* (From the History of the Organs of State Security of Uzbekistan). Tashkent: Izdatel'stvo Uzbekistan 1967.

Bednenko, A.B. "Administrativnye voprosy organizatsii inostrannogo turizma v Sotsialisticheskikh stranakh" (Administrative Questions of the Organization of Foreign Tourism in Socialist Countries). *Kandidat* dissertation, Irkutsk State University 1972.

Belov, G.A., et al., ed. *Iz istorii Vserossiiskoi Chrezvychainoi komissii 1917–1921 g.g.: sbornik dokumentov* (From the History of the All-Russian Extraordinary Commission 1917–1921: Collection of Documents). Moscow: Gosizdat 1958.

Blokhin, L. *Chekisty ognennykh let: Iz istorii organov bezopasnosti Tadzhikistana* (Chekists of the Fiery Years: From the History of the Organs of State Security of Tajikistan). Dushanbe: Izdatel'stvo Irfon 1968.

Britvin, N. "Na strazhe Sovetskikh rubezhei" (On Guard at the Soviet Frontier). *Agitator*, no. 10 (May 1987): 28–30.

Bukharin, Nikolai I. *Izbrannye proizvedeniia* (Selected Works). Moscow: Ekonomika 1990.

– *Problemy teorii i praktika sotsializma* (Problems of the Theory and Practice of Socialism). Moscow: Izdatel'stvo politicheskoi literatury 1989.

Chugaev, D.A., et al., eds. *Petrogradskii Voenno-revoliutsionnyi Komitet: dokumenty i materialy* (The Petrograd Military-Revolutionary Committee: Documents and Materials). 3 vols. Moscow, 1966–67.

Chugunov, A.I. *Bor'ba na granitse* (Struggle on the Border). Moscow: Izdatel'stvo Mysl 1980.

– *Granitsa nakanune voiny 1939–1941* (The Border on the Eve of War 1939–1941). Moscow: Voennoe izdatel'stvo 1985.

Danilov, V.P., ed. *Ocherki istorii kollektivizatsii sel'skogo khoziaistva v soiuznykh respublikakh* (Sketches of the History of Collectivization of Agriculture in the Union Republics). Moscow: Gosizdat 1963.

Dinis, Georgii Georgevich. "Mezhdunarodno-pravovaia osnova prigranichnykh otnoshenii SSSR s Evropeiskimi stranami-chlenami SEV" (The International-Legal Basis of Border Relations of the USSR with CMEA Member States). *Kandidat* dissertation, Kyïv State University 1988.

Dumbadze, E. *Na sluzhbe Cheka i Kominterna: lichnye vospominaniia* (At the Service of the Cheka and Comintern: Personal Memoirs). Paris: Izdatel'stvo Mishen' 1986.

Elistratov, A.I. *Administrativnoe pravo* (Administrative Law). Moscow: Gosudarstvennoe izdatel'stvo 1929.

Fateev, P.S. *Kh.G. Rakovskii: kratkii ocherk zhizni i deiatel'nosti* (K.G. Rakovskii: A Short Sketch of his Life and Work). Kyïv: Obshchestvo "Znanie" Ukrainian SSR 1989.

Fel'shtinskii, Iurii. *K Istorii nashei zakrytosti: zakonodatel'stvye osnovy Sovetskoi immigratsionnoi i emigratsionnoi politiki* (Towards a History of Our Enclosure: Legislative Bases of Soviet Immigration and Emigration Policy). London: Overseas Publications International Limited 1988; Moscow: Terra 1991.

Fomin, F. *Zapiski starogo chekista* (Notes of an old Chekist). Moscow: Izdatel'stvo politicheskoi literatury 1964.

Frenkin, M.S. *Revoliutsionnoe dvizhenie na Rumynskom fronte* (The Revolutionary Movement at the Rumanian Front). Moscow: Izdatel'stvo "Nauka" 1965.

Frunze, Mikhail V. *Krasnaia armiia i oborona Sovetskogo Soiuza* (The Red Army and the Defence of the Soviet Union). Moscow: Gosudarstvennoe voennoe izdatel'stvo 1925.

Gertsenzon, A.A., and A.A. Piontkovskii. *Ugolovnoe pravo: osobennaia chast'* (Criminal Law: Special Part). Moscow: Iuridicheskoe izdatel'stvo NKIu SSR, 1939.

Gladkov, Teodor, and Mikhail Smirnov. *Menzhinskii*. Moscow: Izdatel'stvo TSK VLKSM 1969.

Goliakov, I.T. *Sbornik dokumentov po istorii ugolovnogo zakonodatel'stva SSSR i RSFSR, 1917–1952* (Collection of Documents on the History of Criminal Legislation of the USSR and RSFSR 1917–1952). Moscow: Gosudarstvennoe izdatel'stvo iuridicheskoi literatury 1953.

Golichenko, V.D. *Partiyne kerivnytstvo orhanamy derzhavno bezpeky: na materialakh Ukrany* (Party Leadership by Organs of State Security: From Ukrainian Materials). Kyv: Vydavnytsvo Kivs'koho Universiteta 1968.

Il'inskii, I.D. (I.D. Bruk). *Gosudarstva zapadnogo rubezha SSSR* (States on the Western Frontier of the USSR). Leningrad: Gosizdat 1925.

Ippa, S. "Kontrabanda i dela tamozhennye." (Contraband and Customs Matters) *Rabochii sud*, no. 39–40 (1925): 1481–8.

Iurovskii, L.N. *Denezhnaia politika Sovetskoi vlasti (1917–1927)* (Monetary Policy of Soviet Power 1917–1927). Moscow: Finansovoe izdatel'stvo 1928.

Ivanchishin, General-Major P. "Na strazhe granits Sovetskoi otchizny" (On Guard of the Borders of the Soviet Homeland). *Politicheskoe samoobrazovanie*, no. 4 (1978): 48–54.

Ivanov, V.S. *Chasovye Sovetskikh granits: kratkii ocherk istorii pogranichnykh voisk* SSSR (Sentries of Soviet Borders: A Short Sketch of the History of Border Troops of the USSR). Moscow: Izdatel'stvo politicheskoi literatury 1984.

Kareva, D.S., ed. *Ugolovnoe zakonodatel'stvo* SSSR *i soyuznykh respublik, Sbornik* (Criminal Law of the USSR and Union Republics: Collection). Moscow: Gosudarstvennoe izdatel'stvo iuridicheskoi literatury 1957.

KPSS *o vooruzhennykh silakh Sovetskogo Soiuza: dokumenty 1917–1981* (The CPSU on the Armed Forces of the Soviet Union: Documents, 1917–1981). Moscow: Biblioteka ofitsera 1981.

KPSS *v rezoliutsiiakh i resheniiakh s'ezdov, konferentsii, i plenumov* TSK (The CPSU in Resolutions and Decisions of Congresses, Conferences and Plenums of the Central Committee). Moscow: Izdatel'stvo politicheskoi literatury 1984.

Khrabskov, V.G. *Tamozhniia i zakon* (Customs Administration and Law). Moscow: Iuridicheskaia Literatura 1979.

Koldaev, V.M. "Istoriia i sovremennye sposoby bor'by s kontrabandoi v SSSR" (History and Contemporary Means of Struggle against Contraband in the USSR). *Kandidat* dissertation, Leningrad State University 1972.

Kolosova, V.I. *Otvetstvennost' za kontrabandu. Bor'ba apparatov* BKHSS *so spekuliatsiei kontrabandnymi tovarami* (Responsibility for Contraband: Struggle of the Apparatus of BKSS with Speculation in Contraband Goods). Gorky: MVD USSR 1987.

Krasin, L. B. *Planovoe khoziastvo i monopoliia vneshnei torgovli* (The Planned Economy and the Monopoly on Foreign Trade). Moscow: Izdatel'stvo "Planovoe khoziaistvo" 1925.

– "Gosudarstvennyi khoziaistvennyi plan i monopoliia vneshnei torgovli" (The State Economic Plan and the Monopoly on Foreign Trade). *Planovoe khoziaistvo*, no. 5 (May 1926): 7–34.

– *Voprosy vneshnei torgovli* (Questions of Foreign Trade). Moscow: Izdatel'stvo "Mezhdunarodnye otnosheniia" 1970.

Kustovtsev, P. "Nelegal'nye ukhody iz SSSR" (Illegal Departures from the USSR). *Posev* (Munich), no. 7 (1978): 24–8.

Lenin, V.I. *Pol'noe sobranie sochinenii* (Complete Collected Works). Moscow: Izdatel'stvo politicheskoi literatury 1964.

– *V.I. Lenin on the Soviet State Apparatus.* Moscow: Progress Publishers 1969.

Makotinskii, M. "Bor'ba s kontrabandoi i nadzor prokuratory" (The Struggle with Contraband and the Role of Procuracy Control). *Vestnik Sovetskoi iustitsii* (Kharkov), no. 8 (42) (1925): 329–31.

Maksimova, M. "Ot imperskogo soiuza k sodruzhestvu nezavisimkh gosu-
darstv" (From an Imperial Union to a Commonwealth of Independent
States). MEMO, no. 4 (1992): 5–20.

Markov, L.N. *Ocherki po istorii tamozhennoi sluzhby* (Sketches on the History of the Customs Service). Irkutsk: Izdatel'stvo Irkutskogo Universiteta
1987.

Mezhdunarodna politika RSFSR *v 1922 g.: otchet Narodnogo Kommissariata
po Inostrannym Delam* (The International Policy of the RSFSR in 1922:
Report of the People's Commissariat of Foreign Affairs). Moscow: Narko-
mindela 1923.

Mukhachev, Iu. V. "Krakh burzhuaznogo restavratorstva v SSSR" (The Failure
of the Bourgeois Restoration in the USSR). *Voprosy istorii*, no. 8 (1982):
94–105.

Muradov, A.M. *Patrioticheskie podvigi trudiiashchikhsia Turkmenistana pri
okhrane gosudarstvennoi granitsy SSSR (1939–1945 g.g.)* (The Patriotic
Deeds of the Workers of Turkmenistan in Defending the State Border of the
USSR 1939–45). Ashkhabad, 1985.

Novikov, Aleksei Sergeevich. "Rol' kooperatsii v razvitii vneshnetorgovoi
deiatel'nost' Sovetskogo gosudarstva (oktiabr' 1917–1925 g.g.)" (The Role
of Co-operatives in the Development of Foreign Trade Activity in the Soviet
State, October 1917–1925). *Kandidat* dissertation, Ivanovskii State University 1987.

Parsadanova, V.S. "Deportatsiia naseleniia iz zapadnoi Ukrany i Zapadnoi
Belorussii v 1931–1941" (The Deportation of the Population from Western
Ukraine and Western Belarus in 1931–1941). *Novaia i noveishaia istoriia*,
no. 2 (1989): 26–44.

Pashkov, A.M. *Stranitsy geroicheskoi letopisy: istoricheskii ocherk o Sakhalin-
skom ordenom Lenina pogranichnom otriiade* (Pages of the Heroic Chroni-
cles: A Historical Sketch of the Sakhalin Order of Lenin Border Detachment). Iuzhno-Sakhalinsk: Sakhalinskoe otdelenie Dal'nevostochnogo
knizhnogo izdatel'stva 1975.

Petrov, I.I. "Zabota partii ob ukreplenii pogranichnykh voisk (1939–1941
g.g.)" (The Party's Task in Strengthening Border Troops 1939–41). *Voprosy
istorii* no. 5 (1968): 94–9.

Pilniak, Boris. *Tadzhikistan: Sed'maia Sovetskaia: ocherki materialy k romanu*
(Tajikistan, the Seventh Soviet Republic: Sketches towards a Novel).
Leningrad: Izdatel'stvo pisatelei 1931.

Pirozhkov, V.P. *V.I. Lenin i VChK: sbornik dokumentov (1917–1922)* (Lenin
and the Cheka: Collection of Documents). Moscow: Izdatel'stvo politicheskoi literatury 1987.

Platonov, V,. and A. Bulatov, cols. "Pogranichnye voiska perekhodiat v nastu-
plenie" (Border Troops Approach the Advance). *Voenno-istoricheskii zhurnal* 7, no. 8 (1965): 11–16.

Pochs, K. *Sanitarnyi kordon* (Cordon Sanitaire). Riga: Zinatne 1985.

Radulgin, N.V. "Sovetskie organy gosudarstvennoi bezopasnosti v gody voiny" (Soviet Organs of State Security in the Years of War). *Voprosy istorii*, no. 5 (May 1965): 20–39.

– "Razvitie zakonodatel'stva ob obespechenii gosudarstvennoi bezopasnosti sssr" (The Development of Legislation for State Security of the ussr). *Sovetskoe gosudarstvo i pravo* 16, no. 5 (May 1988): 23–9.

Resheniia partii i pravitel'stva po khoziaistvennym voprosam (Decisions of the Party and Government on Economic Questions). Moscow: Izdatel'stvo politicheskoi literatury 1967.

Rubanov, V. "Ot kul'ta sekretnosti k informatsionnoi kul'ture" (From the Cult of Secrecy to an Information Culture). *Kommunist*, no. 13 (1329) (Sept. 1988): 24–36.

S'ezdy Sovetov Sovetskikh Sotsialisticheskikh Respublik. Sbornik dokumentov (Congresses of Soviets of the Soviet Socialist Republics: Collected Documents). Vols. 1–3.

Shaposhnikov, Evgenii. *Vybor: zapiski glavnokomanduiushchego* (Choice: Notes of the Head of Command). Moscow: Nezavisimoe izdatel'stvo PIK 1993.

Shevardnadze, Eduard. *Moi vybor: v zashchitu i svobodu* (My Choice: In Defence of Freedom). Moscow: Novosti 1991.

Shiriaev, Iu. "Sotsialisticheskii transnatsionalizm i mirovoi rynok" (Socialist Transnationalism and the World Market). *Kommunist*, no. 5 (May 1989): 107–15.

Sistematicheskoe sobranie deiustvuiushchikh zakonov sssr (Systematic Collection of Existing Laws of the ussr). Moscow, 1926.

Soldatenko, O.K. "Sotsial'no-politicheskaia priroda gosudarstvennykh granits i territorial'nyi suverenitet sotsialisticheskikh stran (avtoreferat)" (The Socio-political Nature of State Borders and the Territorial Sovereignty of Socialist Countries). *Kandidat* dissertation, Leningrad State University 1975.

Tamozhennyi kodeks sssr (The Customs Code of the ussr). Moscow: Iuridichekoi literatury 1983.

Tarle, Galina Yakovlevna. "Uchastie zarubezhnykh trudiiashchikhsia v vosstanovlenii narodnogo khoziaistva sssr (1920–1925 g.g.)" (The Participation of Foreign Workers in the Establishment of the National Economy of the ussr). *Kandidat* dissertation, Moscow State University 1965.

Trainin, A. N. *Ugolovnoe prava rsfsr: chast' osobennaia, prestupleniia protiv gosudarstva i sotsial'nogo poriadka* (Criminal Law of the rsfsr: Special Section, Crimes against the State and Social Order). Leningrad: Gosizdat 1925.

Tsvetkov, A., and L. Kozlov. "Sovetskie pogranichniki v Velikoi Otechestvennoi voine" (Soviet Border Troops in the Second World War). *Voenno-istoricheskii zhurnal* 10, no. 6 (June 1968): 80–8.

Vasiliev, V. I., et. al. *Leninskie dekrety 1917–1922* (Lenin's Decrees 1917–22). Moscow, 1974.

Verkhovnyi Sovet sssr. *Stenograficheskie Otchety Sovmestnogo Zasedanie*

Soveta Soyuza i Soveta Natsional'nostei sssr (Stenographic Records of the Joint Section of the Council of the Union and Council of Nationalities of the ussr). 1989–1991.

Vinogradov, V.S., et. al. *Krasnoznamennyi pribaltiiskii pogranichnyi* (The Red Banner Baltic Border). Riga: Avots 1988.

Vinokur, A.P., ed. *Praktika tamozhennogo dela* (Practice of the Customs Service). Moscow: Izdatel'stvo Narkomtorga sssr i rsfsr 1927.

Vladimirskii, Mikhail Fedorovich. *Organizatsiia Sovetskoi vlasti na mestakh* (The Organization of Soviet Power in the Localities), Moscow: Gosizdat 1919.

Yakovlev, Aleksandr. *Muki prochteniia bytiia. Perestroika: nadezhdy i realnosti* (The Pain of Reflection: Restructuring, Hopes and Realities). Moscow: Progress 1991.

Zaboletnyi, Lt-Gen. "Polveka na strazhe Sovetskikh granits" (A Half-Century of Guarding Soviet Borders). *Kommunist vooruzhennykh sil*, no. 9 (1968): 35–41.

Zyrianov, P.I., et al. *Pogranichnye Voiska sssr: sbornik dokumentov i materialov* (Border Troops of the ussr: A Collection of Documents and Materials). 1: 1918–28; 2: 1929–38; 3: 1939–41. Moscow: Izdatel'stvo Nauka 1973.

PERIODICALS

Arkhiva samizdata
Biulleten' Verkhovnogo Soveta sssr.
Biulleten' Narkomtruda
Biulleten' rvva
Bil'shevik Ukraïny
Bol'shevik
Chronicle of Current Events
Commersant
Current Digest of the Soviet Press
Dekrety Sovetskoi vlasti.
Ekonomika i zhizn'.
Ezhenedel'nik Chrezvychainykh Kommissii po Bor'be s Kontrrevoliutsiei i Spekuliatsiei (Moscow), nos. 1–6 (22 Sept.–27 Oct. 1918).
Finance and Development.
Foreign Broadcast Information Service, *Daily Report, Central Eurasia*
Foreign Broadcast Information Service, *Daily Report on the Soviet Union*
gatt *Focus*
International Monetary Fund, *Economic Review*
Izvestiia tsk
Kommersant
Kommunist
Kommunist vooruzhennykh sil

Krasnaia zvezda
Materialy samizdata/Arkhiva samizdata
MEMO
Moscow News
Ogonek
Planovoe khoziaistvo
Pogranichnik
Pravda Ukraïny
RSFSR, *Sessii Vserossiiskogo Tsental'nogo Komiteta*
Rabochii sud
Radio Free Europe/Radio Liberty *Research Report*
Radio Liberty, *Report on the* USSR
Revoliutsiia i natsional'nost'
Rossiiskaia gazeta
Sbirnik uzakonen' ta rosporiadzhen' (Ukraïna)
S'ezdy Sovetov SSSR, *Stenograficheskie otchety.* Moscow: Izdanie TSK Soyuza SSR
S'ezdy VKP(b). *Stenograficheskie Otchety.* Moscow/Leningrad: Gosizdat. Ninth
   to Eighteenth Congress, 1920–39
Sobranie zakonov i rasporiiazheniia rabochego i krest'ianskogo pravitel'stva,
   1924–38
Sobranie zakonov i rasporiiazhenii SSSR
Sobranie postanovlenii pravitel'stva SSSR
Sobranie uzakonenii RSFSR
Sovetskoe stroitel'stvo
Spravochnik partiinogo rabotnika
Tamozhennyi vestnik
Vedomosti Estonskoi Respubliki
Vedomosti Verkhovnogo Soveta Respubliki Gruzii
Vedomosti Verkhovnogo Soveta i Pravitel'stva Litovskoi Respubliki
Vedomosti Verkhovnogo Soveta Litovskoi Respubliki
Vedomosti S'ezda Deputatov i Verkhovnogo Soveta Rossiiskoi Federatsii
Vedomosti Verkhovnogo Soveta SSSR
Vedomosti Verkhovnogo Soveta Ukraïny
Verkhovnyi Sovet SSSR, *Stenograficheskii otchet*
Vestnik Sovetskoi iustitsii (Kharkiv)
Vestnik TSIK, *Sovnarkoma i Soveta Truda i Oborony* SSSR
Vlast' Sovetov
Vneshniaia torgovlia
World Bank, *Studies of Economies in Transition*

NEWSPAPERS

Argumenty i fakty
Business in the USSR

Chekist na strazhe (Birzul)
Chervonyi kordon (Mogilev)
Ekonomika i zhizn'
Izvestiia
Kazakhstanskaia pravda
Klinok pogranichnika (Mogilev)
Kolhospnik prikordonnia (Yarmolinsti)
Kommersant
Komsomol'skaia pravda
Literaturnaia gazeta
Militsioner prikordonnia (Vinnitsa)
Moscow News
Na granitse (Harbin)
Na krasnom rubezhe (Shepetevo)
Na strazhe (Pskov)
Nedel'ia
New York Times
Pogranichnik (Luga)
Pogranichnik Dnestra (Mogilev)
Pogranichnik-Kommunar (Pokrovka)
Politicheskoe obrazovanie
Pogranichnaia pravda (Sebezh)
Pravda
Pravda Ukraïny
Pravda vostoka
Pravitel'stvennyi vestnik
Prikordonnyi Bil'shevik (Pauzhnia)
Prikordonnyi kommunist (Berezdiv)
Prikordonna pravda (Slavutsk)
Prikordonna zirka (Yarun')
Rabochii sud
Rossiiskaia gazeta
Sovetskaia Rossiia
Sovetskaia torgovliia
Torgovo-promyshlennaia gazeta

SPECIALIZED LIBRARIES

While I was researching my dissertation, I had the privilege of visiting the following libraries and reading rooms: Institute of State and Law of the Russian Academy of Sciences library, Moscow; INION Library, Moscow; the Lenin Library, Moscow; the New York Public Library.; and the Tsentral'na Nauchna Biblioteka Akademii Nauk UKSSR im. Vernadskogo, Kiev, Ukraine.

Index